Whom God Has Called

Whom God Has Called

The Relationship of Church and Israel in Pauline Interpretation, 1920 to the Present

CHRISTOPHER ZOCCALI

☙PICKWICK *Publications* • Eugene, Oregon

WHOM GOD HAS CALLED
The Relationship of Church and Israel in Pauline Interpretation, 1920 to the Present

Copyright © 2010 Christopher Zoccali. All rights reserved. Except for brief quotations in critical publications or reviews, no part of this book may be reproduced in any manner without prior written permission from the publisher. Write: Permissions, Wipf and Stock Publishers, 199 W. 8th Ave., Suite 3, Eugene, OR 97401.

Scripture quotations, unless otherwise indicated, are from the New Revised Standard Version Bible, copyright © 1989, Division of Christian Education of the National Council of the Churches of Christ in the United States of America. Used by permission. All rights reserved.

Pickwick Publications
An Imprint of Wipf and Stock Publishers
199 W. 8th Ave., Suite 3
Eugene, OR 97401

www.wipfandstock.com

ISBN 13: 978-1-60899-571-2

Cataloguing-in-Publication data:

Zoccali, Christopher

    Whom God has called : the relationship of church and Israel in Pauline interpretation, 1920 to the present / Christopher Zoccali

    xii + 224 p. ; 23 cm. Includes bibliographical references and index.

    ISBN 13: 978-1-60899-571-2

    1. Paul, the Apostle, Saint—Criticism, interpretation, etc. 2. Judaism (Christian theology)—History of doctrines—Early church, ca. 30–600. I. Title.

BS2655 .J4 Z75 2010

Manufactured in the U.S.A.

Dedicated to my parents, Guy and Mary Zoccali

Contents

Acknowledgments / ix
List of Abbreviations / x

1. What's in a Name? / 1
2. From Dodd Forward: A Developing Debate / 23
3. Exegetical Investigation, Part I / 55
4. Exegetical Investigation, Part II / 91
5. Negotiating Perspectives, Part I / 119
6. Negotiating Perspectives, Part II / 145
7. Conclusion / 171

Bibliography / 179
Index of Ancient Documents / 199
Index of Modern Authors / 221

Acknowledgments

This book was originally submitted as my PhD thesis for the University of Wales, Lampeter, UK, in March 2009. I owe an enormous debt of gratitude to my doctoral advisors, Professors William S. Campbell and Kathy Ehrensperger for their critical guidance and support throughout this project. Professor Campbell's own work on the subject matter was essential to the very shape of the thesis, and Professor Ehrensperger's work on Paul also played a significant role in my thinking.

I would additionally like to express my appreciation for two other persons whom I believe were integral to the writing of this book. My first pastor, Reverend Joseph M. Burress, initially encouraged me to study the Bible and, eventually, to pursue formal training. Professor J. Richard Middleton was my Old Testament instructor during my graduate studies at Colgate Rochester Crozer Divinity School and soon became a trusted mentor and good friend. Both men continue to be a source of encouragement and inspiration.

I would be utterly remiss if I did not thank yet two other crucial figures in my life, my parents, Guy and Mary. Their unwavering support for all of my endeavors I could simply not do without. It is to them that this book is dedicated.

Abbreviations

AAJ	Approaches to Ancient Judaism
AB	Anchor Bible
ABD	*Anchor Bible Dictionary* (ed. D. N. Freedman; 6 vols.; New York, 1992)
ABR	*Anglican Biblical Review*
ANTC	Abingdon New Testament Commentary
Bib	*Biblica*
BibInt	*Biblical Interpretation*
BR	*Biblical Review*
BZNW	Beihefte zur Zeitschrift für die neutestamentliche Wissenschaft
CBQ	*Catholic Biblical Quarterly*
CCWJCW	Cambridge Commentaries on Writings of the Jewish and Christian World, 200 BC to AD 200
CTJ	*Calvin Theological Journal*
EvT	*Evangelische Theologie*
ExAud	*Ex auditu*
HeyJ	*Heythrop Journal*
HTKNT	Herders theologischer Kommentar zum Neuen Testament
HTR	*Harvard Theological Review*
IBC	Interpretation: A Biblical Commentary for Teaching and Preaching
ICC	International Critical Commentary
Int	*Interpretation*

JBL	*Journal of Biblical Literature*
JETS	*Journal of Evangelical Theological Studies*
JRS	*Journal of Religious Studies*
JSJ	*Journal for the Study of Judaism*
JSJSup	Supplements to the Journal for the Study of Judaism
JSNT	*Journal for the Study of the New Testament*
JSNTSup	Supplements to the Journal for the Study of the New Testament
JTS	*Journal of Theological Studies*
LD	Lectio divina
MNTC	Moffatt New Testament Commentary
NAC	New American Commentaries
NCBC	New Century Bible Commentary
NIB	New Interpreter's Bible
NICNT	New International Commentary on the New Testament
NIGTC	New International Greek Testament Commentary
NovTSup	Supplelments to Novum Testamentum
NT	*Novum Testamentum*
NTM	New Testament Monographs
NTS	*New Testament Studies*
OTL	Old Testament Library
PRSt	*Perspectives in Religious Studies*
PSBSup	*Princeton Seminary Bulletin Supplements*
RB	Revue Biblique
RevQ	*Revue de Qumran*
SBLDS	Society of Biblical Literature Dissertation Series
SBLSP	*Society of Biblical Literature Seminar Papers*
SNT	Studien zum Neuen Testament
SNTSMS	Society of New Testament Studies Monograph Series
SP	Sacra pagina
TNTC	Tyndale New Testament Commentaries
WBC	Word Biblical Commentary
WMANT	Wissenschaftliche Monographien zum Alten und Neuen Testament
WUNT	Wissenschaftliche Untersuchungen zum Neuen Testament
ZTK	*Zeitschrift für und Kirche Theologie*

1

What's in a Name?

THE RELATIONSHIP OF CHURCH and Israel according to the apostle Paul is an issue of considerable debate in contemporary New Testament scholarship. For centuries, beginning in particular with Justin Martyr's *Dialogue with Trypho* in 160 CE, mainstream Christian interpretation held that Christianity was the fulfillment of Judaism and that the church was the rightful inheritor of all the promises of God made to the historical nation of Israel in Scripture. In the earlier part of the contemporary era perhaps the most cogent articulation of this perspective is that of C. H. Dodd. In Dodd's interpretation of Paul the Christ event signals the abrogation of Torah. Accordingly, the legalism of Judaism was deemed anathema, having been replaced by the "Christian religion" of God's grace accessed solely by faith and therefore available to all. Thus, in Paul's theology, the people of God, Israel, are transformed—or ultimately realized—as the universal church.

REAPPRAISAL OF THE QUESTION IN MODERN PAULINE SCHOLARSHIP

Yet while Dodd's overarching view of the church as a "new Israel" represented the dominant understanding in Pauline scholarship for some time, aspects of his reading were already called into question. F. C.

Baur, for example, had previously argued that Rom. 9–11, understood by Dodd as something of an excursus and ultimately inconsistent with Paul's theological program, was rather an integral part of the argument of the entire letter. Though understanding a similar antithesis between the particularism of Judaism and the universalism inherent in the Christ movement, this assertion by Baur that was subsequently taken up by many later scholars, along with other developments in New Testament scholarship, would soon bring about interpretations that would challenge the majority view.[1]

Helping to lay the foundation for such was Albert Schweitzer's study of Paul (1912), which sought to re-establish Paul's thoroughly (apocalyptic) Jewish worldview against years of scholarship that read him as embracing Hellenistic ideals of universalism over against Jewish particularism. While Schweitzer called attention to the similarities between Paul and apocalyptic Jewish literature, W. D. Davies (1948) drew important parallels between Paul's teaching and that found in rabbinic Judaism. Following this, Johannes Munck's reading of Rom. 9–11 (1959, 1967) demonstrated a Paul who was centrally concerned about the fate of historical Israel.

And deeply contributing to a change of perception among New Testament scholars, Krister Stendahl's provocative lecture "Paul and the Introspective Conscience of the West" (cf. Stendahl 1976a: 78–96), given in 1961, pointed out that, contrary to the Lutheran/Protestant perspective, Paul's doctrine of justification by faith had nothing to do with an internal struggle to keep the law and the solution to a guilty conscience—a view inherited from Augustinian theology—but concerned rather the joining of gentiles together with Jews as peoples of God.

But perhaps most significantly, the reappraisal of first-century Judaism proposed by E. P. Sanders (1977),[2] in which it was shown to be nothing like the traditional Lutheran/Protestant understanding of a "religion of works-righteousness" (in contrast to the emergence of

---

1. Like Dodd, Baur (1876) read Paul in the context of a dispute with the Jewish faction of the church. However, as pointed out, his recognition of the importance of Rom. 9–11 within the letter as whole was an impetus for later scholarship that would rethink the supposed irreconcilability of first-century Judaism and the emergence of (Pauline) Christianity, contrary to Baur's dialectical perspective on the matter, which became the central thesis of the Tübingen school of historical criticism.

2. Prior to Sanders, Moore (1921) and Schoeps (1961) similarly challenged the traditional Christian view of first-century Judaism.

Christianity as a "religion of grace through faith"), further precipitated a rethinking of the role of Israel in Pauline theology.[3] What would eventually develop from here into the so-called New Perspective assisted many scholars in the conclusion that for Paul the church could not simply be characterized as a "new Israel." Historical Israel in its own right still played a significant role in God's purposes that was in no way terminated by the coming of Christ.

POST-HOLOCAUST SCHOLARSHIP AND THE RECOGNITION OF THE INTEGRITY OF JEWISH IDENTITY

Unquestionably, the movement in this direction was intensified by the increasing acknowledgment among New Testament scholars that in light of the horrifying events of the Holocaust one could no longer carelessly speak of historical Israel as the negative counterpart and foil to the (largely non-Jewish) church. As Kathy Ehrensperger (2004: 16) comments,

> Scholarship and the enterprise of biblical interpretation in particular are contextual, 'conducted by real people who are concretely located in the historical process' [Brueggemann 1997: 734]. Therefore, we cannot ignore the fact that this enterprise is undertaken in a post-Shoah situation. Since theological supersessionism and practical Christian teaching of contempt for Jews contributed to the emergence of political anti-Semitism and its unthinkably brutal realization in the Third Reich, Christian theology has lost its innocence and cannot go on doing business as usual.

This heightened sensitivity to the Jewish origins of Christianity, but also to the integrity of Jewish identity, has influenced new theological formulations concerning the relationship of church and Israel. In the most extreme example of this development, pushing beyond the claims

---

3. Sanders' basic thesis describing first-century Judaism's understanding of the law in terms of the now well-established label "covenantal nomism" contains eight key aspects: (a) God has elected Israel; (b) God has given the law to Israel; (c) the law includes God's promise to maintain Israel's election; (d) Israel is responsible to obey the law; (e) God punishes transgressions but rewards obedience; (f) the law provides a means for atonement for transgressions; (g) the measures for atonement allow for one to maintain one's covenant status; (h) "All those who are maintained in the covenant by obedience, atonement, and God's mercy belong to the group which will be saved. An important interpretation of the first and last points is that election and ultimately salvation are considered to be by God's mercy rather than human achievement" (Sanders 1977: 442). Cf. more recently Sanders 2008.

of the New Perspective, scholars such as Stendahl, Lloyd Gaston, and John G. Gager have proposed that Paul's teaching should be understood in terms of two covenants.[4] Here, God's historical covenant with the Jewish people stands unaltered, and the Christ event represents a way of salvation only for the other nations. In a more traditional view, in that Christ is still seen as essential to Jews and gentiles alike for salvation, but nevertheless born of the same concerns as the scholars who suggest a two-covenant approach, both William S. Campbell and Mark D. Nanos have forcefully argued that Israel remains a distinct entity from the church.[5]

At the same time, however, still other scholars, while accepting of the insight yielded by the New Perspective and taking seriously the centrality of Israel in Paul's theology, cannot ignore what they believe to be strong implications in the relevant texts that Paul did in fact view the church as in some way "Israel." Characteristic of this viewpoint, James D. G. Dunn suggests that while historical Israel retains a continuing significance in Pauline thought, there is also present a notion of the church in which it is necessarily identifiable as "Israel." An even stronger position along these lines is that held by N. T. Wright. Quite similar to the view of Dodd, Wright has argued that for Paul Jesus takes upon himself the identity of "true Israel," which is then transferred to those "in Christ," the church of Jews and gentiles.

RELIGION OR ETHNICITY? JEWISH IDENTITY IN THE FIRST CENTURY

Though the scholarly debate described above is focused primarily upon the theological and contemporary ethical implications derived from the Pauline corpus, recent discussion on how Jewish self-understanding in the first century should be construed must be taken into consideration.[6] Scholars such as Shaye Cohen (1999), Philip F. Esler (2003), and

---

4. Cf. Stendahl 1976a, 1976b; Gaston 1987; Gager 2002a, 2002b; see also Stowers 1994 and Johnson-Hodge 2007. Stendahl had since distanced himself from this reading; cf. Stendahl 1995: x–xi.

5. Other scholars emphasizing the retention of Jewish identity in Paul include (in addition to those listed in n. 4 above) Eisenbaum (2000), Esler (2003), Zetterholm (2003), Ehrensperger (2004), Kinzer (2005).

6. Cf. the excellent discussion of this issue in Miller 2007, on Professor David A. Miller's blog, online: http://gervatoshav.blogspot.com. Miller similarly, though in greater detail, reviews the hypotheses of Cohen, Esler, and Mason.

Steve Mason (2007) have raised important issues surrounding the notion of ethnicity in antiquity and, in particular, the proper meaning of Ἰουδαῖος.

Cohen specifies three possible definitions for the Greek term in antiquity, arguing that originally Ἰουδαῖος connoted a geo-ethnic meaning, i.e., "Judean" (1999: 69). Around the period of the Maccabean revolt in the second century BCE, a "political" meaning of the term developed, in which citizenship could be granted to foreigners. "Such newly franchised citizens themselves became *Ioudaioi* or Judaeans. They still retained their prior ethnicity and much of their prior religion and culture, but they joined the Judaean people and declared loyalty to the God of the Judaeans" (1999: 105). It is only following the Maccabean revolt that a meaning of the term in a religious-cultural sense, i.e., "Jew," emerged (cf. 2 Macc. 6.6; 9.17).

In some distinction, Esler argues that, at least prior to 135 CE, Ἰουδαῖος should be *consistently* understood and translated as "Judean," a geo-ethnic designation, given especially the common Greek practice "to name ethnic groups in relation to the territory in which they originated" (2003: 63), as well as the tight connection made in Judean sources between the people and their homeland and its temple (2003: 64). According to Esler, in light of the fact that expressions of ethnic boundaries change over time, first-century "Judeans" must be viewed in critical discontinuity with contemporary Jews,[7] and "the words 'Jews', 'Jewish', and 'Judaism' now carry meanings indelibly fashioned by events after the first-century" (2003: 66–67).

Moreover, the translation of Ἰουδαῖος as "Jew" to denote especially a "religious" identity, as Cohen asserts, is further indicative of the anachronism such a translation presents. Esler (2003: 73) points out that the concept of "religion," as a dimension of life that can be separated from "ethnic and geographic realms," is a post-Enlightenment construct that would have been completely foreign in antiquity. It is illusory to suggest that non-Ἰουδαῖοι of the period wishing to convert were in fact converting to a religious system, i.e., "Judaism," and thus would be "Jews"

---

7. Cf. Esler 2003: 62: "[A]lthough they may be a group that has maintained a sense that it is a group for millennia, the cultural indicia used in delimiting its boundaries may have changed dramatically over time. This means that to treat modern understandings of Jews as equally applicable to the Ἰουδαῖοι of the first century CE—on the basis that the people has remained essentially the same across the centuries—runs the risk of ignoring features of the identity of this ancient people that they themselves saw as foundational for their sense of self."

rather than "Judeans," and it is also to ignore the very real phenomenon of nested or multiple ethnic identities that individuals or groups may possess. In his 2007 article on the matter, Mason affirms much of what Esler has proposed, similarly suggesting that, from an emic perspective, the terms Ἰουδαισμός and Ἰουδαΐζω have reference not to the practice of a religious system but to that of a particular ethnic group.

Notwithstanding these important observations, I have chosen to employ the conventional English translation "Jew" for Ἰουδαῖος as it appears in Paul (and will similarly use expressions such as "Jewish," etc.).[8] Though the concerns of scholars such as Esler and Mason can in no way be summarily dismissed, and bring needed attention to accurate historical reconstructions of the identity of first-century Ἰουδαῖοι, I justify my choice on the following reasons.

First, the obvious should nevertheless be pointed out that this is not a question of the appropriateness of an etic term (as when the term "Christian" is employed in relation to the Pauline corpus; see below) but of how a term present in the relevant texts themselves should best be translated into English.[9] While there are undeniable differences between the self-understanding of the first-century group labeled Ἰουδαῖοι and modern Jews, and thus the main difficulty with the common translation, this surely does not mean that legitimate lines of continuity cannot also be drawn, as they indeed are by contemporary Jewish groups.[10]

Moreover, an emphasis upon the historical otherness of the former in relation to the latter, as is indicative of the translation "Judean," is also not unproblematic. Consider Amy-Jill Levine's assertion (2007: 160) that in Esler's reading the "Jew is replaced with the Judean and thus we have a *Juderein* ('Jew free') text, a text purified of Jews." It would seem, then, that whatever English translation is employed, at least some explanation concerning the semantic significance of Ἰουδαῖος is necessary.

Cohen's suggestion aside,[11] the English terms "Jew" and "Jewish" connote *both* religious and ethnic meanings. And while Judaism as an

8. In keeping with the common nomenclature I will mostly employ the English translation "gentiles" for ἔθνη.

9. This point is similarly made by Barclay (2007: 110–12) who supports the translation of Ἰουδαῖος as "Judeans."

10. For a discussion concerning the historical continuity of Judaism, cf. Levine 2007: 159–66; see also Johnson-Hodge 2007: 14–15.

11. As Johnson-Hodge (2007: 54) points out, Cohen's assertion that ethnic origination, i.e., kinship, is fixed and non-transferable, while other aspects of identity, namely

abstracted "religious system" did not exist in antiquity, that Paul is particularly concerned with what may best be described (however in etic fashion) as the "religious" dimension of Jewish identity—i.e., allegiance to the God of Israel expressed in terms of submission to the requirements of Torah—even if inextricably connected to other aspects of ethnicity (not least a myth of shared ancestry; cf. Rom. 4.1; 9.3ff.; 11.1; Phil. 3.5; Gal. 1.14; 2.15; 1 Cor. 10.1), seems evident from the relevant texts under investigation in this study.

Thus, while appreciating the notion of ethnicity as it applies to the Ἰουδαῖοι of the first-century Greco-Roman world, contrary to anachronistic perceptions of "religion" divorced from other expressions of group boundaries—especially by way of a comparative religion approach to Paul, in which Christianity is compared to (and often set against) Judaism—the question that occupies this study remains whether or in what sense Paul can claim the identity of "Israel" for the multiethnic Christ community,[12] and what premise(s) either allows or disallows him from doing so.

In this light, I have chosen to employ the phrase "historical Israel" or simply "the (historical) nation" when referring to the Israel defined

---

beliefs and practices, are malleable and transferable, is untenable. All aspects of ethnic identity are subject to negotiation and change (even when the former is perceived by group members as immutable; cf. esp. on this point Buell 2005: 6–10; see also Lieu 2006: 99–100; Johnson-Hodge 2007: 19–42), and the distinction between heritable and achievement-orientated dimensions of identity can never be completely separated.

12. While it is safe to conclude that Paul's letters (save, of course, Philemon) were addressed in each case to a majority gentile audience, I find it highly unlikely that in these communities collectively there were not the presence of Jews, according to which Paul's Christ gospel equally applied. Specifically, I argue that neither the empirical or encoded audience of the letter to the Romans, in which Paul thoroughly explicates the implications of his gospel, is *entirely* non-Jewish.

Further, by employing the phrase "multiethnic" I am affirming that the self-perception of early (i.e., first- and second-generation) Christ followers was *neither* one in which prior ethnic identities were thought to be wholly transcended nor one in which ethnicity itself had become irrelevant—i.e., "non-ethnic" (this latter notion in particular being a literal impossibility, despite the assertion of such in later Christian writings). More to the point, I suggest Paul's vision of the church is one of communities that stand in historical continuity with God's people "Israel" (sharing in the Jewish symbolic universe), but which nevertheless consists by necessity of multiple people groups. On both counts the church is for him emphatically not a "third race" that is *neither* Jewish nor gentile, nor even less an entity altogether void of ethnic ascription. Rather, the church is in one sense *entirely* "Jewish," and yet in another sense *both* Jewish and gentile.

according to traditional ethnic markers,[13] in distinction to the proposal that Paul may also define Israel such that it is coextensive with the Christ community in its entirety, that is, the church.[14] It is also to draw a distinction between another possibility—that Paul may refer to "Israel" such that only a subset of the larger group, i.e., Jewish Christ followers, are included. Ostensibly, this sort of reference would be indicative of a conviction that those who are true to the implications of Jewish identity would embrace his gospel.

It would do well to also point out here that, whereas I have decided to stress historical continuity in my use of the English translation "Jew," I will not employ the term "Christian" when referencing first-century individuals or groups, except if in reference to other scholars' views. I will refer instead to the "Christ follower" or "Christ community." The reason for this is quite simple: the name Χριστιανός does not appear in the Pauline corpus, and it is my aim to interpret Paul, to the extent I am able, on his own terms.

CONTINUITY VS. DISCONTINUITY: DIFFERING THEOLOGIES IN ADDRESSING THE QUESTION

Clearly impacting the question at hand is the decision by scholars whether Paul's teaching demonstrates a fundamental continuity of salvation history, or if the coming of Christ and subsequent formation of the church

---

13. I am not suggesting here that these boundaries were fixed or univocal throughout the greater Jewish, or specifically, Diaspora community (cf., e.g., the discussion in Lieu 2006: 98–146), but only that Paul possesses a particular understanding of what makes one Jewish, explicitly referring to two primary aspects of this ethnic boundary: kinship and Torah submission, both of which are, generally speaking and despite the ambiguities it presented for women, interconnected to the rite of circumcision (cf. Cohen 1999: 109–39 for a discussion on the preeminence of circumcision in Jewish self-understanding beginning in the second century BCE).

Without attempting to gloss over the complexity of first-century Judaism, it would seem quite safe to conclude that most orientations of Judaism in this period regarded circumcision as a primary marker of Jewish identity and inextricable to other aspects of such (cf. Nanos 2002a: 89–91)—though Paul is apparently alone in using this rite as a synonym for the Jewish people as a whole. As I will argue in the following chapters, while Paul may redefine what it means to descend from Abraham, "fulfill" the Torah, and be circumcised, this redefinition does *not* supplant the prior definition, but remains parallel to it; contra Lieu (2006: 128) who remarks that Paul chooses to draw a particular line of demarcation for Jewish identity only to then erase it.

14. I suggest that this broad definition of "church" does have a basis in Paul (cf. Gal. 1.13; 1 Cor. 10.32; 15.9), and will be the one assumed throughout this study.

stands in radical discontinuity with the period before. But what either of these approaches would suggest in terms of the relationship of church and Israel is also a matter of considerable debate. One finds in Dodd's reading, for example, an emphasis on continuity. In contrast, following Schweitzer in asserting the pervasiveness of apocalyptic thought in the theology of Paul, Ernst Käsemann emphasizes discontinuity and holds therefore that the church is foremost an entity distinct from Israel. Yet, according to Käsemann, as a distinct entity the church nevertheless supersedes the historical nation along with all aspects of the former age in God's redemptive plan. And in this respect he paradoxically reaches the same essential conclusion as Dodd. Thus, advocates of both continuity and discontinuity can propound supersessionism.[15]

Käsemann's influence is far reaching, and several aspects of his reading of the relationship of church and Israel in Paul's thought have been subsequently incorporated by a wide spectrum of scholars. And several recent scholars have attempted to articulate similar "apocalyptic" approaches but without the supersessionist notion that characterizes Käsemann's reading.[16] One finds, then, a somewhat peculiar phenomenon in current scholarly debate as to which paradigm, "salvation history" or "apocalyptic," is more inherently supersessionist.

And within a variety of interpretive schemes, scholars have argued from the basis of both continuity and discontinuity in regard to the significance of the Christ event in order to demonstrate that historical Israel retains its theological and sociological integrity in Paul. Yet, there are those who have continued to understand Paul as teaching that the church is in some way "Israel," while affirming that there is nothing necessarily anti-Jewish to be found in such a conclusion.

---

15. It should be observed that the notions of "continuity" or "discontinuity" can be construed in different ways. For example, one might view the two-covenant reading as representing an emphasis on discontinuity, because the Christ event inaugurates an entirely new way of salvation for the gentiles, as distinct from God's dealings with Israel. However, it could very easily be argued that this interpretation actually points in the direction of continuity, in that historical Israel continues to relate to God in precisely the same way after Christ's coming as before. The decisive factor is thus whether one is defining these notions primarily in terms of the significance of the salvation accomplished by the Christ event or that of the historical election of Israel. In what follows, I will employ these notions according to the former.

16. Cf., e.g., Harink 2003, D. A. Campbell 2005.

THE POSITION ADVOCATED HERE

I find agreement with those scholars who hold that Israel *is not* to be identified with the church in Paul's thought. However, I also agree with those who interpret Paul to mean that, at least in a certain respect, the church *is* Israel. What would seem to be two irreconcilable views can, I believe, be held together when one fully appreciates Paul's different tracks of thought on the relationship of church and Israel.

This contextual nature of Paul's thought is sometimes disregarded, as when some scholars, in an apparent desire for coherence, extend an otherwise valid thesis about what Paul says in some texts to the point where it no longer can be sustained without doing injustice to other Pauline texts. In my opinion this is the problem with most scholarly views on this question. Of course, there are those who have suggested that many of Paul's statements that pertain to the question are in fact inconsistent, and that Paul is at these points either seemingly unconcerned to construct a reasonable argument or simply did not himself possess a coherent understanding (cf. Sanders 1983: 123–35; Räisänen 1986: 94–119, 264; see also Watson 1986: 170).[17] I do not agree with this conclusion. Indeed, a coherent Pauline view of the relationship of church and Israel can be found, but such a view needs to adequately account for the complexity of the question.

THE PROBLEM OF IMPOSING EXTRABIBLICAL NORMS IN PAUL: TWO CASE STUDIES

As suggested in the quotation from Ehrensperger above, the context of the interpreter will and should have an affect on interpretation. However, in some current New Testament scholarship certain ethical and theological premises formulated independently from the text have been observed in the interpretation of Paul. As these premises become the parameters for legitimate interpretation, they begin to encroach upon matters of the

---

17. It is Paul's view of the role of Torah in light of the Christ event—integral to the matter of the relationship of church and Israel—that is the main target of such accusations. But see further Räisänen's treatment of Rom. 9–11 (1988: 182, 192–96), which he (wrongly, in my view) understands to be internally contradictory. Also see Cosgrove 1997 for a discussion concerning the apparent contradictory statements in Romans concerning "the identity and election of Israel and God's impartiality toward all" (ibid., 21). I believe Cosgrove overstates the ambiguity present in the letter and the apparent antithesis between Rom. 1–4 and 11.

historical plausibility of Paul's meaning. Further, their imposition upon the relevant texts has prejudiced the question surrounding the ethical and theological appropriateness of Paul's teaching in a contemporary context. Bearing on the matter of the relationship of church and Israel, Ehrensperger's view (2004: 18–19) is indicative. She asserts:

> The interpretation of Scriptures is a crucial issue that we must address in the process of reformulating Christian identity without anti-Judaism. Theologies grappling with Auschwitz have developed several general hermeneutical rules as guidelines for looking afresh to our biblical heritage, to find meaning and guidance for contemporary problems of everyday life as well as world politics.

She continues by articulating these "hermeneutical rules," among which is that "any form of displacement theory concerning Israel, or the Jewish people, has to be abandoned." While it is not made explicit what exactly would constitute a "displacement theory," the implication is that *any* view that would understand the church as Israel would fall under such a category.

I affirm much of the same concerns that Ehrensperger expresses. Certainly, the sociopolitical, cultural, and historical location as well as the theological and ethical commitments of the interpreter invariably affects the way in which s/he will read a text.[18] Further, how one articulates an interpretation should be sensitive to the contemporary context in which it will be received.[19] Nevertheless, to the extent that New Testament scholars are in the business of discerning what New Testament texts say, it is, in my mind, incumbent upon them to respect the alterity of the text. I do not refer here to the distinction to which Stendahl (1962: 418–32) pointed between historical exegesis and contemporary application, which has since been erroneously understood to mean that the first is an objective, "scientific" enterprise, and the latter,

---

18. As the only viable means by which the hermeneutical process can take place, human subjectivity is thus a positive value that should not itself be cause for misgiving. It is precisely one's preunderstandings that allow for a point of engagement with the text.

19. Cf. Cosgrove 1997: 100: "We ought to bear in mind that many past Christian interpreters whose discourse about Jews and Judaism now appears to us to contain anti-Jewish content did not regard themselves as anti-Jewish and in some cases saw themselves as defenders of the Jewish people. The question of anti-Jewishness in the canonical Paul must therefore be kept open. As definitions of anti-Jewishness change, fresh analysis of the semantic potential of Paul's text is required."

a subjective one.[20] It is clear to me that valid interpretation is always an intersubjective,[21] dialogical engagement with the text. However, this is different from how one may further negotiate a reading according to one's own beliefs and agenda. To simply collapse these two matters is to fail to respect the text's own integrity and otherness.

Case Study #1: Charles H. Cosgrove

An example in which Pauline interpretation pertaining to the matter at hand is self-consciously directed by an external ethic is found in Charles H. Cosgrove's *Elusive Israel: The Puzzle of Israel's Election in Romans* (1997). Cosgrove suggests that Rom. 9–11 employs two instances of co-deliberation, Rom. 9.22ff. and 11.15ff., whereby the text itself invites the reader to be self-involved in determining the meaning of the text, and as such requires "the guidance of an ethic of interpretation" (p. 39). Yet, pointing out that there are ultimately only a limited number of plausible interpretations for any given text,[22] he continues to explain a method whereby the meaning of Romans as part of the Christian canon can be adjudicated,[23] implementing an internal principle from the canon itself

---

20. Nor am I naively suggesting that biblical scholarship is wholly prior to and should thus be unaffected by biblical, systematic, or practical theology. Rather, I am indicating an insistence on taking seriously the text on its own terms, which would include its contemporary relevance, despite the potential for it to conflict with one's own sensibilities and commitments.

21. To characterize hermeneutics as "intersubjective" means that the text cannot be reduced to merely an "autonomous object" (cf. Grenholm and Patte 2000: 13), but is itself a "speaking" partner in the interpretive process. Rather than a "hermeneutical circle," interpretation is better characterized therefore as a spiral, whereby the interpreter through an encounter with the text (as well as other readings of it) may find her/himself in a different perspectival location from where s/he had begun.

22. As Cosgrove also notes here, the determination of what the borders for this range of plausibility should be are, of course, open to debate and, I would add, can never be legitimately established in a priori fashion. Although requiring, then, subjective judgments from interpreters, that such a finite range exists is necessarily the case. A failure to recognize this and to thus assign equal validity to any and all readings is invariably to affirm academically and ethically irresponsible interpretations. I would also point out that absolute claims derived from biblical readings (however broadly defined) are not anymore intrinsically violent or oppressive than relative ones (contra Ehrensperger 2004: 14ff.); they are, moreover, inevitable, for the notion of complete relativity is itself an absolute claim in competition with others. See Middleton and Walsh 1995.

23. Many have, like Cosgrove, noted that it is precisely Paul as he is read in the context of the New Testament that has mostly contributed to a supersessionist interpretation of him. But in contrast to the corrective strategy offered by Cosgrove, it is

as a guide for such deliberation. He finds this principle in Matt. 22.37–40: to love one's neighbor as one's self.

Thus, Cosgrove concludes of his interpretation of the identity of Israel in Romans that it is "a constructive adjudication, informed by moral judgments lying largely outside the conceptual frameworks of Paul." He explains,

> I am not claiming that Paul was dealing with modern concerns, much less that he was guided by the same insight into human identity that inform modern discussions of this complex subject. Rather, I have used my own ethical sense informed by modern discussions, to justify a specific interpretation—or integrated complex of interpretive decisions—as most conducive to a humane use of Romans by the church in the late twentieth century. (pp. 79–80)

But I find some difficulty with this approach. First, I question whether the sort of co-deliberation that Cosgrove suggests is truly warranted by the text.[24] Again, while all interpretation is dialogical—"meaning," then, residing neither wholly in the text or the interpreter—such a co-deliberation seems to me to encroach on the real contribution of the text as a meaning-making participant apart from the interpreter. Second, it is one thing to relativize, qualify, or contextualize Paul's teaching in light of a greater canonical/moral principle or new historical context, e.g., a post-Holocaust one, but it is quite another by this means and in virtue of the supposed indeterminacy of the text to arrive at a legitimate interpretation. I am not suggesting that external voices, including the history of both latent and explicit anti-Judaism in the church, should not be heard, as if interpretation in isolation from the interpreter's own context would be viable or desirable (which it is neither), or further that they cannot awaken interpreters to more plausible readings of the rel-

---

frequently proposed, as Gager (2002b: 59) asserts, that Paul be loosed from his New Testament moorings, and be read "in his own settings, in his own times, not as he was read later in totally new settings and times." But I would suggest that this is a false antithesis. Despite the problems evidenced in the history of interpretation in the church, Paul can be read *both* historically and canonically—indeed an informed canonical reading must take seriously Paul's historical context—and one can arrive at an ethically responsible interpretation that is not intrinsically anti-Jewish.

24. It is hardly the case that these rhetorical questions are inviting the reader to make up his/her own mind, but to propel the reader toward the conclusion provided in the text itself.

evant texts (which they have).[25] But in my view, despite his elucidating of the various ways in which Paul could arguably be read on this matter, Cosgrove overstates the "plasticity" of the probable meaning of the texts in question in their own right,[26] which serves as his rationale for subsuming them to what he presupposes to be the more ethical reading.

However, most contemporary scholars addressing the relationship of church and Israel in Paul, while striving for an ethically responsible interpretation, are doing so, largely, on the basis of the historical-critical method, and not the approach outlined above. Yet, in my estimation, several of those advocating a Paul who understood an ongoing distinction between Israel and the church have argued for this in significant part, similar to the example from Cosgrove above, in terms of an a priori assumption (however influenced by legitimate concerns) that to hold otherwise is intrinsically anti-Jewish. This is not to say that the view whereby the church is not to be identified with Israel is exegetically unsupportable from the relevant texts; as noted above, I believe that it does have merit. But subtle indications of uncritical bias are nevertheless present, with the result that Paul's own sensibility is collapsed with that of the interpreter.

Case Study #2: John G. Gager

Illustrative is the analysis of Paul's apparent contradictory statements in Gager's *Reinventing Paul* (2002a: 5–6; cf. Gager 2002b: 68–69). Gager

---

25. It is worth pointing out here that it would seem Paul employs a similar hermeneutic when he quotes from Scripture to support his gospel, thus giving these texts, however arguably consistent with their original context, new significance in light of the Christ event. See further Grenholm and Patte 2001: 26: "Biblical critics should learn from theologians that the interpretations of biblical critics are framed by theological categories that they brought to the text.... Positively, they should learn about the role that theological, cultural, and value judgments played in focusing their critical interpretations upon certain features of the text that had been overlooked because their significance was not clear without such focus.... It takes a confrontation with feminist and other advocacy scholars to discover the androcentrism and Eurocentrism of one's interpretation; when one acknowledges that one's interpretation is subtly framed by specific cultural categories that one brings to the text, it becomes possible to envision that our own theological or ideological categories had a similar role in the interpretive process."

26. It is important to acknowledge that this is equally a subjective construct affected by the interpreter's own context. And while I do not delimit this "historical voice" to authorial intent, I believe that it is nevertheless instructive to reconstruct what Paul in his historical location would have likely meant by what he actually writes, however tentative all such historical reconstructions ultimately may be.

constructs two categories of Pauline texts. He labels one set of texts, including Rom. 3.1, 31; 7.7, 12; 9.4; 11.1, 26; and Gal. 3.21, "pro-Israel." He labels the other set of texts, which include Gal. 3.10–11; 6.15; Rom. 3.20; 9.31; 11.28; and 2 Cor. 3.14ff., "anti-Israel." As consistent with a two-covenant approach, Gager proposes that the apparent contradiction created by these two sets of texts can be resolved when it is realized that the "anti-Israel" passages are not actually directed towards Israel at all, but concern "the new redeemed status of Gentiles-in-Christ" (2002b: 70).

He thus concludes that the historical Paul cannot properly be labeled the father of anti-Judaism, despite this traditional view of him. Though I agree with this final conclusion reached by Gager, I do not read Paul along the lines of his two-covenant interpretation. In any respect, what is pertinent here is that Gager simply presumes that those passages to which he refers, if indeed directed towards Jews as well as gentiles, would in fact be anti-Jewish; a point for which he nowhere argues or discusses in any sustained critical fashion.

The implication from Gager and others is that Paul is either wrong to identify the church as Israel, and thus in need of critique, or, as in this case, needs to be defended against anti-Jewish accusations because Paul does not actually make this equation. But seemingly disallowed is to responsibly maintain that Paul does claim the identity of Israel for the church while not recognizing any necessary negativity to be associated with this notion.

Can this development in the scholarly debate on the question be understood, then, as anything but the new dogma of post-Holocaust scholarship? And if not, the continuing appearance of such dogmatism is nothing short of paradoxical given that it now arises amidst the postmodern trend in much contemporary New Testament scholarship that has sought to undermine the objectivist presuppositions and consequent hegemony characteristic of older scholarship.

One might note the similarly dogmatic response of Käsemann (1971: 60–78) to Stendahl's thesis in "Paul and the Introspective Conscience of the West" (Stendahl 1976a: 78–96) that it was a threat to the very existence of Protestant Christianity in its challenge to the then mainstream view of justification, and further that Stendahl's emphasis on salvation history was, ironically enough, dangerously akin to Nazism.[27] Yet, what

27. Käsemann's reaction here is understandable in view of the Third Reich's self-

would become the New Perspective has now gained majority acceptance among Pauline scholars. Protestant Christianity is alive and well and, I would add, has profited greatly from this reappraisal of the historical, decidedly Jewish context of Paul's apostolic mission and theology.

VIEW OF THE SCHOLARLY DEBATE ON THE QUESTION

But whether what is at stake is the traditionally received view or more recent challenges to this, it is in my mind an unfortunate development whenever scholarly debate over biblical texts takes place foremost on the grounds of ethical and/or theological sensibility, and is occupied with reactionary polemics and extrapolation of interpretive motives rather than exegetical argumentation premised upon the givenness and alterity of the text, however informed this process is by one's ethical or theological presuppositions. In as much as this can potentially silence scholarship that interprets Paul in contentious ways, and even more dangerously the Pauline texts themselves, it can thwart the possibility of quite constructive implications that may otherwise be had.

As such, I do not deny a place for a hermeneutic of suspicion, whereby perceived threads of violent or oppressive ideologies contained in the biblical text are exposed.[28] Yet, I propose that a hermeneutic of trust, which, as Richard B. Hays (2005: 197–98) explains, "is a faithful struggle to hear and discern" and "a readiness to trustingly receive," should occupy a primary role.

My intention here is not to create a guise behind which I can secretly affirm a positivistic view of scriptural interpretation, nor, once more, to claim that moral/theological judgments cannot legitimately guide this process—indeed they must, but to (quite contrarily) affirm that what is and what is not an ethically or theologically appropriate reading should not be heavy-handedly presumed, as I believe it commonly is in this matter.[29] Thus, as indicated above, I hold that there is something positive

---

understanding, which, as Käsemann (1969: 64) asserts, was a "conception of salvation history which broke in upon us in secularized and political form."

28. Cf. Schüssler Fiorenza 2000: 51: "In short, an ethics of interpretation that does the work of a public health department in Pauline studies would require that scholars problematize the hermeneutics of identification with Paul and critically investigate the 'public health' aspects of Paul's rhetoric and politics of meaning."

29. Acknowledging the obvious potential for Paul to have made assertions with which one disagrees or finds distasteful, even scandalous, is clearly necessary if one is to affirm the integrity of the text. And illustrative in advancing interpretations of Paul that

to be heard from both the view that understands the church as an entity other than Israel, as well as that which understands church and Israel to be the one and same entity.³⁰

MY APPROACH TO THE QUESTION

Though vitally interconnected to the practical missionary experience and social reality Paul faced, this study is foremost concerned with the theological underpinning for Paul's understanding of this matter, as extrapolated from the most relevant texts.³¹ And this is in the context of (a) the monumental shift of paradigms in modern scholarship (beginning here with C. H. Dodd), that is, the movement from the "old" to New Perspective on Paul, as well as (b) the unquestionable significance that it

---

stand in a certain tension with the values and religious commitments of the interpreter are Segal 1990, Boyarin 1994, Nanos 1996, and Eisenbaum 2000. But it is nevertheless interesting to observe the apparent ease with which some scholars concede the inappropriateness of integral aspects of Paul's teaching in contemporary dialogue.

So, for example, Wasserberg (2001) who after interpreting Rom. 11 to indicate that Paul hoped other Jews would come to salvation through accepting the gospel of Christ, notes: "If my reading of Paul has merit, then his paradigm cannot provide the model for Jewish-Christian relations.... While I have great respect for scholars such as Stendahl, Gaston, and Nanos—I have learned much from them—I suspect that despite all their efforts to criticize anti-Jewish interpretations of Romans, they take too easy a way out of a fundamental problem inherent in Christianity. How can we resolve this problem, or at least leave it open in a way that respects both Judaism and Christianity? Despite all, what we learn from Paul is to be reminded that Israel's election remains valid. How, then, to define Christianity in a way that does not deny Judaism the Torah as God's way of salvation for Jews? Or, in the phrasing of Rosemary Radford Ruether (1974), how to affirm Christian Christology without at the same time affirming its 'anti-Judaic left hand?'" (pp. 184–85).

30. Cf. Wright 2001: 451: "On the one hand, we are urged to reject non-Jewish styles of Christianity, to recover the Jewish roots of our faith, and to cherish and nourish such echoes of Jewish ways, Jewish rituals, Jewish understandings, as we can. Christian versions of Seder meals have become common. This, it seems to me, is a healthy corrective to the many ways in which Christians so easily slip into non-Jewish modes of thought, taking their color and agenda instead from the pagan world around. On the other hand, the same people who urge this agenda regularly also press upon the church the need to renounce all claim to be 'the Jew,' 'the circumcision.' 'Supersession' is the magic word here, or perhaps we should say the demon-word. It is wheeled out again and again, implying that in such a view the church has taken Israel's place in God's plan, leaving no room any longer for non-Christian Israel, Israel (in Paul's phrase) 'according to the flesh.' This double position is grossly inconsistent."

31. By "theological underpinning" I basically assume the definition provided by Scroggs (1991: 212): "Paul's theology is what he thinks about the transcendent and its intervention into immanent reality."

holds for contemporary Christian self-understanding vis-à-vis Scripture, along with its accompanying theological and ethical implications.

It would be a grievous error to fail to consider the socio-historical contingencies that give rise to and surround Paul's writings, and the following will give due attention to these factors where necessary and/or especially useful. But it is nevertheless not the purpose here to explore social-scientific questions of identity or ethnicity in regard to Paul and his addressees (or early Christianity in general) in their own right.[32] Again, the primary focus will be to uncover the theological grounding from which Paul can equate the church with Israel while simultaneously suggesting a distinction between these two entities.

OUTLINE OF THE FOLLOWING CHAPTERS

It is, I believe, an analysis of the major viewpoints that have been advanced in modern scholarship to date that will provide the best vantage from which to look afresh at this question. Thus, chapter 2 will survey this scholarship, attempting to provide both a fair and balanced presentation of the relevant views of key scholars who have addressed the matter, and further demonstrating the underlying rationale for the exegetical decisions that have been made.[33]

First will be the views of C. H. Dodd and Ernst Käsemann, "old perspective" Pauline scholars who in like fashion emphasize the doctrine of justification as central to understanding the relationship of church and Israel. Yet, in contradistinction to one another, Dodd emphasizes continuity in Paul's theology, while Käsemann discontinuity. Both, however, articulate views that have since been deemed supersessionist by more contemporary scholars.

Following this will be James D. G. Dunn, N. T. Wright, and Terence L. Donaldson. As New Perspective scholars, all three understand that the church is to be in some way identified with Israel. Central to Dunn's

---

32. Though not the focus of this study, the important insights offered by social identity theory (cf. Tajfel 1978, Tajfel and Turner 2001), particularly as they have been adapted to the study of the Pauline literature in Esler 1998 and 2003, will be considered at several points throughout.

33. There are certainly numerous scholars who have addressed the question of the relationship of church and Israel in Paul. But the particular scholars whose work I will review in ch. 2 were chosen because each has, in my view, contributed a sufficient body of work on the subject, and collectively represent a broad range of interpretive options. They thus will provide a contextual basis from which to explore this question.

thesis is the eschatological tension initiated by the Christ event, resulting in a temporary bifurcation of Israel during the course of the present age prior to the eschaton. This bifurcation is between the unbelieving portion of the historical nation (which still has right to the title "Israel") and the church of Jews and gentiles (which is nothing other than "Israel"). Similarly, Donaldson holds that with the advent of Christ, Israel has been redefined, its boundaries no longer determined by the ordinances of Torah but by Christ faith. Yet, Paul continues to ascribe the title "Israel" in its full covenantal sense to the historical nation irrespective of Christ faith. In contrast to Dunn and Donaldson, Wright understands that by virtue of Christ Israel has been wholly transformed into the church of Jews and gentiles.

Next are William S. Campbell and Mark D. Nanos, both of whom suggest that the church is not to be identified with Israel, but is, theologically speaking, a larger entity that encompasses Israel and the other nations. However, both argue that in actual terms the church communities Paul established existed under the "umbrella" of Judaism and thus can be best described as subgroups within the greater Jewish community. Nanos presses this thesis the furthest, suggesting a thoroughly open relationship between the Pauline communities and the synagogue.

Finally, the views of Lloyd Gaston and Douglas Harink will be discussed, both of which emphasize the discontinuity between the salvation inaugurated by the Christ event and the prior dispensation. Gaston advocates a two-covenant reading, in which Israel and the church are entirely distinct entities, the Christ event and subsequent formation of the church having primary significance only for the gentiles. Harink suggests that while the apocalypse of Christ has accomplished the redemption of all of creation, including both Israel and the other nations, Israel's historical election, as a guarantee of salvation, stands and is applicable to Jews irrespective of their assent to the gospel of Christ. There is here, then, a distinction to be drawn between the church and Israel, though, in as much as Christ is ultimately the means of salvation, these entities are not to be set apart as radically as in Gaston's reading.

The following four chapters will serve as a critical assessment of the viewpoints presented in chapter 2. Chapter 3 will consist of exegetical analyses of two Pauline texts that I believe are integral to the question: Rom. 2.29 and Gal. 6.16. It will be shown from these texts that (a) Paul applies the titles "Jew" and "Israel" to members of the Christ community, that is, to a superordinate group status inclusive of both Jews (traditionally/non-christologically defined) and non-Jews, and according to which subordinate ethnic distinctions are therein preserved while also transformed; and that (b) it is "new covenant" and "new creation" conceptions that allow Paul to make such applications.

Chapter 4 will focus on Rom. 11.26, the climax to Paul's argument in chapters 9–11, which has been generally recognized by scholars since Munck as of central import in addressing this matter. I will first critique the various interpretive options for this text that have been advanced to date. I will then suggest that here Paul is articulating how God has not in fact turned away from historical Israel despite appearances. But God is in the *present time* fulfilling his promise to save the Jewish people by means of their acceptance of the Christ gospel. It will be seen that throughout this section Paul still assigns the title "Israel" exclusively and in total to the Jewish people, though in the context here of an eschatological tension between the "already" and "not yet." For Paul, in the eschaton only Jews who have placed their trust in God's act in Christ will retain right to this identity.

While there are certainly other passages that bear on the question at hand, I propose that none deal as directly with, or reveal in themselves the fundamental theological grounding for, Paul's understanding of the relationship of church and Israel comparative to the three texts I have chosen for detailed analysis. Together Rom. 2.29, Gal. 6.16, and Rom. 11.26[34] form a sufficient interpretive matrix by which these other relevant texts may be judged in terms of what they actually speak to this matter.[35]

And thus in chapters 5–6 I will summarily engage other relevant Pauline texts (cf., e.g., Gal. 1.13–14; 3; Rom. 4; 7; 14; 15.8–12; Phil. 3;

---

34. Each of these texts forms a conclusion to the extent argument in key sections of their respective letters, and the ensuing analysis of them will of course engage these larger contexts.

35. To argue this point here would seem to be rather superfluous. As the old saying goes, "the proof of the pudding is in the eating." Thus, an implicit question in chs. 5–6 will be whether the exegetical conclusions gathered from chs. 3–4 successfully construct a complete picture of Paul's theology concerning the relationship of church and Israel that can both stand in the face of other relevant Pauline texts (in dialogue with the various readings presented in ch. 2) and, further, serve to illuminate them. I believe that the following will meet this burden.

1 Cor. 7.17–20)³⁶ while in dialogue with and evaluation of the views presented in chapter 2. As such, chapter 5 will further endeavor to demonstrate that, rather than a sectarian, Paul was a Jewish reformer who understood the church as standing in continuity with the Jewish community and not as a replacement for it. Chapter 6 will concern the Israel-centeredness and yet universality of the gospel of Christ, as well as the relationship between apocalyptic and salvation history conceptions in Paul. In other words, how the "apocalypse of Christ" is for Paul the fulfillment of the prophetic promises to both Israel and all creation that have been made manifest in, through, and for the church. The ethical implications of this reading, as per charges of supersessionism and anti-Judaism, will also be confronted. I then discuss the central matter of divine election, which, when viewed from Paul's perspective, affirms the continuity between Israel, Christ, and the church.

Lastly, in chapter 7 I will offer my final conclusions on the relationship of church and Israel in Paul, as informed by the scholarly contributions discussed throughout.

---

36. This study will proceed on the assumption that, in addition to the seven undisputed Pauline texts, Colossians and 2 Thessalonians were likewise written by Paul. The letter to the Ephesians may also be cited in the conviction that the author of this text, as an early interpreter of Paul, may help to illuminate aspects of his thought found in the authentic letters.

2

From Dodd Forward: A Developing Debate

THE FOLLOWING WILL EXPLORE the various understandings of the relationship of church and Israel in modern Pauline interpretation, beginning in 1920 with the work of C. H. Dodd. Nine scholars have been chosen and categorized into four primary viewpoints on the question: (a) church and Israel before the New Perspective, (b) the church is Israel, (c) the church is not Israel, and (d) church and Israel beyond the New Perspective. Within each category I will discuss the main thesis of each of its representative scholars and explicate common and distinctive aspects between them.

Regarding category (a), it is no mere exercise in curiosity to examine how this question was addressed prior to the advent of the New Perspective, under the assumption that such views are antiquated and distorted in their reconstruction of Paul's socio-historical context, including most critically the practice and beliefs of first-century Jews. It will be seen that while, indeed, much has fallen by the wayside from the "old perspective," there are many notions that have nevertheless survived and continue to be expounded in more current scholarship.[1] Thus, following the exposition of the scholars in category (b), I will compare

---

1. Expositing the views of these scholars also functions to elucidate what some later scholarship addressing the question has specifically reacted against.

their collective views with those from (a) in order to better situate the effect the New Perspective has had on this question.

And to clarify the fundamental divergence on this question that exists within the New Perspective itself, after expositing the views contained in category (c), I will compare them directly against (b). Finally, the survey will conclude with category (d), which represents how some quarters of Pauline scholarship have sought to move beyond the New Perspective, in the conviction that Paul must be liberated from perceived anti-Jewish sentiment found in varying degrees in much of the foregoing scholarship.[2]

In all, this presentation of the wide spectrum of scholarship concerning the relationship of church and Israel in Paul—in addition to demonstrating the sheer complexity of the matter—will both establish a context for the exegetical investigations to be conducted in chapters 3–4 as well as form the basis for a negotiation of perspectives on the question in chapters 5–6.

CHURCH AND ISRAEL BEFORE THE NEW PERSPECTIVE: C. H. DODD AND ERNST KÄSEMANN

> [F]or Paul to accept Jesus meant that he was outside the Law, and therefore on common ground with Gentiles, and hence . . . the true Church of Christ must rest upon the principle—'there is no distinction'; 'in Christ there is neither Jew nor Greek'. In one sense this already means the universality of the Christian religion. Yet we must define more closely what Paul's new position is. According to I Thess. ii.16, 'the Wrath' has fallen *finally* on the Jews—εἰς τέλος implying that this sentence of reprobation cannot ever be reversed. Similarly, according to Gal. vi.15–16, the Israel of God is co-extensive with those who believe in Christ and excludes all those who make circumcision and the Law necessary to salvation. Unless he has expressed himself incautiously in the heat of controversy, not only Jews, but even Jewish Christians who enforce the Law are 'anathema.' . . . To be committed to the Law is to fall under this condemnation, and outside the sphere of grace and election. (Dodd 1954: 120–21)

> Paul is obliged to destroy those claims of Israel which are grounded in its own history in exactly the same way as those of the

---

2. As the exposition of these viewpoints will demonstrate below, my use of the title "beyond the New Perspective" is, in short, indicative of any reading of Paul that does not see allegiance to Christ as necessary for the redemption of the Jewish people.

individual religious man. The express fashion in which he does this shows that Israel has exemplary significance for him; in and with Israel he strikes at the hidden Jew in all of us, at the man who validates rights and demands over against God in the basis of God's past dealings with him and to this extent is serving not God but an illusion. . . . [I]f real salvation comes only from the Judge of our illusions, then there can be authentic promise only for the broken, for those who have been thrown back on to the true human condition of guilt, of waiting and of suffering. It is just this that Paul finds illustrated in the Old Testament; this is what is stamped on the covenant-history which is there rehearsed and which thus preserves the character of the history of promise pointing the way to the Cross of Jesus and yet at the same time pointing beyond the Old Covenant to God's dealings with all people. (Käsemann 1969: 186)

Two significant figures among those representing modern New Testament scholarship prior to the advent of the New Perspective on Paul are C. H. Dodd and Ernst Käsemann. Their respective views are characteristic of the majority understanding of the relationship of church and Israel in Pauline thought for this period, beginning with Justin Martyr. Dodd is perhaps best known for his central thesis of "realized eschatology" and his emphasis on the historicity of the Christian religion.[3] In some contrast, Käsemann's reading develops from a broader "apocalyptic"[4] perspective.

3. Dodd interpreted Pauline thought as shifting clear away from futuristic, unfulfilled expectations onto a focus on the here and now—the present realities made possible through the resurrection of Christ. Accordingly, Paul's original "futurist eschatology" evident in 1 Thessalonians was eventually replaced by the notion of "Christ mysticism," or the present communion of believers with the Lord via the Spirit, evident in Paul's later letters. Dodd's view of "realized eschatology," which presupposes the historical character of Christianity, is clearly seen in his explanation of the Pauline kerygma. It is the "proclamation of the facts of the death and resurrection of Christ in an eschatological setting which gives significance to the facts. They mark the transition from 'this evil Age' to the 'Age to Come.' The 'Age to Come' is the age of fulfillment. . . . [T]he fulfillment of prophecy means that the Day of the Lord has dawned: the Age to Come has begun. The death and resurrection of Christ are the crucial fulfillment of prophecy. By virtue of them believers are already delivered out of this present evil age. The new age is here, of which Christ, again by virtue of His death and resurrection, is Lord. He will come to exercise His Lordship both as Judge and as Saviour at the consummation of the Age" (Dodd 1964: 13).

4. For a detailed analysis of the meaning and centrality of "apocalyptic" in Käsemann's study on Paul, cf. Matlock 1996. Though widely debated by contemporary scholars, the definition of apocalyptic provided by Beker (1984: 136) is instructive here,

Centrality of Justification by Faith

Despite these different approaches, for both scholars primacy is placed upon the doctrine of justification (as understood, of course, in terms of the classic Reformation model) as the defining context for understanding the relationship of church and Israel in Paul (cf. Dodd 1932: 163; Käsemann 1980: 264ff.). It is abundantly clear that a largely negative view of the Torah and its incompatibility with faith is a guiding force in their readings (as with old perspective Pauline scholarship in general) (cf. Dodd 1932: 177; Käsemann 1971: 147). As Dodd (1920: 70ff.) explains, Paul came to the realization that the law, with its "awful principle of retribution," was incomplete, incapable of "exhaust[ing] the whole truth about God and man." Even the way God had dealt with Israel's patriarchs in the past suggested that God's activity was not confined to retributive justice, and thus the need for a "different principle to be disclosed."

Though having inwardly struggled with his failure to keep the law, Paul discovered through his experience with Christ a new perception of God different from that of the Pharisees. No longer was God seen by him as standing "aloof from the world," allowing the law to "take its course," and not now "deal[ing] with individual sinful men" (1920: 74). Accordingly, Dodd's Paul challenged his pharisaic opponents to "interpret the law by the prophets, and to find, even in the books of the law itself, statements suggesting a personal relation to God over and above the merely legal relation to Him as governor of the universe." He thus argued "that the Christian revelation of God is the fulfillment of a logical necessity in the heart of the old religion" (1920: 76–77).[5]

---

as it is the one Käsemann presumes, and has been the conventional understanding in modern scholarship since Schweitzer: Apocalyptic revolves around the basic ideas of (a) historical dualism, (b) universal cosmic expectations, and (c) the imminent end of the world (cf. Matlock 1996: 14–15).

5. Dodd's comments on Rom. 3.21-26 (1932: 50) are noteworthy here, as he explains that though the "new revelation of God's righteousness is apart from the law, in so far as the law is a code of commandments," it is not so in the broader sense, in which the law refers to the whole revelation of God in the Old Testament. Paul can thus say that God's righteousness is attested in the law and the prophets. While on the surface this may seem to be inconsistent with Paul's assertion that Christ brings the law to an end (Rom. 10.4 according to Dodd's reading), Dodd notes Paul's insight in recognizing distinct strands of tradition within the Old Testament. Other concepts of God that move beyond that found in the "legalistic Judaism" of Paul's day, and represent "the direct antecedent of Christianity," are present in the Prophets and Psalms, and "even embedded within the Pentateuch itself."

In Dodd's reading, then, the law has been "abolished in Christ" and replaced with "a law written on the heart," a feature of the new covenant prophesied in Jer. 31.31-34 and now representative of the "Christian religion" (1951: 69-70). He concludes that all members of the church must surrender claims to moral superiority and exclusive privilege. "For the Jew, entrance in the Christian community meant the surrender of the ancient institutions of the law of Moses, which he had been taught to consider a mark of God's special favor" (1952: 25; 1965: 14).

Käsemann addresses this matter quite similarly in his essay "Paul and Israel" (1969). He first points to the contradiction posed by the apparent anti-Jewish sentiment expressed in 1 Thess. 2.15-16 in comparison to both Rom. 9.1-5 and Rom. 11, according to which Paul asserts respectively that Israel is in particular "the bearer of the promise," and that the ultimate purpose of his apostolic mission is the "winning of Israel for Christ." Käsemann then affirms that it is only the doctrine of justification of the ungodly that can make sense of Paul's (i.e., the church's) relationship with Israel.

In support of his conclusion Käsemann first turns to Phil. 3.4-9, whereby Paul, reflecting on his past as a devout Jew, declares the worthlessness of his former pursuit of a "righteousness of his own," which was predicated upon obedience to the law, in light of the righteousness found in Christ. And this is precisely how Paul describes Israel's destiny in Rom. 10.2-4. It is therefore evident for Käsemann that Paul's "real adversary" is not Israel per se, but rather "the devout Jew," which is "the reality of the religious man" (1969: 184). At stake for Paul was the question, "Who really is God?" The answer for him was found only in the necessity of the atonement provided by Christ. No human can glory in their own achievement; none are righteous before God. Thus, the "real God is the enemy and judge of every human illusion—especially every pious illusion" (1969: 185).

And it is this conviction where Käsemann's Paul comes into conflict with Israel (cf. 1980: 33). For him true righteousness can no more arise from "religious achievement" than from any previous distinction or privilege conferred by God. Rather, "Right and righteousness can only be ours in so far as God gives them anew every day—i.e. in faith" (1969: 185).

Both Dodd and Käsemann proceed by extending this intrinsic antithesis between faith and law to the relationship of church and Israel.

Historical Israel is identified by the misguided and invariably impossible attempt to merit the status of righteousness through the keeping of the Torah,[6] and stubbornly refuses the grace of God as ultimately manifested in the Christ event (cf. Dodd 1920: 44, 49; Käsemann 1980: 285–86). By contrast the church represents the realization of salvation by faith and not works, and as such supersedes the historical nation as demarcating the community of the redeemed. Israel cannot thereby have any continuing theological significance (save perhaps the notion of its final salvation).

Universalism vs. Particularism

Interconnected to this is a second point of commonality between these scholars: the mutual exclusivity and irreconcilability of universalism and particularism. Here Paul sets over against the particularity of historical Israel the universality of the church; the former being replaced by the latter in God's purposes (cf. Dodd 1920: 44–45; 1954: 119–20, 122–23; 1932: 186–87; Käsemann 1971: 88–89, 108, 273, 310). Again it is the Torah (as practiced in first-century Judaism) that is the culprit, and which must be abandoned as a prerequisite for entrance into the people of God (or, as Käsemann [1971: 109] prefers as the central motif in Paul's ecclesiology, the "body of Christ").

That Israel had been set apart from the other nations by virtue of its possession of the Torah resulted in a (false) notion of Jewish superiority, and an exclusionary understanding of redemption at the expense of the gentile world. In light of the revelation of Christ Paul came to understand, rather, that God's salvation is not restricted to Israel and on the basis of Torah, but available to both Jews and gentiles on the sole ground of faith.

THE FINAL SALVATION OF "ALL ISRAEL"

A third point of commonality is found in Dodd's and Käsemann's respective readings of Rom. 11, in which Paul postulates the final salvation of historical Israel. Given the above two premises it is perhaps not surprising that this notion presents a certain challenge for both scholars. Paul's apparent presumption that "all Israel" must be saved stands in some tension to his doctrine of justification and his rejection of the

---

6. Though in both Dodd and Käsemann νόμος is translated as "law," I will translate the term in most instances more appropriately as "Torah," and so throughout.

assumed special privilege afforded Israel in first-century Jewish thought (following here Dodd and Käsemann's understanding). Though Dodd and Käsemann similarly accept that Paul does, nevertheless, hold to the certainty of Israel's eventual salvation, they take two distinct routes by which to explain the relationship between Paul's assertion here and the central viewpoint each has maintained for him.

For Dodd this notion cannot in fact be successfully reconciled with what Paul has previously established in the letter to the Romans and elsewhere (1932: 183ff.). Paul's commitment to historical Israel's salvation represents merely the remnants of an invested national interest that had not yet given way to the full implications of his theological program (1932: 151). Yet Dodd also suggests that Paul's thought was moving towards a universal notion of salvation, and that if "all Israel" is to be saved it is because God's plan of redemption ultimately encompasses all people (1932: 184).

Käsemann, however, interprets the seeming reversal in Rom. 11 in terms of a dialectic through which Paul understands the relationship between the continuity of God's promise to the historical nation with the "true Israel" that God has elected in accordance with the doctrine of justification (1980: 308ff.). This apparent paradox can only be resolved if one accepts God's free and sovereign will over creation. Still, the salvation of "all Israel" is not on different terms than that of the gentiles, but only at a different time. Historical Israel's salvation is accomplished through its incorporation into the church at the Parousia and the close of the age (1980: 310–11, 314).

Salvation History vs. Apocalyptic

In addition to these areas of commonality there are, however, important distinctions between the perspectives of Dodd and Käsemann. The following two main points of contrast may be noted. First, Dodd maintains a salvation history approach, as being at the center of Paul's understanding of the relationship of church and Israel (cf. 1951: 9; 1953: 111–13; 1964: 62). The church of Jews and gentiles represents the eschatological fulfillment of the prophetic promises given to historical Israel and the climax of a continuous salvation history. As consistent with God's absolute freedom, Israel is thereby transformed, being now defined strictly in terms of Christ. Dodd can then refer to the church as the "true Israel" and/or "new Israel" (1932: 154–55, 160, 183).

But Käsemann (1971: 87, 108-9; 1980: 261-63) maintains that such a "linear" approach is secondary in Paul's understanding. Käsemann's Paul views the relationship of church and Israel primarily in discontinuous and antithetical terms; the secondary and primary approaches are then held together in dialectical and paradoxical fashion. The notion that the church stands in continuity with historical Israel arises largely in Paul's polemical discourse against Judaism in which he attempts to prove the church is the "true Israel," as anticipated in Scripture. And yet Käsemann also emphasizes that to the extent Paul holds such a perspective it is premised upon the conviction that the church finds its origin in historical Israel and does not simply replace it (1980: 261).

Nevertheless, though the continuity of church and Israel is an indispensable concept for Paul, it is not foremost in his thought as it was with "Jewish Christianity" in general. Rather, Paul understands the church to represent a (new) people of the new covenant age that has dawned in Christ. In contrast, Israel is representative of the old covenant age—of the fallen creation that has now been superseded by the new (1971: 108-9). That Paul can hold to both concepts is, again, a function of his dialectic approach. Though bringing him to the point of self-contradiction, maintaining such a paradox was a necessary corollary to Paul's conviction of God as Creator, who "establishes his claim to the world by fulfilling his promise" (1980: 309). It is only accordingly that Paul affirms the salvation history of Israel (albeit in modified form), which will be brought to eschatological completion at the Parousia.

Romans 9-11

The second point of contrast concerns the role historical Israel's present rejection and ultimate salvation plays in Paul's theological program. For Dodd it is tangential at best, if not altogether inconsistent. But Käsemann believes it to be fundamental. Illustrative here is the way each scholar understands the relationship of Rom. 9-11 to the rest of that letter. For Dodd it is an independent sermon that functions largely as an apologetic for what Paul has established in chapters 1-8 as being central to his gospel; namely, the principle of "no distinction" in the new dispensation of Christ, and thus the abrogation of special privilege for historical Israel despite their "special part in the divine plan" (cf. 1932: 150-51). In contrast, for Käsemann Rom. 9-11 is an essential part of the letter, in which Paul, by "using the special case of Israel," can "exemplify God's dealings with the whole world" (1980: 82). Israel's guilt and yet God's ultimate faithfulness to the promises are typological representations of the plight and yet ultimate hope of "religious humanity."

TOWARD A NEW PARADIGM

It is important to once more point out that the similarities and differences between the positions of Dodd and Käsemann on the question of the relationship of church and Israel in Paul are all contained within a larger framework characteristic of the scholarship prior to the New Perspective. And many Pauline scholars have since been highly critical of this framework as a form of supersessionism or "replacement theology."

It is asserted that if the Torah is rendered obsolete by the Christ event it can only mean exclusion from the community of salvation of the historical people whose self-identity is inextricably bound by such. It is asked, moreover, whether, theologically speaking, Israel can be rightfully reduced to a mere forerunner for the church in the course of salvation history. Does the historical nation serve now only as a type of the church? Or is it perhaps merely a premier illustration of the plight of religious humanity at large? Could any of these views possibly represent the perspective of Paul?

Indeed, the advance of Pauline scholarship in the contemporary era has led to a greater sensitivity to the significance of historical Israel for the apostle (something that can, despite the above criticism, be seen in several respects already in Käsemann as compared to Dodd). With the advent of the New Perspective and thus a new appraisal of Paul's understanding of Judaism and the Torah—that they should no longer be viewed as foils against which he makes his "Christian" claims—this has continued to develop. That being said, many aspects of Dodd and Käsemann's respective interpretations do surface in those of several New Perspective scholars. And clearly indicative here are James D. G. Dunn, N. T. Wright, and Terence L. Donaldson.

THE CHURCH IS ISRAEL: JAMES D. G. DUNN, N. T. WRIGHT, AND TERENCE L. DONALDSON

> A Christianity which does not understand itself in some proper sense as "Israel" forfeits its claim to the scriptures of Israel. Likewise, so long as Jewish-Christian dialogue remains a dialogue

> between "Judaism" and "Christianity," it cannot really begin to engage with the arguments of Paul. (Dunn 1998: 508)

> [T]he list of Jewish privileges in [Romans] 9:4f. is not arbitrary, but echoes precisely those privileges which, throughout Romans up to this point, Paul has shown to be transferred to the Jews' representative Messiah, and, through him, to all those who are "in him," be they Jewish or Gentile. Sonship, glory, covenants, law, worship, promises, patriarchs: all has become the glory of the church in Christ. This intensifies the irony—and, for Paul, the agony—of the present situation. (Wright 1991: 237)

> In his first-generation situation, expecting the return of Christ and the consummation of salvation to occur soon, he could insist, as his basic conviction impelled him to do, that membership in Israel was determined by Christ, not Torah, while at the same time continuing to take for granted—in accordance with another of his core convictions—the traditional, Torah-based distinctions between Jew and Gentile. But there was at least a latent tension between these core convictions which Paul, even with the full panoply of his rhetorical powers deployed in the task, could not fully overcome. (Donaldson 1997: 306)

As is often noted, it was James D. G. Dunn in his 1982 Manson Memorial Lecture who coined the phrase, "the new perspective on Paul," designating this movement in New Testament scholarship. And committed to the New Perspective's reappraisal of Second Temple Judaism, and thus Paul's understanding and treatment of the Torah, Dunn, Wright, and Donaldson also hold in common the notion that for Paul the church is to be in some way identified with Israel. Of course, each demonstrates in their reading a particular way in which this is the case.

According to both Donaldson and Dunn, Paul ultimately redefines Israel in terms of Christ, but he nevertheless continues to uphold the abiding theological significance of the historical nation. For Wright, however, historical Israel relinquishes its role in God's redemptive program. This role is taken up by Christ and thus by those "in Christ"—i.e., the church.

Two "Israels"?

Central to Dunn's view of the relationship of church and Israel is the eschatological tension between the "already" and the "not yet," in which the identity of Israel has been bifurcated (cf. 1988: 526; 1998: 519–20, 523,

525). While in the present time historical Israel as a corporate whole has rejected the gospel, many—Jews as well as gentiles—have come to Christ faith. As representing God's elect people, the identity of "Israel" belongs to them. But despite this development in the course of salvation history, the historical nation—irrespective of Christ faith—cannot be severed from its historic status as God's elect people. They can neither, therefore, be properly understood as anything other than Israel. It will not be until the eschaton when historical Israel in total will come to accept Jesus as the Messiah. And at that time Israel will be one, the eschatological tension being finally resolved (cf. 1988: 527).

Donaldson's analysis (1997) sees the notion of two "Israels" arising from the hypothesis that Paul conceives of his gentile converts as proselytes[7] to an "Israel" defined by Christ faith rather than the observance of Torah. Yet, Donaldson equally maintains that "Israel" as traditionally demarcated by Torah remains a significant category for Paul. Like Dunn, Donaldson affirms on the basis of Rom. 11 that historical Israel's failure in large part to accept the Christ gospel will continue only until the Parousia, at which time it will experience its promised eschatological salvation (cf. 1997: 193, 216ff.). Such could only be maintained if Paul assumed a continuing role for the historical nation during the present dispensation.

In Wright's view, for Paul, historical Israel's role as God's elect people is wholly taken up and fulfilled by its redeeming, representative Messiah, the "true Israel," who took upon himself the curse of exile and exhausted it (cf. 1991: 151, 155; 1997: 95). Accordingly, Paul "system-

---

7. The concept of proselytism in Second Temple Judaism has its roots in the preexilic category of the גר, or resident alien, who in the Torah is seen largely as standing in equality to the native Israelite before the law. The LXX renders the term גר as προσήλυτος, and "in rabbinic usage גר (sometimes with the addition of צדק) refers to the proselyte proper" (Donaldson 1997: 55). Donaldson (pp. 57–58) notes the wide distribution of references to proselytism in the literature of the period: Palestinian pseudepigrapha (cf., e.g., Jdt. 14.10; Tob. 1.8; 2 Bar. 41.4); Josephus, referring to Fulvia in Rome (*Ant.* 18.82), Helena and Izates in Adiabene (*Ant.* 20.34–53); Philo (cf., e.g., *Virt.* 102; *Spec. Laws.* 1.51–52; 4.178); Tannaitic sources (cf., e.g., *m. Bik.* 1.4; *b. Pesah.* 87b; *m. 'Abot* 1.12; *b. Šabb.* 31a; *Sipre Num.* 108; *Mek.* on Exod. 20.10; *b. Sanh.* 97b; the thirteenth benediction in the *Shemoneh Esreh*); Christian literature (cf., e.g., Matt. 23.15; Acts 2.11; 6.5; 13.43; Justin, *Dial.* 122); Greek and Roman authors (cf., e.g., Dio Cassius, *Hist. Rom.* 37.17.1; 57.18.5; 67.14.1–3; Juvenal, *Sat.* 14.96; Horace, *Sat.* 1.4.142–43). The profile of proselytism that arises from these texts includes (a) exclusive devotion to the God of Israel, (b) incorporation into the people of Israel, and (c) circumcision as an entry requirement for male converts.

atically transfer[s] the privileges and attributes of 'Israel' to the Messiah and his people" (1991: 250; 2001a: 689–90). While there continues to exist, then, an Israel defined by traditional ethnic markers including the observance of Torah, there is also now an "Israel according to promise"; a "worldwide family" that singularly represents the people of God (1991: 238; cf. 2001a: 636).

The Role of Torah in the Dispensation of Christ

Though it is evident that Donaldson and Dunn possess quite similar views on the question at hand, Donaldson suggests that Dunn's perspective presents a certain inconsistency. Dunn asserts as a priori problematic for Paul, in light of the Christ event, the emphasis placed by historical Israel upon "physical and national factors, on outward and visible enactments" with the result that the covenant was distorted and its promise destroyed (1990: 227). And this is where Dunn finds basic agreement with Wright (see below). But for Donaldson, that Paul supplants the Torah with Christ is not the consequence of a notion whereby the Torah, as practiced by first-century Jews, is fundamentally antithetical to God's covenant purposes.

Donaldson notes the exception Dunn takes with both the traditional Protestant approach, as well as Sanders' "solution before plight" reading, which in the end trades a Lutheran Paul for a Paul who is inexplicable and idiosyncratic. While it would seem that he understands Paul's critique of the Torah to be primarily (though not entirely) relevant only to the period following Christ's coming (in some distinction to Donaldson's suggestion otherwise, but in any case, more strongly indicated in Dunn 1998: 143–55), Donaldson (1997: 341) remarks that Dunn's

> solution to this unpalatable set of alternatives is to argue that by using the Torah as an ethnic boundary marker the Jews were misapprehending the nature of the covenant. But surely the idea of a family of Abraham's descendants, marked out by circumcision, food laws, and so on, is an essential part of the covenant itself. Thus the price Dunn pays to render Paul more explicable is ethnic Israel itself.

Although Dunn's reading affirms the historical nation's continuing right to the title of "Israel" in the full "covenantal" sense, seemingly inconsistent with this is Dunn's simultaneous contention that Paul wholly rejects the ongoing function of the Torah in setting Israel apart from the other nations. Donaldson observes, rather, that there exists in Paul a "certain element of category-confusion: the boundary of Abraham's family being marked here by Christ (e.g., Gal 3:29) and there by circumcision (e.g., Rom 11:25); Gentiles being equal members with Jews of the former but categorically differentiated from Jews in the latter; and so on" (pp. 160–61).

But despite this difference and the distinct approaches taken between Dunn and Donaldson, it is evident that an even greater disparity exists between their respective views and that of Wright. With particular regard to Donaldson's position, there are two primary and interconnected points of contention noted by him that ultimately lead to the disparity between his reading and that of Wright's on this question. First is Wright's assertion that for Paul Jesus—in his life, death and resurrection—has brought to a complete fulfillment Israel's role as God's elect people. Second is his notion that Paul understood God's redemptive program as having as its fundamental goal a "worldwide family" void of the Jew/gentile differentiation rendered by Torah. These notions are prominent features of Wright's interpretation of both Romans (cf. 1991: 238–41; 2001a: 636; 1997: 108) and Galatians.

Illustrative is Wright's analysis of Gal. 3.10ff., in which central to Paul's argument is the understanding of Israel's present experience of exile due to their covenant infidelity, as predicted by the Torah. Accordingly, Wright comments, "The Torah looks as though it might render the promise to Abraham, and to his worldwide family, null and void" (1991: 142; cf. Donaldson 1997: 154–55). But "the death of Jesus, precisely on a Roman cross which symbolized so clearly the continuing subjugation of the people of God, brought the exile to a climax" (Wright 1991: 146). And in doing so Christ makes possible Israel's subsequent covenant renewal, which was likewise predicted by the Torah. It is by virtue of this renewal that Israel's elect purpose of being the means through which the nations would be blessed can finally be fulfilled, as per the original promise to Abraham (p. 153).

The Torah, then, functioning to demarcate Israel from the other nations, has reached its intended conclusion. It cannot continue to stand as it is at odds with the ultimate covenant purpose of God, which, as Wright concludes from his reading of Gal. 3.15–18, "always envisaged a single family, not a plurality of families" (1991: 163–64; cf. Donaldson

1997: 155–56). Thus, the implications of the Christ event are summed up in Rom. 3.22 and 10.12: "there is no distinction between Jew and Greek."

Donaldson, in basic agreement with Wright, affirms that Paul (a) relegates the Torah to a preparatory role prior to Christ, and (b) understands Christ as "the representative individual of the representative family, [and thus the] . . . representative of all" (1997: 245).[8] However, he parts company with Wright in his readiness on these premises to deny the legitimacy of a distinct role for historical Israel apart from the church in God's redemptive plan, or even as being a distinct entity within the church itself, as (Donaldson holds) the logic of Wright's reading demands. Donaldson suggests that Paul's *Heilsgeschichte* is a "significant reconfiguration of traditional expectations, not the smooth continuation of them" proposed by Wright (Donaldson 1997: 244). The Christ event ushers in an unexpected "interim period" (cf. Schweitzer 1968: 90ff.) that brings the era of Torah to its close. It does not inaugurate the final age of salvation, but provides, rather, a limited period of time "during which gentiles are provided an opportunity to enter the covenant community," before the final salvation of historical Israel (1997: 244).

Donaldson further points out that Paul's assertion of "no distinction" should not be understood in an unmitigated sense, but as an affirmation of the gentiles' equal status with Jews in the covenant on the basis of Christ faith. In all, he appeals to three key aspects that demonstrate the ongoing significance of historical Israel for Paul: (a) his conviction concerning their final salvation at the eschaton; (b) the theological significance he assigns to an identifiable Jewish remnant within the church; and (c) his self-conscious apostolic mission to the gentiles in particular. Donaldson (1997: 157) concludes therefore of Wright's reading:

> Israel, as a Torah-delineated, ethnic group, gets squeezed out of the picture. For Wright, the role of Israel is taken over by Christ without remainder, so much so that any hope of the eschatological salvation of ethnic Israel is eliminated from Romans 11, "all Israel" being read to mean "all in Christ." In order to preserve a Paul who stands in greater continuity with Israel's traditions, Wright is prepared to abandon ethnic Israel itself.

But in defense of his own position, Wright (2001a: 451–52) notes,

---

8. Donaldson agrees, moreover, with Wright's thesis regarding the function of Torah in concentrating the sin of humanity that would ultimately be borne by Israel's Messiah.

The more we examine the Jewish roots of the Christian faith, the more we are bound to discover that all the early Christians known to us defined themselves with joy as God's Israel, living in and seeking to share the blessings of the messianic age that had dawned with Jesus, the new age for the whole world that began when Jesus rose from the dead. This is hardly supersessionism, unless we are to charge Isaiah, Ezekiel, Deuteronomy even, and figures like John the Baptist, and indeed the Essenes, with that crime as well. Making the totally Jewish claim that God will renew, or has renewed, the covenant, throwing its membership open as far and wide, was unpopular when the prophets did it, when Jesus did it, when Paul did it.

Historical Israel is not, Wright asserts, superseded or replaced by a "superior group" in his reading. Rather, Israel is transformed by virtue of its Messiah so that it now includes members of the historical nation *and* representatives of the other nations as well. Israel is thus, "as was always promised, both less and more than the physical family of Abraham: less, as in 9:6–13; more, as in 4:13–25" (2001a: 690).

THE IMPACT OF SHIFTING PARADIGMS

As New Perspective scholars, Dunn, Wright, and Donaldson read Paul with a very different understanding of "justification by faith," while the traditional understanding of this doctrine is integral to both Dodd and Käsemann's interpretations of the relationship of church and Israel. Nevertheless, there are several similarities to be found in a comparison of Dodd and Käsemann's reading with that of these scholars.

Salvation History

Similar to the views of Dodd, Dunn, Wright, and to a somewhat lesser extent Donaldson, all demonstrate in their readings an emphasis on the continuity of salvation history, more than discontinuity, which is a prominent feature of Käsemann's reading.[9] It is, however, only Wright

---

9. Dunn (1998: 145–50) does stress the epochal contrast between the periods before and after Christ, as apparent in Rom. 5.12–21; Gal. 4.21–31; and esp. 2 Cor. 3.4–18. But the eschatological division of time marked by the coming of Christ is maintained within a larger salvation-historical—"promise and fulfillment"—schema, rather than antithetical to such. Wright shares a similar understanding. Dunn remarks: "For Paul the gospel of Christ would have been impossible to understand except as a means of fulfilling the promise to Abraham and as marking a line of continuity with God's saving purpose for Israel" (1993: 41; cf. 1994).

who, like Dodd, arrives on this basis at the conclusion that the church is Israel in total. Though decrying the "psychologizing" of Dodd in his treatment of Paul and the law (as one of several casualties of the old paradigm's faith vs. works antithesis), it seems evident that Dodd's view is still of significant influence to Wright. Wright employs the very same language of "climax" as Dodd in order to articulate the significance of the Christ event in relation to Israel's salvation history. Both clearly point to a realized eschatology manifest in the understanding of Christ as the full embodiment of the prophetic promises to Israel. Though not following through with precisely the same implications, the notion of an eschatological climax in Christ is likewise integral to Dunn's view.

Jewish Privilege?

Both Dunn and Wright also share to a certain degree Dodd and Käsemann's assessment of first-century Judaism in terms of special privilege over the gentile world—what Dodd referred to as a "national arrogance" that was fostered from their commitment to the Torah. Though Dunn's reading is grounded in the notion of covenantal nomism, and thus distinct from Dodd and Käsemann, Dunn (1990: 200) notes similarly that Paul came to take exception to the "works of the law," as they were understood in terms of "Jewish prerogative and national monopoly." He comments, "It is this attitude which Paul attacks in criticizing Jewish 'boasting,' their misplaced emphasis on the outward and physical, their claim to an exclusive Jewish righteousness" (1990: 231). To insist upon the continued observance of the traditional practices prescribed by Torah as a basis of covenant righteousness "was to ignore both the way the covenant began and the purpose it had been intended to fulfill in the end." Through Christ "God's covenant purpose had reached its intended final stage in which the more fundamental identity marker (Abraham's faith) reasserts its primacy over against the too narrowly nationalistic identity markers of circumcision, food laws and Sabbath" (1990: 197–98).

The "Righteousness of God"

In agreement with Käsemann, and contrary to Dodd, all three of the above scholars (as generally consistent with New Perspective thought) understand the notion of "God's righteousness" not as an absolute ethical standard on the basis of which God metes out reward or punishment,[10] but as primarily God's own faithfulness. Yet, contrary to Käsemann, they each understand this faithfulness specifically in the context of God's covenant with Israel, rather than the redefinition of such in terms of all creation (as a consequence of Käsemann's rejection of Jewish particularism).[11]

That Paul links God's righteousness with the salvation of the gentiles is, according to Donaldson (1997: 95), a feature of Paul's reworking of Jewish universalism rather than a rejection of particularism. Wright's view here, as similarly true of the respective positions of Dunn and Donaldson, stresses the ultimate purpose of the covenant in Paul's thinking: that "the promises were both *to* Israel and *through* Israel to the rest of the world" (2001a: 747).

The Final Salvation of "All Israel"

Both Dunn and Donaldson largely follow Käsemann's reading of Rom. 11 with respect to the final salvation of historical Israel. Such will take place through an eschatological miracle at the time of the Parousia. Again, this is integral to the notion that historical Israel retains its salvation-historical significance throughout the new age inaugurated by the resurrection of Christ. And this is despite the simultaneously held view of Dunn and Donaldson that Paul has redrawn the covenant boundary marker around Christ in place of Torah.

It is only Wright who so thoroughly redefines Israel in terms of Christ faith that he, like Dodd, holds such a proposal to be entirely antithetical to Paul's theological program, which is centered on the premise of "no distinction" between Jew and gentile. Unlike Dodd, however, Wright does not then discount Rom. 11 as a sudden resurgence of national

---

10. Dodd understands δικαιοσύνη in Paul, typically translated as "righteousness," to bear this sense. Cf. the translation of the term as "justice" in *The New English Bible, New Testament* (ed. C. H. Dodd; Cambridge: Cambridge University Press, 1961).

11. According to Käsemann (1971: 108) in Paul's theology the covenant itself is universalized—transformed from "Moses and Sinai" to the "creation of the world." Paul understands God's righteousness to be revealed in the founding of a wholly new covenant, not in a renewal of the old (cf. 1980: 79–80). Rather than a historically continuous relationship between them, the old and new covenants stand, therefore, in an antithetical one. It is the contrast of ages—of "Adam and Christ, of fallen and redeemed creation"—that represents the center of Paul's ecclesiology.

patriotism. Instead, he advances an exegetical alternative to the majority interpretation in support of his thesis that the church *is* Israel.

AN "ISRAEL-CENTERED" INTERPRETATION?

It would seem that Dunn, Wright, and Donaldson have sought to establish a more thoroughly Jewish-thinking Paul. But questions still remain for many scholars as to the critical theological difference developed by their respective interpretations. It would seem that an "Israel" no longer identified by traditional ethnic makers, particularly the practice of Torah, becomes the focal point of God's redemptive program—at least with respect to the period between the cross and the Parousia. And it is therefore asked if historical Israel is then rendered, if not obsolete, as has been suggested of Wright's reading, effectively irrelevant all but until the eschaton, as is arguably implicit in the reading of Dunn. Even if not at the expense of Torah observance, as per Donaldson's position, does equating the church with Israel inevitably mean the marginalization of the historical nation? Thus, the leading question becomes, once more, whether this could indeed be representative of Paul's perspective.

For several other contemporary scholars, such interpretations do not properly relate and/or reconstruct the sociological context from within which Paul the missionary worked. Nor do they accurately reflect the theological matrix within which the early Christ movement understood itself. But perhaps more to the point, it is held by some that any reading that seeks to identify the church with Israel, despite attempts to explain otherwise, serves ultimately to disinherit God's historically elect people, a notion that Paul categorically rejects (cf. Rom. 11.1, 11, 29). Two such scholars are William S. Campbell and Mark D. Nanos.

The Church Is Not Israel: William S. Campbell and Mark D. Nanos

> We must continue then to stress that the "church" in Paul's perspective is inseparably related to Israel—through Christ as Israel's Messiah and through the righteous remnant of Israelites, that nucleus of Christ followers through and from whom, the church grew and developed. But however related to Israel, the church is not Israel; Israel's identity is unique and cannot be taken over by gentile Christ-followers, or even completely shared by them. . . . All Christ-followers have a shared identity in that all of them are together one in Christ, but oneness is not sameness and they dif-

fer in that some are and remain Israelites and some are of gentile extraction. (Campbell 2006: 170)

Interpreters continue to miss the central point of Paul's instructions in [Rom. 9–11], in fact, throughout the letter, when they assert that Paul saw the church replacing or becoming Israel, or gentiles as "true Jews," etc. Paul would have responded to these suggestions as he did to the suggestion that the Law was obsolete, "May it never be!" Paul insisted that Israel's distinctive role not only was maintained, but was still the priority. The church was a new entity that consisted of Jews and gentiles coming together in Christ equally, but this meant Israel and the nations had come together to give glory to the God of the whole world (8:18–21; 11:25–36; 15:5–12; 16:25–27), not that Israel alone, as now represented by the church, would give glory to God. (Nanos 1996: 149)

The views of both Campbell and Nanos stress the centrality of historical Israel in Paul's theology and apostolic mission. Integral to each of their readings is the premise that Paul in no way redefines Israel in terms of Christ or Christ faith. Torah-observant Jews, who alone constitute Israel, retain their ethnic distinctiveness as well as their priority in salvation history, and this is not contrary to the gospel of Christ. Rather, Paul affirms that righteousness is now determined by Christ faith, and thus gentiles qua gentiles can on this basis share with Jews qua Jews in God's covenant with Israel.

Equality Is Not Sameness

Campbell and Nanos each point to the Shema as fundamental to Paul's thought, in which the differentiation between Jew and gentile is inextricably connected with the notion of monotheism, for God is the God of *both* Jews and gentiles. Additionally stressed in their respective interpretations is the social reality faced by Paul, whose primary aim was to bring and hold together in one community Jewish and gentile Christ followers in a context of mutual respect and equality.

The very success of his missionary endeavor was dependent upon the degree to which each group could accept the legitimacy of the other's ethnic identity and practice, however qualified by Christ faith. As such, Paul encouraged Torah obedience on the part of Jews as being fully consistent with his gospel. Moreover, he insisted upon halakhic requirements for his gentile converts as consistent with traditional "righteous gentile" conceptions in first-century Judaism that, in accordance with the apostolic decree, "enable[d] voluntary social relations with Jewish Christ-followers" (Campbell 2006: 58).

A Non-Sectarian Paul

Further, both Campbell and Nanos argue that Paul was *not* a sectarian who sought to establish socially distinct groups from the greater synagogue community.[12] Of particular note in this regard is Paul's collection project for the Jewish Christ followers in Jerusalem. This "witnesses against a sectarian mentality in Paul because in it he manifests hope rather than the despair typical of sects who withdraw from the larger group" (Campbell 2006: 48). Paul should thus be viewed as a Jewish reformist who understood that the eschatological age had dawned with the appearance of Israel's Messiah, and on this basis gentiles could participate as full and equal members in the community of salvation without becoming Jewish proselytes. Campbell (2006: 66) asserts,

> Pauline Christ-followers were at one and the same time related in some sense to a Jewish symbolic universe but simultaneously, required to remain distinct from Jews. This was essentially the crux of Paul's problem as we understand it. But even as presented in this way, this does not mean that Paul wished his communities to develop an entirely separate identity from Judaism.

The failure of certain Jews to share Paul's conviction notwithstanding, historical Israel is the only "Israel" of which Paul knows. Instead of a transfer of identity, then, from one group to another, the largely gentile churches Paul established were for him subgroups within Israel. They consisted of a faithful Jewish remnant and representatives from the nations who had turned from idolatry in worship of Israel's God. And Paul's hope was that Israel's complete restoration, signaled by the rem-

---

12. Campbell (2006: 47) points out that even if it be granted that the Pauline communities were in fact socially distinct from the synagogue, this still "does not deny some contact," and perhaps could "presuppose some positive links between diverse groups, as in the case of modern political parties." It is clear, moreover, that Paul himself "maintained his links with synagogue worship," and, to the extent that Acts represents an accurate historical portrayal, "even with the Temple." In agreement with Sanders, Campbell further notes that "punishment implies inclusion. . . . That Paul suffered under Jewish discipline is one of the best attested aspects of his life and letters, indicating the apostle's rugged determination to cling to his ancestral faith. A sectarian apostle would have no such struggle [cf. 2 Cor. 11.24]" (p. 48).

nant, would eventually come to fruition in fulfillment of the prophetic promises.

Campbell (2006: 52) suggests, moreover, that "identity precedes theology, and that theological constructions emerge to solve the problem of identity rather than create it" (cf. Lieu 1996: 47–51, 277–90; 2002a). Thus, why would it have taken so long for the eventual schism between Christianity and Judaism to occur if already at the time of Paul's writing the church understood itself as Israel? Campbell concludes that such an identification could not have yet been realized, and only developed after the schism had occurred, long after the time of Paul.

DIVERGENCE WITHIN THE NEW PERSPECTIVE

Both Campbell and Nanos observe along with Dunn, Wright, and Donaldson that Paul's overarching concern, particularly in Galatians and Romans, is the relationship between Jews and gentiles now that the eschatological age has been inaugurated in Christ. Common in most respects to all five scholars is that Paul's criticism of Jewish practice has nothing to do with a misguided attempt to merit the status of righteousness with God. It concerns, rather, an attachment to ethnocentric covenant entrance requirements; a refusal to see Christ as the new basis of covenant membership, and thus the equal standing of gentile Christ followers with Jews in the community of salvation. Moreover, all five scholars read Paul primarily in terms of a salvation history approach, emphasizing the continuity of God's purposes.

Yet, in contrast to Dunn and Wright, Campbell and Nanos suggest that Paul's critique of Jewish practice on these grounds is not an a priori rejection of traditional covenant identity markers. Nanos (2002a: 98–99) asserts that the debate in which Paul should be situated is whether other covenant identity markers suitable for the new age, namely trust in God's act in Christ and concomitant reception of the Spirit, should be recognized among the gentile Christ followers by Jews. While Paul may insist upon Christ faith for the Jew and gentile alike, he does not deny in any way the validity of Torah-prescribed practices for Jews, but only that they should not be imposed upon gentiles in Christ (1996: 178, 183–84). Closer to this view is Donaldson, who holds that Paul presupposes and thus positively affirms the Torah's continuing role in demarcating Israel from the nations.

To the extent that Dunn and Donaldson view historical Israel as possessing an ongoing theological significance for Paul, they are in basic agreement with the positions of both Campbell and Nanos. In further agreement with Campbell (1992: 92; 1993b: 445), though contrary to Nanos' interpretation, is Dunn and Donaldson's readings of Rom. 11, in which Paul postulates the final salvation of "all Israel" after the ingathering of the gentiles, and at or just prior to the Parousia.

But this is where the similarities on the matter at hand largely end. *While there is broad consensus that a central issue for Paul is the Jew-gentile relationship in God's redemptive program, the fundamental ground of disagreement between each set of scholars are the terms in which Paul defines God's people in the dispensation of Christ.*

Could Paul have viewed the church outside of the category of "Israel," the historic title for the people of God? On the other hand, could Paul have thought of God's historically elect people, Israel, as any other but the ethnic group who practices Torah? For Dunn and Wright the answer is apparently "no" to the first question and "yes" to the second. Campbell and Nanos would answer oppositely. Donaldson would seemingly answer "no" to both questions. It is these disparate frameworks from within which each scholar reads Paul that result in several specific points of contention.

The Context of Paul's Rhetoric: "Intra-Christian" or "Intra-Jewish"?

No doubt instructive to many readings that equate the church with Israel, scholarship has generally understood Paul's argument in both Galatians and Romans in the context of a dispute between rival Christ-following factions. On this point Dunn (2001: 310) notes, "Paul's treatment of the law in his letters was formulated in dialogue and dispute not with non-Christian Jews, but with fellow Christian Jews." Implicit in this, a view held by the majority of scholars, is a sectarian understanding of the communities Paul founded that more easily lends itself to an ecclesiological redefinition of Israel. It is Nanos' contention, however, that the proper context in which to read the letter to the Galatians is that of an inter- and intra-Jewish debate (2002a: 75–76, 97–98; 2002b; 1998; cf. also Campbell 2006: 64–67). And he holds that Romans is likewise addressed to a synagogue subgroup (1996: 31, 68–75).

Nanos's reading of both letters, unlike Dunn, Wright, or Donaldson, emphasizes an "Israel-centered" worldview for Paul within a social and institutional context, rather than a purely theological or conceptual one (cf. esp. Nanos 2002a: 96–100; 2002b: 397). The synagogue did not cease representing for him the covenant community, despite the failure of certain Jewish groups, even if the majority, to recognize Jesus as Israel's Messiah, and embrace the theology and praxis of Paul and the Christ-following coalition. The central question in dispute for Paul is therefore the proper relationship between the greater Jewish community, which remains "Israel," and subcommunities of gentile Christ followers who possess an equal share in Israel's election privileges without themselves becoming part of Israel.

The interpretation of Gal. 6.16 is an important test case. Is the "Israel of God" none other than the historical nation, as asserted by Campbell and Nanos, or the church of Jews and gentiles as per the readings of Dunn, Wright, and Donaldson? In Campbell's view (2006: 49), if "gentiles are so designated, even if only in association with Jewish Christ followers, they may then separate from Jewish Christ followers and yet retain title to Israel and her heritage independently, a possibility Paul warns against in Rom. 11." It cannot be, then, that Paul in any way refers in Gal. 6.16 to gentiles, as this would seemingly contradict Paul's concern over historical Israel's theological and sociological integrity. Similarly debated is the reference to a "true Jew" in Rom. 2.29. Does this represent a subset of historical Israel, so Campbell and Nanos, or does Paul redefine this title to include gentile Christ followers as well, as both Dunn (1988: 125) and Wright (2001a: 448–49) propose?

"Children of Abraham"

Likewise divergent is the implication drawn from Paul's argument concerning the children of Abraham in Gal. 3 and Rom. 4. Is Paul's claim that gentile Christ followers are children of Abraham equivalent to the suggestion that they are therefore proselytes to an Israel redefined around Christ? In Donaldson's assessment (1997: 104, 126–27), if covenantal nomism is indeed foundational to Paul's thought, Paul could not have conceived of gentile Christ followers as both remaining gentiles and also as full and equal members of Abraham's family, these being contradictory categories. Wright similarly presupposes this dichotomy in his reading of these texts. But because Donaldson also observes that Paul continues to affirm a distinction between Jew and gentile within the covenant boundaries that he has redrawn around Christ, he is forced to recognize a certain degree of "category confusion" on Paul's part.

Unlike Donaldson, however, Campbell and Nanos understand "eschatological pilgrimage" and "righteous gentile" patterns of universalism to explain Paul's underlying justification for gentile inclusion.[13] Thus, the ethnic distinctions assumed by Paul, not least within his argument for gentile inclusion in Abraham's family (cf. Rom. 4.11-12, 16), precisely demonstrate that he could quite readily conceive of gentiles qua gentiles as such.

Campbell (2006: 62-63) remarks that Paul's identification of Christ as the singular seed of Abraham in Gal. 3 could be understood "to deny any role to Judaism after Christ and to claim only individual linking to Christ by faith alone without any communal influence being necessitated." However, Rom. 4 offers "a fuller picture of Abraham's significance for Paul" as "the father of both descendents by his blood and also those by adoption through incorporation into Abraham's blood descendent, Christ." And thus in Rom. 4 Paul's redefinition of "children of Abraham" as inclusive of gentile Christ followers does not, then, imply that they are in any way "Israel." Rather, it suggests only that they have been made acceptable before God and coparticipants with Jews in the community of salvation.

Romans 9-11

Campbell takes similar exception to Wright's approach to Rom. 9-11, in which historical Israel's role in God's covenant purposes has culminated

---

13. Donaldson (1997: 85, 147-48) contends that righteous gentile notions are ruled out as Paul does not differentiate the way the Torah is to be observed for gentiles over against Jews, nor does Paul hold the Torah to be still in effect and sufficient for Jews. In contrast, Nanos argues that not only did Paul believe Jews should continue to submit to Torah, but he also expected gentile Christ followers to observe the halakhot befitting righteous gentiles, which Nanos links to the phrase "the obedience of faith" (Rom. 1.5; 16.26).

Further, Donaldson (1997: 193) understands eschatological pilgrimage notions to be ruled out primarily by Paul's assertion in Rom. 9-11 concerning Israel's present failure and future restoration at the time of the Parousia, only *after* the full inclusion of the gentiles. And this utterly fails to comport with the logic that lay behind the eschatological pilgrimage notion, which calls for the restoration of Israel as the impetus for the conversion of the gentiles to Israel's God. However, Nanos' reading of Rom. 11.25-27 circumvents this objection by postulating Israel's restoration as a present phenomenon for Paul.

in Christ, with the result that "Israel" has been transformed into the church of Jews and gentiles. In this reading Paul conceives of a transfer of identity from the historical nation to its Messiah and then to the Messiah's people.

Absent in Campbell's interpretation is any sense that Israel's election was understood by Paul as functional in character (not least in terms of being the place wherein God concentrated the problem of sin; cf. Wright 1991: 239-40), and brought to its completion by Christ.[14] Here, the notion that Israel's covenant privileges are now made equally available to gentiles is subordinate to the fact that they are enjoyed first by the historical nation, however dependent upon Christ faith. Thus, historical Israel inalienably represents God's elect covenant people, though gentiles too are being called to share in their inheritance.

Campbell's Paul begins in Rom. 9.6 by pointing strictly to a selection from within the nation (1992: 44, 143; 1993b: 442-43). But Wright (1991: 238; 2001a: 636) reads this verse as drawing a radical distinction between two "Israels": the historical nation and the church of Jews and gentiles. In 9.24-29 Campbell (1992: 47-48) understands the focus to remain upon the historical nation. Gentiles enter the discussion only in a secondary manner. As such, the Hosea citations in vv. 25-26, traditionally taken as a prooftext for gentile inclusion in the people of God, is read by Campbell as a reference exclusively to historical Israel. He argues that this is consistent with both the original context of those passages, as well as the citations from Isaiah in vv. 27-29, which Paul unquestionably applies to the present circumstances of the nation. Campbell (2000: 199) explains,

> Rejected Israel, like the northern tribes, will be restored. This is Paul's primary thesis, but in and with the restoration, another "non-people," the Gentiles, will also be blessed. Paul does apply the Hosea citation in a secondary sense, typologically, to Gentiles also, but only after he has first used it to refer to Israel. Like Hosea, he envisages the reuniting of the twelve tribes into one people, that is, the hardening and the remnant parts of Israel will one day be reunited.

---

14. Cf. Campbell 2006: 170: "We can accept that Jesus may rightly be described as the true Israelite who alone fulfilled the divine destiny. But that does not allow us to displace an historic people by even the most righteous of her sons in whom the promises of Israel's restoration have allegedly been fulfilled. Representation is one thing, but displacement is quite another."

In Wright's view (2001a: 642–43), however, the thrust of the passage concerns not the restoration of historical Israel as in any way distinct from the inclusion of gentiles, but rather the creation of one multiethnic people—the church. He explains that the quotations from Hosea "speak of the restoration Israel can expect after exile: it will be a strange reversal of judgment, in which a new word of grace will be spoken to a new people." And this "new people" are the people of the new covenant, the "children of promise who are 'reckoned as seed'" (Rom. 9.8; cf. 8.12–30), which includes gentiles as well as Jews.

Both scholars understand this passage to be anticipatory of what Paul will eventually assert in 11.26. Campbell reads "all Israel" as a corporate designation for the nation, both the "remnant" and those once "hardened." Wright understands "all Israel" as God's whole people, both Jews and gentiles.

IS TRUST IN GOD'S ACT IN CHRIST INDISPENSABLE?

While there are clear differences between the views of Campbell and Nanos with those of Dunn, Wright, and Donaldson, common to all of them is the understanding that Paul insists upon trust in God's act in Christ for Jews and gentiles alike. Christ is the ultimate basis, then, for covenant membership. It seems fair, moreover, to infer from the readings of Campbell and Nanos that while the church existed for Paul under the umbrella of Israel, in as much as it consists of Jewish and gentile Christ followers it can equally be seen as a larger entity encompassing both Israel and the nations (cf. Nanos 2000: 221; Campbell 2006: 138).

Indeed, both scholars stress in their respective interpretations the salvation-historical priority of Israel, the abiding nature and positive valuation of Jewish identity, and thus the perpetual role of the Torah in God's covenant purposes. However, such is viewed as interdependent with God's act in Christ, and subsequent formation of the church. As Campbell (2006: 131) notes, "In our reading the distinctiveness of Jew and gentile in Christ is safeguarded and abides but in a common transformation in Christ. Whilst a new covenant is offered in Christ, we do not see this as a second covenant, but more as a renewal so that continuity in the divine purpose is thereby ensured."

But is the notion that the failure to recognize Jesus as Messiah will ultimately disqualify Jews from the community of salvation incompatible with God's sovereign election of the Jewish people? And is this, therefore, a premise that Paul himself could *never* have entertained, even if only for rhetorical purposes?[15] Further, is it possible that Paul held God's historic covenant with Israel, as established in and through the Torah alone, to be in its own right proficient for their salvation in accordance with divine faithfulness?

In question here is more than the validity of Israel's distinctiveness from the gentile world. It is not merely a matter of distinguishing Israel from the church, in the conviction that God's purposes for historical Israel are not yet fully realized (cf. Campbell 2006: 99). But it is whether (or in what sense) Israel and the (predominately gentile) church—however interrelated as representations of God's people—are nevertheless entities mutually distinct from one another in Paul's theology.

It has been proposed that interpretations that (a) understand the Christ event as being in some way the fulfillment of God's promise to (or covenant with) Israel, and/or (b) are suggestive of a necessary requirement for Jews to convert to "Christianity" in order to be saved, are implicitly anti-Jewish as well as un-Pauline. Two scholars who have argued along these very lines are Lloyd Gaston and Douglas Harink.

CHURCH AND ISRAEL BEYOND THE NEW PERSPECTIVE: LLOYD GASTON AND DOUGLAS HARINK

> As long as Judaism is understood as a kind of Christian heresy to be combated, there will never be an end to Christian anti-Judaism. Is there room in Pauline thought for such a concept as "two religions, two chosen people"? The one who said in another context, "I wish that all were as I myself am" (1 Cor 7:7), probably hoped that all Jews would come to share his faith. . . . Paul is of course concerned to argue for the full right of Gentiles to be equal members of the people of God, and it is to this issue, where Christ language is important, that all of his words are directed (whereas other God language, as in Romans 11, would be more appropriate). But now that that battle has been won, and in the light of subsequent history, Pauline interpreters today need to emphasize the other side, the right of Israel to remain Israel, without being defined by someone else's "mystery," as equal but elder recipients of the grace of God. (Gaston 1987: 33–34)

---

15. That is, if it be supposed he was convinced on the grounds of their special election Jews would necessarily in the end come to trust in God's act in Christ.

> Both liberal and evangelical theologies continue to occlude Israel and the Jews in important ways, either by relativizing Judaism (and Christianity) as one religious path among many (the liberal option) or by continuing to view Christians and the church as replacing the Jews and the synagogue in God's purpose (the traditional and evangelical "supersessionist" option). . . . But I am convinced that any such occlusion of Israel, the Jews, and the synagogue, and relativizing of their constitutive role in Christian theology, whether of the liberal or evangelical kind, is not only a kind of anti-Judaism, but also and more importantly for the present work, fundamentally un-Pauline. (Harink 2003: 151–52)

Emphasizing the theological and ethical implications of historical and contemporary understandings of the relationship of church and Israel in Paul, Gaston and Harink share in many respects the concerns of Campbell and Nanos, but each develop alternative solutions by which to address the matter.

In his *Paul and the Torah* (1987) Gaston points to the "church's centuries long 'teaching of contempt'" towards Judaism, and proposes that the task of the exegete in the context of the post-Auschwitz era is to "expose the explicit or implicit anti-Judaism inherent in the Christian tradition, including the New Testament itself" (p. 2). Harink's *Paul among the Postliberals* (2003) challenges the so-called supersessionist perspective of N. T. Wright, providing a counter-reading of Israel's election based largely on an analysis of Rom. 9–11 (cf. pp. 153–203). Harink condemns what he deems Wright's rigorous supersessionist reading, which if correct makes Paul "the most significant enemy of Judaism in the history of Christianity" (p. 153). He elaborates upon his own reading of Paul on this question in "Paul and Israel: An Apocalyptic Reading," a paper presented at the 2005 Society of Biblical Literature annual meeting.

The Guarantee of Salvation for Historical Israel

Clearly fundamental to the respective views of Gaston and Harink is that Paul presupposes the special election of historical Israel, such that the Jewish people in their entirety, and irrespective of their assent to the Christ gospel, are the primary constituents of God's people and thus possess the assurance of salvation. Each stresses the intrinsic qualities of God—sovereignty, faithfulness, grace, and mercy—and thus divine action over against human response or disposition, whether of works or faith, as the grounds for this reading. Moreover, they both point out that such an emphasis on God's own person and purpose is necessary, because it is only upon this that the (predominately gentile) church possesses any assurance of salvation.

Discontinuity: Two-Covenant vs. Apocalyptic

Additionally, both emphasize a certain discontinuity wrought by the Christ event. For Gaston this means that Paul's soteriology is best understood in terms of two distinct covenants, the one established at Sinai with Israel and another through Christ for the gentiles (cf. esp. pp. 143–44). For Harink it is the sharp antithesis between the old world and new creation inaugurated by the advent of Christ.

But while Harink and Gaston have arrived at several similar conclusions regarding the question at hand, there is, nevertheless, a good deal of variance between their respective positions. The differences between them ultimately arise from Harink's apocalyptic understanding of the Christ event over against Gaston's interpretation of the singularly gentile necessity and purpose for Christ in Paul's theology. Again, while agreeing with Gaston that Jews are saved irrespective of whether they acknowledge the Christ event, Harink asserts that it is nevertheless through Christ that this deliverance is accomplished. It is only because "God has finally and decisively invaded the old cosmos with the advent of Christ," that *both* Israel and the nations can be liberated from the enslaving cosmic powers of sin and death, which "oppose God's good purpose for all creation" (2003: 68).

Grounding much of his understanding from a reading of Rom. 9–11 (cf. 2003: 168ff.), Harink does not fully explicate the logical relationship in Rom. 11 between Israel's hardening/stumbling/disobedience and their final salvation as it further relates to Christ faith. However, he simultaneously maintains that (a) these descriptions of Israel's present condition signify a "failure" (though primarily God's doing) to trust what God has accomplished in Christ; (b) God will, in the end, deliver Israel from this condition; (c) the basis for this deliverance is Israel's special election; and (d) while Jews living in the interim possess an irrevocable place in the community of salvation, there exists a "remnant" who "respond in faith to [the liberating word of Christ]" (2005: 25).

In contrast, Gaston understands neither Israel's hardening nor the remnant as relating in any way to the recognition of Christ as accomplishing Israel's own salvation. Rather, Israel's hardening as described in

Rom. 11.7ff. consists of a certain blindness regarding the fulfillment of God's righteousness in providing through Christ a means of salvation for the gentiles (p. 147). The "remnant" represents those who have not failed to appreciate this, and have thus undertaken the gentile mission with Paul. The cosmic powers to which Paul refers in his letter to the Galatians (cf. 4.3, 8) have brought only the gentile world into enslavement and therefore in need of redemption (cf. pp. 10, 42). No such condition exists for the members of the Sinai covenant.

Both Gaston and Harink (cf. 2005: 17, 21–24) affirm: (a) ethnic distinctions are consistently maintained by and are of continued importance to Paul, and thus an ongoing role for the Torah among Jews is presupposed by him; (b) Paul continues to hold to the theological integrity and legitimacy of Israel as a distinct body from the church; and (c) Paul thinks in terms of one people of God.[16] Yet, the thoroughly separate but equal "religious" differentiation suggestive of Gaston's two-covenant approach—"a gentile church that is an equal partner alongside of Israel" (p. 149)—stands largely antithetical with the implications of Harink's reading.

For Harink, circumcision, the preeminent sign of Torah submission and covenant identity setting Israel apart from the nations, and thus the "first principle" bringing order to the world, is "rendered powerless and invalid *in its world-ordering function*" by virtue of Christ (cf. Gal. 5.6). "The cross of Jesus Christ is now the 'first principle' and the Holy Spirit is the power of the new creation . . . in which Paul finds himself. On the cross the old world order . . . constituted by the ruling principle of circumcision/uncircumcision ceased to exist for him, and he ceased to exist for that old world order" (cf. Gal. 6.14–15) (2005: 5; cf. 2003: 71–72, 80–81). As such, while "covenantal callings, social, economic and political orders, or bodily particularities" are not erased in Christ, they are recontextualized such that they testify and are made subordinate to the gospel (2005: 23).

The Role of Torah in the Dispensation of Christ

Encapsulating the key differences between them are Gaston and Harink's respective views of the relationship of Israel, Torah, and Christ, as particularly found in Rom. 9.30—10.4. In Harink's understanding

---

16. Gaston (p. 33) does, however, also speak here of two chosen peoples.

this section concerns Israel's misguided conviction (a consequence of their hardened condition) that the status of righteousness is attained through dedication to Torah rather than in the resurrection of Christ. He explains,

> [T]o think thus is *sarkikos*—it is for Israel to participate willingly but unknowingly in her own enslavement under the cosmic regime of Sin and Death. Sin lays hold even of the Torah and uses it in the unholy service of the regime of Death, even against the very nature of Torah as "holy and just and good" (7:12). Thus the Torah itself is weak, of no help whatsoever in the war against the enslaving powers. (2005: 14–15)

However, Gaston interprets this section as explicating only Israel's failure to recognize that the goal of the Torah was the expression of God's righteousness found in Paul's gospel of inclusion for the gentiles through Christ. Thus, there is in this reading "no criticism of Torah [or] of Israel for pursuing it. Nothing whatsoever is said about the fulfillability of commandments or the inappropriateness of seeking righteousness in the Torah" (p. 128).

TOWARD A CONCLUSION

The above investigation of the relationship of church and Israel in modern Pauline interpretation has revealed a quite complex picture, involving the perception and interplay of Paul's native (Jewish) context and his Christ convictions. In pursuing this question, what has been central in each of the major viewpoints, as Dunn (2001: 328) has rightly suggested, is the precise character of continuity/discontinuity in the divine activity through history and accompanying sociological realities, as reflected in Paul's letters. No position analyzed here consistently maintains complete continuity or discontinuity, and it is generally agreed that at least in some respects Paul understands a certain measure of both (cf. Dunn 1994: 378).

While it is clear, however, that different emphases have been chosen, it is not simply a matter of a choice of emphasis by which one then arrives at a singular conclusion. The above has demonstrated that "continuity" can be used to argue quite opposing perspectives (e.g., the salvation history reading of Wright, as compared to that of Nanos), and so too "discontinuity" (e.g., the two-covenant reading of Käsemann, as compared to that of Gaston). In either case, ultimately in view is how the several texts upon which all such constructs stand are interpreted and related to one another.

And while it is presupposed here that a coherent Pauline perspective on the question at hand can be found, it unquestionably arises from the midst of distinct rhetorical and/or socio-historical contingencies that must be carefully considered and given due justice before the formulation of any comprehensive hypothesis. The challenge is to arrive at this end without resorting to uncritical, prejudicial use of certain texts at the expense of others. Further, it is to present a coherent conclusion without artificial harmonizing and "forced exegesis," as one encounters throughout the Pauline corpus assertions that collectively propose what may seem, however more apparent than real, an inconsistent—even contradictory—position. What has clearly been shown to be the result of such disparate argumentation by Paul is several equally disparate ways in which his writings can plausibly be understood on the matter.

Thus, chapters 3 and 4 will investigate three primary texts directly addressing the question of the relationship of church and Israel: Rom. 2.29; Gal. 6.16; and Rom. 11.26. The exegetical conclusions gathered here will produce an interpretive matrix for Paul's view of the matter from which a negotiation of the variegated perspectives presented in this chapter may be conducted in chapters 5 and 6.

3

Exegetical Investigation, Part I

> Is Paul a radical Jewish sectarian who redefines Israel "spiritually" as those from all nations who believe the gospel and live "in Christ?" Or is he a rabbi who affirms the ongoing election of ethnic Israel but holds that God has sent Jesus Christ as a special way of salvation for the gentiles? Perhaps the truth about Paul lies between these two extremes or combines them is some way.
> (Charles H. Cosgrove 1997: 1)

IN THE OPENING CHAPTER of his book *Elusive Israel: The Puzzle of Election in Romans* (1997), Cosgrove portrays an imaginary dialogue between three Roman Christ followers living at the time shortly following Paul's death; one is a gentile and the other two are Jews. In debate is the meaning of Paul's letter to the Romans with respect to the identity of Israel. Through the ensuing discussion, Cosgrove is able to demonstrate the multiple and even contrary ways in which Paul's teaching on this matter can be plausibly construed.

Chapter 2 of this present study functions in much the same way, exhibiting an array of both common and conflicting interpretations of the relevant texts that inform these various perspectives on the relationship of church and Israel in Paul. Thus, in this and the following chapter I will set out to analyze three key texts that bear directly on this question: Rom. 2.29; Gal. 6.16; and Rom. 11.26. It is my contention that the exegetical conclusions to be gathered here will allow the greatest degree of clarity in a final negotiation of the question (for purposes of this study) to be taken up in chapters 5 and 6.

THE AUDIENCE OF PAUL'S LETTER TO THE ROMANS

Clearly, Romans has been the primary letter of appeal in addressing the question of the relationship of church and Israel, and the matter arises first in 2.25-29. But an initial concern here is the identity of the audience of the letter. In fact, much of the two-covenant interpretation, particularly the reading of the first person plurals in chapters 5-8 (where Paul explicates the implications of Christ faith) as "we/us gentiles" (cf. Stowers 1994: 255-82; Gager 2000a: 122-27), rests on the notion that the implied or encoded audience of the letter to the Romans (irrespective of the original empirical audience) is exclusively non-Jewish (cf. Stowers 1994: 21-33).

But Esler (2003: 119), in agreement with the current majority opinion that Rom. 16 is an original part of the letter (cf. Gamble 1977; Donfried 1991: 48-52; Fitzmyer 1993: 55-65; Moo 1996: 5-9; Jewett 2007: 4-9), has cast considerable doubt on this conclusion, asserting that "of the twenty-six people greeted by Paul [in 16.3-16] the most prominent four were Judeans,[1] while overall the proportion of Judeans may have reached 50 percent." He points out, therefore, the high improbability that Paul would not have also addressed the letter to Jews, particularly given the fact that to deliberately ignore this group would have been a cause for shame to them, something that the content of the letter suggests he would have avoided at all cost.

Though 1.1-15 is frequently cited as evidence for a gentile audience,[2] as Paul refers here to his apostolic mission among the gentiles (vv. 5-6; vv. 13-15; cf. 16.4), Esler (2003: 113) argues that such a view "depend[s] on both an insensitivity to the ethnic implications of Paul's language . . .

---

1. As pointed out in pp. 4-6 above, "Judeans" is Esler's preferred translation of Ἰουδαῖοι.

2. Romans 11.13 is also cited as support for this conclusion, but Wagner (2002: 268) rightly notes, "Although Paul turns in v. 13 to address his remarks specifically to the Gentiles in his audience, we must be wary of naively reading this rhetorical move as evidence that Paul envisions his audience to be composed entirely of Gentiles. The hypothesis of a mixed Jewish/Gentile audience or of multiple intended audiences may actually make better sense of Paul's decision to single out the Gentiles among his listeners" (cf. Rom. 7.1; 15.1; contra Das 2007: 67-68).

and a faulty grasp of the meaning of his mission in its socioreligious context." While it is reasonable to suggest Paul's primary concern was to bring non-Jews to faith in Christ, one cannot "exclude a geographic dimension from Paul's mission [cf. Cranfield 1977: 20]. His apostleship entailed preaching the gospel outside Judea in the lands inhabited by idolatrous non-Judean peoples (but which also contained a minority population of Judeans)."

> When Paul speaks, first, in 1.5–6, of his mission being "among all the foreigners, among whom are you also," he is referring to his work among the non-Judean peoples of the region, now extending to Rome. Nothing in this excludes the fact that Judeans regularly formed part of this congregation. Nor would any Judean or non-Judean Christ followers in Rome listening to the letter as it was read deduce from this expression that the Judean members were excluded. . . . Similarly, when in v. 13 Paul explains that he wants to come to them "in order that he might reap some fruit also among you just as also among the rest of the foreigners," this simply constitutes an acknowledgment that he wants to have a successful mission in Rome, just as he has had elsewhere, even though his congregations were often composed of Judeans as well as non-Judeans. (pp. 114–15)

I am not persuaded by the arguments put forward by Das (2007: 54–63, 97–102) to the contrary. The assertion that Paul's mission among the gentiles was strictly occupied with non-Jews is clearly belied by 1 Cor. 1.22–24; 7.17–20; 9.20–21. Further, Rom. 16 cannot be simply dismissed as shedding some light on the composition of the *entire* Christ-following community in Rome, which one would have every reason to suppose was in Paul's mind as he wrote the letter (cf. 1.7). Too much should not be made of the second-person form of greeting (cf. esp. v. 16; see also 1 Cor. 16.20b; 2 Cor 13.12), as we see the same form in Phil. 4.21; 1 Thess. 5.26–27; and Col. 4.15–16. In each of these cases those to be greeted are unquestionably included in the letter's implied audience, and do not represent a third party. There is little reason, then, to hold that this is not also true for the people named in Rom. 16.

Given this preliminary observation, the following will begin with an analysis of Rom. 2.29.

ROMANS 2.29: A TRUE JEW

Does this passage indicate that for Paul gentile Christ followers have a right to the name "Jew"? Käsemann (1971: 145-46; 1980: 75), Dunn (1988: 125), and Wright (2001a: 448-49) read the passage in this way. I will conclude similarly. And if indeed a convincing reading can be advanced along these lines then it may serve to support a Pauline view in which the church is, at least in a certain sense, to be identified with Israel.[3]

Though articulated in various ways, it has been largely recognized that Rom. 1.18—3.20 demonstrates the equality of Jews and gentiles in relation to sin and accountability toward God.[4] But that the case Paul makes in chapter 2 is thought to be valid, persuasive, or consistent with other of his statements in Romans and elsewhere engenders considerably more debate.[5] Specifically, 2.17-29 has been characterized as an almost desperate and half-hearted attempt on Paul's part to portray Jewish sinfulness (cf. Donaldson 1997: 139-41; Esler 2003: 152-53). The suggestion has also been made, however, that Paul's rhetorical motivation in this section of the letter has little or nothing to do with a predicament shared by Jews, but that it concerns only the situation of the gentiles who stand outside of God's covenant with Israel (cf. Gaston 1987: 138-39; Stowers 1994: 143-58). In order to draw conclusions as to the identity of the "true Jew" it will be helpful to examine the first half of Paul's critique in 2.17-24, which establishes the primary context for understanding this notion appearing in vv. 25-29.

---

3. Although Ἰουδαῖος and Ἰσραήλ are not synonymous, each term within first-century Judaism could similarly function to demarcate the people of God from the other nations (cf. Gal. 2.15). Paul's readiness to apply the former term to gentile Christ followers would seemingly lend to a readiness to apply the latter in similar fashion.

4. Cf., e.g., Dodd 1932: 45; Bruce 1966: 81-83; Cranfield 1977: 104; Kasemann 1980: 33-36; Bassler 1984: 43-58; Achtemeier 1985: 34; Dunn 1988: 50-51; Elliot 1990: 105-57; Fitzmyer 1993: 296; Stuhlmacher 1994: 33; Thielman 1994: 168-80; Moo 1996: 91-94; Byrne 1996: 79-80; Donaldson 1997: 131-33; Wright 2001a: 448-49; Esler 2003: 143-44; Witherington 2004: 77; Keck 2005: 56-57; Jewett 2007: 148.

5. Cf., e.g., Sanders 1983: 123-35; Räisänen 1986: 94-119. Both have argued that Rom. 2 fails on all the above accounts, a likely result of the fact that Paul's thinking on the matter is retrospective, beginning with the "solution" and only in this light fabricating the "plight" (cf. Sanders 1977: 442-47; see further nn. 14 and 17 below).

Romans 2.17–24: The Reality of Jewish Sinfulness

There is here some measure of consensus among current scholarly opinion. Romans 2.17–24 continues the diatribe style that began in 2.1, following the indictment of the idolatrous gentile world in 1.18–32. Paul questions an imaginary Jewish interlocutor with a series of claims concerning the privileged "religious" status to be found in Jewish identity, and the presumed role in relation to non-Jews fostered by such a position.

But in vv. 21–23 Paul advances several rhetorical questions to the Jewish interlocutor regarding hypocritical behavior; the climactic fifth question in v. 23 asks in summary if he has transgressed Torah. Paul follows this final question with a scriptural proof in v. 24, citing in modified form Isa. 52.5 LXX, which in Paul's rendering exclaims the despising of God's name among the gentiles as a direct result of such hypocrisy.[6]

---

6. The wording of Isa. 52.5 in the LXX is "on account of you my name is continually blasphemed among the gentiles," and concerns Israel's experience of Babylonian exile (cf. Ezek. 36.20–21). Byrne (1996: 101), Hays (1989: 45), Käsemann (1980: 71), Fitzmyer (1993: 318–19), and Jewett (2007: 230–31) understand Paul to have recontextualized the passage such that what was originally a word of compassion and hope for Israel is turned into one of reproach. However, Hays (1989: 45–46) also suggests that this "provocative misreading of Isa. 52.5 is only provisional." He explains, "If [Paul] reads Isa. 52.5 as a reproach, it is a reproach only in the same way that the historical event to which it refers was a reproach; a heightening of the tension of grace, a painful reminder of the discrepancy between human unfaithfulness and the faithfulness of God who will never abandon his covenant people" (cf. 3.1–4; 9–11). Wright (2001b: 142; 2001a: 447–48) similarly looks to the original context of the passage as suggestive of the quotation's function here, which is to point to Israel's ongoing state of "exile" as a consequence of her corporate sins, its end being found only in Christ.

Due consideration should be given to Stanley's assertions (2004: 40–61, 145–50) that (a) many, if not most, of Paul's addressees, and even perhaps Paul himself, would not have been aware of the original context of his scriptural quotations; (b) if such awareness was present in either party, it is still not at all clear there was any intent to communicate such "intertextual echoes"; and (c) authorial intent is not, in any case, the governing criterion of "meaning," but one must take into account the way in which the text may have been received by the audience. Yet the good sense brought to Rom. 2 by the original context of Isa. 52 (which Stanley fails to see; cf. 2004: 147–48) cannot easily be dismissed. Wagner (2002: 36–39) has pointed out that Paul's letter to the Romans "was most likely copied, discussed, and even studied by the Roman churches to whom it was sent" (cf. Gamble 1995: 97–99). One might expect, then, that such intertextual echoes did not escape the attention of these first readers of the letter any more than it has for modern interpreters.

On the significance of the original context of Isaiah for Paul's quotation here, cf. Wagner 2002: 177–78. Similar to Hays and Wright, he comments, "In Romans, as in Isaiah, these words of blame serve only as a prelude to the imminent announcement

While this much seems clear enough, there are nevertheless significant variances in the way these verses are understood that undoubtedly affect the interpretation of 2.25–29.

As routinely referenced, Stowers (1994: 143–58) has shown that 2.17–29 employs the language of "philosopher-talk" familiar to ancient audiences of the Greco-Roman world, and is patterned after "the motif of name versus reality in apostrophes to a fictitious addressee" found in Hellenistic literature (cf., e.g., Maximus of Tyre, *Phil. Or.* 33.2b–c; Epictetus, *Diatr.* 2.19.19; 3.7.17; 24.40–43). The section, then, "parodies the philosophical teacher's admonishing censure of a pretentious would-be philosopher" (Stowers 1994: 147; cf. Epictetus, *Diatr.* 4.8–9). But why does Paul adopt this "well-known character type"?

Doubtful is Stowers's assertion that he is attacking other Jewish "missionary" efforts outside the gospel ministry,[7] whereby such "Jewish teachers think that they can make gentiles righteous before God by teaching them to observe certain works from the law" (1994: 151).[8] Similarly problematic is Gaston's assertion (1987: 139) that Paul is being critical of attempts by some Jewish teachers to proselytize gentiles. The notion that Paul is only concerned here with alternative and inadequate approaches to the "gentile problem," whether proselytism or a "righteous gentile" ideal, is unsustainable throughout the scope of the letter, particularly 11.11–15, which will be dealt with in pp. 100–104 below.

---

that God has redeemed his people Israel. Paul quotes Isaiah 52.5 in Romans 2:24 precisely because he believes that without the gospel, Israel is, figuratively speaking, still in exile, still in bondage to the power of sin like the rest of humanity (Rom. 3:9). But just as the word of judgment in Isaiah 52:5 precedes the herald's announcement of the return from exile in Isaiah 52:7–10, so also Romans 2:24 precedes Paul's exposition of the gospel . . . in Romans 3.21ff. . . . If Paul criticizes his fellow Jews, he does so not as an outsider slinging mud, but as a prophet, wounding that he may heal" (p. 178).

7. However, Stowers (p. 151) points out that the notion of a "missionary," particularly in the "Christian" sense, does not accord with first-century Judaism, in which "Jews did not typically think they had to convert gentiles to Judaism in order to save them." Thus, Stowers views vv. 17–29 as suggestive of a "righteous gentile" ideal, which informs the efforts of the Jewish teacher whom Paul here criticizes.

8. Stowers (p. 151) explains this hypothetical perspective further: "If one can train gentiles to keep universally applicable ethical teachings like the Ten Commandments, then they will be righteous, and the Jew will have fulfilled his task of being a light to the nations." He remarks that for Paul such an approach is severely misguided, because God's singular means of dealing with non-Jews is through Christ, "the ultimate expression of mercy to gentile peoples" (p. 152).

More plausible is the view of the majority of commentators suggested above: that 2.17–24 speaks to a negative condition experienced collectively by the Jewish people in parallel to the gentile world. Esler's analysis (2003) of Rom. 1.18—3.20 in terms of an approach within social identity theory known as recategorization is instructive. He understands the section as a concerted attempt on Paul's part to "persuade his Judean and Greek addressees of the significance of what . . . is a new identity derived from the righteousness of God through faith in Christ" (p. 142).

Paul, confronted with the "problem of persisting subgroup loyalties," could not realistically "suggest that his addressees abandon them; nor does he do so, but rather he self-consciously preserves the two social categories, as in the programmatic affirmation of 1:16." Thus, in order to promote a "common ingroup identity," Paul establishes "a common superordinate identity while simultaneously maintaining the salience of subgroup identities" (pp. 143–44).

Esler continues that while Paul attempts to demonstrate the equal status of the two groups, he does so on different terms relative to each group (p. 144). This is necessary because if Paul were to propose this equality by pointing to identical attributes the groups might then be urged to compete with one another, which could in turn destroy the "single ingroup identity to be achieved." Thus, Paul accomplishes his objective in this section of the letter by first relating how each group in particular is under the dominion of sin, and are therefore "precluded from suggesting they will be harmed by the presence of the other."

However, Neil Elliot (1990: 131) has proposed that 2.17–29 represents the "protasis for an argument *a fortiori*," and "substantiates, in a dramatic way, the second half of the legal principle in 2.12–13." This apostrophe, unlike 2.1–5, "does not accuse, but asks—penetrating questions, but not presumptive of the answer." He explains,

> If anyone enjoyed the privilege of exemption from God's wrath, surely it must be the Jew, who "boasts in God" and "relies upon Torah": but for Paul this possession is itself the medium of the Jew's accountability to God, for it is the very revelation of God's will, the "embodiment of all knowledge and truth." The Jew, above all others, cannot plead ignorance. If the Jew, who possesses such privileges as described in 2.17–20, is not exempt from God's judgment when he or she violates the very Torah that constitutes those privileges (2.12b), then how can Gentiles

who have never shared those privileges lay any claim to God's indulgence (2.12a; cf. 2.3-5)?

But though the charges in 2.21-23 remain hypothetical and not presumptive of guilt, by simply raising these questions to the interlocutor the passage brings the reality of Jewish sinfulness to the forefront. And v. 24 moves beyond the hypothetical; it is a "flat out accusation" (Keck 2005: 83). That some Jews have transgressed the Torah is again suggested in 3.3, and emphatically affirmed in 3.9.[9] While Paul's critique of Israel in 2.17-29 is, then, grounded in the notion of universal sinfulness, it is yet set in distinction to that of the gentile world by the fact that they are God's historical covenant people (cf. 9.4-5; 11.1-2), bearers of the Torah (cf. 2.12b; 3.2[10]; see also, e.g., 2 Bar. 48.20-24), and called to be a "light to the nations" (cf. Deut. 4.5-8; Isa. 2.2-4; 11.9-10; 42.1, 6; 49.6; Tob. 13.11; 14.6; see also Sib. Or. 3.195; Wisd. 18.4; 1 En. 105.1; T. Lev. 14.3ff.; 1Q28b 4.27). As Wright (2001a: 445) has therefore observed, "the bearers of the solution have become part of the problem."

The Fulfillment of Torah

Beginning in v. 25 Paul suggests that circumcision is of value—by which he undoubtedly means that it functions as a sign of covenant membership (cf. Dunn 1988: 119-20; Jewett 2007: 231-33)—only if it is accompanied by obedience to Torah. Further, gentiles who are obedient to Torah are reckoned[11] as circumcised—members of the covenant alongside obedient Jews. Paul has already claimed in 2.13-16 that the possession of

---

9. Scholars (cf., e.g., Sanders 1983: 125; Bassler 1984: 54; Räisänen 1986: 99) have persistently read πᾶς in terms of an unwarranted individualism (cf. 3.23; 11.26, 32), when Paul's point here is only that the Jewish people collectively, no less than the gentile world (cf. 1.18-2.16), and thus *all* of humanity, are in bondage to sin (cf. 3.19-20; 5.12-14; 7.7-13; Gal. 3.21-22; see also Stowers 1994: 179-84). The catena of scriptural texts in 3.10-18 (which was possibly compiled independent of and prior to Paul; cf. Keck 1977) that in their original contexts lament the presence of the wicked (and *not* to the exclusion of Israelites/Jews) makes this case precisely: the existence of any such individuals is sufficient to demonstrate a problem affecting the whole; see further below.

10. The "oracles of God" (τὰ λογία τοῦ θεοῦ) entrusted to the Jews, which Paul cites as the primary example of their advantage, likely refers to God's promise of blessing to the gentiles through Abraham's seed, as contained in Scripture (cf. Williams 1980: 266-68).

11. Paul's language of "reckoning" (λογίζεσθαι) here parallels Paul's discourse concerning justification (cf. 4.3ff.), suggesting that the same event is being described (cf. Cranfield 1977: 173-74; Wright 2001b: 136).

Torah has no bearing on justification; it is only the doers of Torah who acquire this status.[12] He asserts moreover that gentiles, who do not by birthright possess the Torah,[13] can nevertheless fulfill its demands.

These gentiles do not represent those who "sometimes fulfill . . . some of the requirements of the law, just as Jews do" (Witherington 2004: 83; cf. Käsemann 1980: 64–65; Dunn 1988: 99; Moo 1996: 148–53; Barrett 1991: 48–50; Keck 2005: 81–82).[14] Neither do they represent a purely hypothetical group who are in actuality a "null set" (cf. Donaldson 1997: 92–93, 133[15]). But they are, as Paul will later reveal, gentile Christ followers (cf. Wright 2001b: 131–50; 2001a: 440–42; Jewett 2007: 212–15; Cranfield 1977: 156–59) who by virtue of Christ faith participate along with believing Jews in the promised covenant renewal (cf. 2 Cor. 3.3ff.; 1 Cor. 11.23ff.) and therefore "show that what the law requires is written on their hearts" (v. 15; cf. 2.25–29; see also

---

12. This assertion does not contradict Paul's statement in 3.20, but carries exactly the same connotation. "Righteous status" is not found in Torah possession, i.e., Jewish identity, as made manifest in the "works of Torah" (cf. esp. 4QMMT C 27–31; see also Wright 2001a: 458–61; Jewett 2007: 265–67), but in God's eschatological act of covenant renewal through Christ, the need for which the Torah itself bears witness: "for through the law comes the knowledge of sin" (cf. Gal. 2.15–16). Wright (2001a: 461) notes, "[Paul's] point . . . was that all who attempted to legitimate their covenant status by appealing to possession of Torah would find that the Torah itself accused them of sin. If 'the Jew' appealed to Torah to say, 'This shows that I am different from the Gentiles' [cf. 1 Thess. 4.5; 1 Cor. 5.1, 9–13; 10.20; 12.2], Torah itself, according to Paul, would say, 'No, it doesn't; it shows that you are the same as the Gentiles.'" See esp. here Deut. 9.4ff. (cf. Rom. 10.6ff.).

13. I take φύσει with what precedes, τὰ μὴ νόμον ἔχοντα, rather than what follows, τὰ τοῦ νόμου ποιῶσιν. That this term should be read as qualifying the identity of the gentiles and not their behavior accords with 2.27, which similarly describes them as those who are "by nature uncircumcised," and is consistent with the vast majority of other occurrences of φύσει in Paul (Rom. 1.26–27; 11.21, 24; Gal. 2.15; 4.8; cf. Eph. 2.3), where it is used adjectively rather than adverbially; cf. Achtemeier 1985: 45; Cranfield 1977: 157; Stowers 1994: 139; Wright 2001b: 145; Jewett 2007: 214; contra Käsemann 1980: 63–64; Dunn 1988: 98; Barrett 1991: 49–50; Fitzmyer 1994: 310; Moo 1996: 149.

14. See also Dodd 1932: 61–62; he holds Paul to be espousing the belief that in both the Jewish and gentile world there are some who will be justified through a life of virtue. Räisänen (1985: 107–8) and Sanders (1983: 123–35) read the passage similarly and find it (wrongly, in my view) to entirely contradict what Paul will go on to claim in Rom. 3.

15. However, Donaldson (1997: 89–90), pointing to Bassler 1982: 141–45, also seems to (rightly) suggest that Paul is anticipating in 2.13–16 what he will eventually conclude in a later stage of the argument: that only the Christ follower can fulfill the requirements of the Torah. But he notes that the "essentially Christian suit becomes apparent, a little ahead of time, in v.16."

Deut. 30.6; Isa. 59.21; Jer. 31.33; 32.39-40; Ezek. 11.19-20; 36.27; Bar. 2.30-35; *Jub.* 1.21-24; CD 3.10ff.; 1QS 1.16-2.25; 1QH 5.11f.; 14.8ff.; 16.15; 1Q34 2.5-7; 4Q504 5.6ff.).[16]

Elliot (1990: 129) is surely correct when he remarks on 2.17-29 that Paul's "purpose is not to pronounce a verdict, but to establish by the vivid illustrative technique of diatribe a legal principle: not *possession* of the Law (or circumcision, or the heritage of the covenant) but *obedience* characterizes the true Jew who is 'justified' (2.13) and rewarded from heaven (2.29)." But equally to be considered is the eschatological context established in 2.2-16, and brought out in Wright's assertion that the "charge against Israel in this passage is not that all Jews steal, commit adultery, and rob temples. That absurd suggestion, and its equally absurd triumphant refutation by some scholars, are quite beside the point. The point is that if Israel was truly redeemed, none of these things would be happening at all" (2001b: 142).[17] Indeed, as Paul

---

16. As Hafemann (1996) has demonstrated, the centrality of the Spirit for Paul, as foundational to his whole ecclesiology, derives from his conviction that the "person and 'work' of Christ" has inaugurated the new covenant, which is what "makes the presence of the Spirit possible" (p. 39) (cf. Ezek. 11.19-20; 36.22-32; 39.29; Isa. 32.15; 44.3; 59.21; Joel 2.28; Zech. 12.10; 1 QH 7.6ff.; 9.32; 12.12; 13.24-25; 14.13; 16.7-15). And it is precisely this understanding that brought Paul "to the conclusion that those truly in Christ will be able to know God directly and respond to him positively with both the desire and ability to keep his covenant stipulations" (p. 39; cf. Gal. 5.13ff.; Rom. 6.1ff.; 8.1-17; 13.8-14; 1 Thess. 4.1-8; 1 Cor. 7.19).

17. As mentioned in n. 14 above, Sanders (1983: 123-35) reads 1.18—2.29 as failing to logically lead to the conclusion reached in ch. 3. He notes that the text would seem, rather, to exhort one to "repent, and obey the law from the bottom of your heart, so that you will be a true Jew" (p. 129). However, when it is understood that Christ as the means by which the law is fulfilled is presupposed throughout the section, such seeming inconsistency vanishes. Paul's concern here is not the individual Jew or gentile and his capacity to fulfill the law, but the hope of Israel's final restoration—the fulfillment of the covenant promises, according to which the gentiles would also be blessed. It is Israel's corporate failure to abide by the covenant that is the premise of 2.17ff. Sanders is not, then, entirely correct, as Wright has aptly demonstrated, when he suggests Paul works strictly from "solution" to "plight" with such supposed contradictions as found in Rom. 2 as the result.

Reading Paul primarily in terms of a systemic shift, i.e., a movement from Judaism to Christianity, rather than a thoroughly eschatological framework from which he understood the Christ event in relation to his native Jewish convictions, seems to be at the center of Sanders's difficulty here (cf. 1983: 176-79; where Sanders admits that it is improper "to speak of Christianity as a new *religion*" [p. 176], but he nevertheless notes that "Paul's view of the church, supported by his practice, against his own conscious intention, was substantially that it was a third entity, not just because it was composed

will later proclaim in 11.32, "God has imprisoned all [that is, both the gentile and Jewish world; cf. n. 9 above] in disobedience, so that he may have mercy upon all."[18]

Thus, the issue at stake in vv. 25–29 is the identity of those who have been conferred membership among the community of the redeemed, God's eschatological "new covenant" people. This identity is not ultimately revealed in the traditional Torah-based markers such as circumcision—i.e., the "works of Torah" referred to in 3.20—but is the sole possession of those who fulfill the Torah, who for Paul are only those in the Christ community (cf. Rom. 3.28-31; 4.16; 7.1-6; 8.1-4; 9.30—10.13; 15.8-9; Gal. 3.23-29; Phil. 3.3). This is additionally demonstrated via the contrast between πνεῦμα and γράμμα that similarly points, as in Rom. 7.6 and 2 Cor. 3.6, to the contrast between Christ fulfillment and Torah independent of Christ (cf. Gal. 3.11-14).[19]

---

of both Jew and Greek, but also because it was in important ways neither Jewish nor Greek" [pp. 178-79]). So also Räisänen (1986: 99), who points to an apparent "double standard" in that transgressions demonstrate the flaw of "Torah religion" but not of "Christ religion." Yet, for Paul, Christ has inaugurated the fulfillment of the covenant (cf. 10.4; 1 Cor. 11.23ff.; 2 Cor. 3.3ff.), according to which sins are finally expiated and will eventually be no more (cf. 11.26-27; 3.25-26; 6.5-6; 8.1-11; 1 Cor. 15.50-57; Phil. 3.20-21). That Christ followers continue to sin is a product of the already/not yet eschatological tension—the interim between Christ's resurrection and that of all believers (cf. 1 Cor. 15.20-28; Rom. 6.1-5; 8.18-23; Col. 3.4; 1 Thess. 4.13-17; 2 Cor. 4.14—5.5), during which time they are "being transformed . . . from one glory [that of the old covenant] to another [that of the (re)new(ed) covenant]" via the Spirit (2 Cor. 3.18; cf. Rom. 8.28-30).

18. The notion of God "imprisoning" (συγκλείω) in disobedience, as Moo (1996: 736) suggests, "involves God's decision to 'confine' people in the state they have chosen for themselves" (cf. Rom. 1.24, 26, 28). Though the specific Jewish disobedience envisaged in 11.30-32 refers in the first place to Israel's refusal to accept the gospel of Christ (cf. 10.16-21), it is nevertheless likely that all Paul has had to say with respect to universal sinfulness comes to its climax here, as also God's mercy (cf. Dunn 1988: 689; Wright 2001a: 694-95; Jewett 2007: 711-12; see also Stowers 1994: 183-84).

19. Contra Käsemann (1971: 146-47) who asserts that the practice of Torah by first-century Jews was a perversion of Torah's original intention to reveal God's sacred will, and is thus identical to the "letter" and "part of fallen humanity which lives in a perverted creation" (cf. 1980: 88), and which "drives men into transgression and hubris." As consistent with "old perspective" scholarship, Käsemann fails to appreciate that Paul does not reject the practice of Torah in itself, nor presupposes its abdication in consequence of Christ faith, but suggests, rather, the failure to understand Torah as necessarily leading to Christ, by which one is stuck in the "letter."

Hafemann (1996: 38) similarly comments on 2 Cor. 3.6: "The problem with the Sinai covenant is not with the law itself, but, as Ezekiel and Jeremiah testify, with the

In my view, Wright (2001b: 138) suggests correctly that Paul understood a priori, based upon texts such as Ezek. 36, Jer. 31, Isa. 32.15; 44.3; 59.21, and Deut. 30, that "members of the new covenant fulfill the law." Therefore, gentile Christ followers who have received the promise of the Spirit (cf. Rom. 8.1-11; Gal. 3.1-5; 1 Cor. 2.10ff.), "as a matter of theological logic," "keep the law" despite being uncircumcised (cf. Gal. 5.13—6.2; Rom. 13.8-10; 1 Cor. 7.18-19; 9.21). In this limited sense, Paul's thinking is retrospective, along the lines of Sanders's premise. The "keeping of the law," irrespective of the "rudimentary details," is here "first and foremost a matter of status," which both Jews and gentiles have now obtained in Christ.

The True Jew: Both Jewish and Gentile Christ Followers?

But the question still remains as to whether Paul is redefining the title "Jew" to include gentile Christ followers or whether he means only that the "true Jew" is one who is so according to traditional ethnic norms as well as who is "in Christ." Though Stowers (1994) is almost certainly incorrect in his assertion that Paul is not describing "an eschatological miracle in 2.25-29 that turns Jews and gentiles into Christians,"[20] his comments on vv. 28-29 bear mentioning:

> Paul is far from saying that the intention alone is enough, but he does stress the inner disposition here. In this regard, Paul was hardly radical or innovative, although his admonitory diatribal language is sharp and forceful. The theme "circumcision of the heart" comes directly from the Jewish scriptures, and many varieties of ancient Judaism emphasized it (Lev 26:41; Deut 10:15, 30:6; Jer 4:4, 9:25-26; Ez 44:7-9; 1QS 5.5; 1QHab. 11:13; 1QH 2:18, 18:20; Philo, *Quaest. Ex.* 2.2; *Spec. Leg.* 1.305). Thus Jews frequently wrote that true circumcision was a matter of the heart without ever supposing an elimination of physical circumcision. (p. 155)

---

people whose hearts remain hardened under it. . . . [T]he letter/Spirit contrast is not a contrast between the law and the gospel as two distinct ways of relating to God. Nor is it a contrast between two distinct ways God relates to us (i.e., externally in the old covenant and internally in the new), since what distinguishes the ministry of the new covenant in Jeremiah 31:31-34 is that the law itself is now kept as a result of a transformed heart. As the expression of the abiding will of God, it is not the law *per se* that kills but the law without the Spirit, i.e., the law as 'letter.'"

20. This statement by Stowers betrays an overwhelmingly anachronistic view of "Christianity" as a "religion" distinct from Judaism.

Accordingly, if the "spirit" in v. 29 refers to that of the human, "then the contrast between circumcision of the spirit rather than 'mere literal circumcision' simply amplifies 'circumcision of the heart.'" But if it refers to God's spirit, then Paul is in keeping with other Jewish sources before him that "had already connected circumcision of the heart with the agency of God's Spirit (*Jub.* 1.23; cf. *Odes Sol.* 11.1–3)" (p. 156).

In response to Stowers's view, I affirm with him that Paul does not advocate the abandoning of the "works of Torah" on the part of Jews, whether Christ followers or not. There is every reason to believe Paul simply presupposed that Jews would continue to submit to these requirements and, as Campbell and Nanos have pointed out, that this was not in any way contrary to his gospel.[21] However, despite this conclusion, it does seem that the logic of the argument suggests gentile Christ followers are to be included under this title in as much as it is shared by God's covenant people, of whom these non-Jews are now fully part.

That Paul understood this to be so is strongly supported by the fact that in 3.1 he advances a retort by his imaginary interlocutor regarding the reality of Jewish advantage, which is a clear attempt to qualify the assertion made in vv. 25–29. Although gentiles in Christ can (at least for the purpose of Paul's argument) lay claim to the title "Jew," this does *not* mean the irrelevancy or dissolution of Jewish identity traditionally (that is, non-christologically) defined: "Circumcision indeed is of value if you obey the law" (v. 25). That is, irrespective of the new relationship gentiles now possess in regard to God's historical people—or rather especially because of it[22]—Christ faith *affirms* and does not eradicate

---

21. This is not to suggest along the lines of Stowers (1994: 158) that Paul continued to believe that *all* ordinances of Torah were still *required* for Jewish Christ followers, even if not for gentile Christ followers. The central point here is that Paul does not stand in the way of Jews who would desire to continue in these traditions. In short, Torah ordinances such as circumcision and food laws are relativized by Paul, but they are not deemed by him as in themselves inconsistent with the gospel (cf. 1 Cor. 7.17–20; Rom. 14.13–23).

22. Contra Dunn 1988: 127–28: "Paul looks for a circumcision of the heart that completely *replaces* the physical rite and does not merely complement it, for a law-keeping which can be completely independent of so much of the law, the ritual law, which Jews regard as fundamental, with all the authority of Moses behind them. But not only is it the law and circumcision that Paul seeks to be removed from the domain of Jewish national pride and self-assurance; even the title 'Jew' itself comes into radical question" (cf. p. 125). In as much as Dunn points here to covenant standing before God, his comments remain valid, but his failure to more carefully explicate the division between Jew and gentile in terms of righteous status in distinction to ethnic diversity is

Jewish ethnicity.²³ "Since God is one . . . he will justify the circumcised on the ground of faith, and the uncircumcised through that same faith" (3.30; cf. 4.16; 15.8–9).

Rom. 2.17–29: A Critique of Ethnocentrism?

It would do well to also address here my view that the attempt by Dunn (1988: 108–28)²⁴ and Wright (2001b: 139–40) to understand throughout this section a critique of "ethnocentricism" or "national righteousness" seems to be overstated.²⁵ Paul's critique of Israel in 2.17–29, and as especially expressed in Rom. 9–11, rests foremost on their failure to accept Christ as the "τέλος of the Torah so that there may be righteousness for everyone who believes" (10.4). By not recognizing that Christ fufills the covenant,²⁶ confirming the promises, unbelieving Israel is unwittingly "seeking to establish [a righteousness of] their own" (10.3), which implies nothing more than a basis of covenant membership other than the one that God has made possible (cf. Phil. 3.9).²⁷

---

problematic. Further, Dunn's language of "national pride and self-assurance" requires qualification; see below.

23. Exactly how the boundaries of Jewish ethnicity were drawn in the first century cannot likely be thought of as monolithic throughout the Diaspora. Despite this degree of ambiguity, the point here is that Paul does not undermine the integrity of Jewish identity as such, irrespective of its precise definition; he suggests only that covenant membership is no longer coextensive with it.

24. Cf. Dunn 1988: 110: "Paul of course makes no (implied) criticism of boasting in God. On the contrary, he makes such boasts himself (5:11; 1 Cor 1:31 and 2 Cor 10:17 both citing Jer 9:23). From the context, however, the implication is that such Jewish boasting tends to be nationalistically exclusive: Jewish boasting in God as theirs alone (cf. 3:27–29). Hence it gathers (by implication) the more negative force which Paul uses in criticizing a boasting based on outward evaluation and physical relationship (2 Cor 5:12; 11:18; Gal 6:13; Phil 3:3)."

25. As equally the case with the traditional reading that finds Paul to be criticizing Jewish legalism; the misguided and utterly futile attempt to merit the status of righteousness.

26. As suggested in n. 17 above, I understand the fulfillment of the covenant to be for Paul inaugurated by the Christ event, though not yet complete.

27. In this respect, despite the misleading and anachronistic language contrasting one "religious system" to another (cf. n. 17 above), I find basic agreement with Sanders' assertion (1977: 552) that what Paul finds wrong with Judaism is that it is not Christianity. However, Wright follows Sanders (1983: 140–41) and reads "their own" in 10.3 as meaning "for Jews and Jews alone," emphasizing the notion of ethnocentrism. While this is clearly the end result of this alternative (false) path to covenant membership, there is little evidence to suggest that Paul thought this to be intrinsically problematic, at least

That there is, as in Wright's understanding (cf. 1991: 239–41), a "meta-level" to Israel's Torah breaking, consisting of the attempt to "confine grace to one race" (p. 240)[28] wrongly posits a secondary implication of Paul's theologizing into a fundamental conviction.[29] First, it should be observed that various forms of universalism were undoubtedly present in first-century Jewish thought, including the notion of the righteous gentile.[30] But particularly given that proselytism was a very real means

---

as a general rule (cf. n. 29 below), but only so in light of the fact that God has provided Christ and Christ alone as the means of righteousness.

28. For the appropriateness or inappropriateness of the term "race" in this context, cf. Buell 2005 and Esler 2003: 51–53, respectively.

29. There is no question that Paul is critical of the refusal of certain Jews (whether unbelievers or otherwise) to come to terms with the implications of his gospel in regard to the equal covenant status of Jews and gentiles in Christ, e.g., the entire argument of Galatians, Phil. 3. But what lay behind this conflict surely had much more to do with a desire by those Jews, however misguided from Paul's perspective, to respect the stipulations commanded in Torah, than an overt desire to limit God's grace to a single people, as Paul, despite his harsh rhetoric, was no doubt aware. Additionally, while perhaps a legitimate critique could hypothetically be made of the failure among at least some Jews to come to terms with the reality that there have always been non-Jews who were righteous before God (a belief that is indeed attested in much Jewish literature; cf. n. 30 below), it nevertheless seems that Paul's critique is specific to the dispensation of Christ. To project a pejorative notion of "national righteousness" for an insistence upon Torah-designated identity markers for the period between "Moses and Christ," as the logic of Wright's reading suggests, imposes a concern that is foreign to Paul (see n. 32 below).

Rather, as suggested in n. 17 above, Paul's argumentation in both Galatians and Romans for the inclusivity of covenant identity is decidedly salvation-historical. It is premised upon, not a principle true for all time, but the inauguration of the eschatological age, however this new state of affairs may indicate a return to God's intention from the beginning (as per Gen. 1–2; cf. Rom. 8.18–25), and reflects the precedent established through Abraham (cf. Gal. 3.6ff.; Rom. 4.1ff). In other words, in dispute is not foremost the question of what has always been the fundamental basis for which God reckons "righteousness," e.g., a proper disposition towards God, but how former boundary markers indicative of this righteous status (none for which Paul indicates any intrinsic dissatisfaction) have now been superseded/transformed in Christ (cf. Gal. 6.14–15; Rom. 4.11–12, 22–25; 7.1–6; 9.30—10.4; 1 Cor. 7.19; Phil. 3.3ff.).

30. Donaldson (2007), in addition to surveying the relevant literature depicting some measure of attachment to Judaism among gentiles whereby they could positively relate to God, i.e., "sympathization" (cf., e.g., Dan. 4.34; 6.26–27; Josephus, *J.W.* 2.201, 340–41, 409–17; 4.181, 275; 5. 15–18, 562–64; *Ant.* 3.318–19; 8.116–17; 11.3–5, 87, 103, 120–32, 331–36; 12.11–18; 13.69–71, 78, 242–44; 14.110; 16.14; 18.122, 286, 288, 309; 20.195; *Ag. Ap.* 2.45, 48, 279–84; 2 Macc. 3.1–3, 12, 33–39; 5.16; 9.11–18; 13.23; 3 Macc. 1.9; 4 Macc. 4.11–12; *2 Bar.* 68.5–6; *Letter of Aristeas* 4–7; Philo, *Embassy* 157, 291–320; *Moses* 2.17–43; Luke 7.2–5; Acts 10.1–33; 13.16–50; 16.13–14; 17.4, 11–12, 16–17; 18.4–7; John 12.20; see Donaldson 2007: 469–82), also employs the term "ethical monotheist"

in first-century Judaism by which gentiles could gain access to Israel's covenant,[31] on what a priori grounds would Paul critique Israel for what would only arguably be their adherence to and insistence upon God-given stipulations in regard to covenant membership?[32] Rather, I hold

---

to describe a pattern of universalism "in which Jews consider it possible for Gentiles to acquire accurate and adequate knowledge of the one true God, or to relate to this God in appropriate ways, without any knowledge of Judaism or association with the Jewish community" (p. 493; cf. pp. 494-98). Accordingly, this notion was arrived at through an appreciation of natural theology and either its alignment with or independence from the law of Moses (cf., e.g., Esther 16.15-16 LXX; Wisd. 1.1-2; 6.9-11; Eusebius, *Praep. ev.* 13.12.6-7; *Letter of Aristeas* 16, 140; *Sib. Or.* 3.545-50, 624-31; 4.24-39; *On Jonah* 216-19; Philo, *Spec. Laws* 2.42-48; *Good Person* 62, 72-74; *Embassy* 245, 291, 294-97, 309-10, 317-20; Josephus, *Ant.* 12.22; *Ag. Ap.* 2.168, 255-57).

31. This is not to claim, however, that proselytism was an uncomplicated matter, that it was necessarily widespread, or that proselytes were viewed by all Jews in a uniformly positive way (cf. Donaldson 2007: 490-91).

32. It may seem that Paul's appeal to the Abraham story suggests a line of argument whereby certain covenant markers prescribed in Scripture, namely circumcision, are relativized in light of texts that suggest other such markers, namely allegiance to the God of Israel and concomitant ethical standards, are paramount. But, notwithstanding the actual merit of such a claim (which seems to underlie "righteous gentile" conceptions; cf., e.g., Josephus, *Ant.* 20.41), the purpose behind Gal. 3 and Rom. 4 is not to validate an enduring principle of "trusting God" over against Torah submission and Jewish identity as the basis of righteous status, but to demonstrate that gentile Christ followers are, along with Christ-following Jews, descendents of Abraham in fulfillment of the promise. The argument in each of these letters is founded upon a notion of shared kinship.

Though I disagree that Paul is strictly referring to gentiles here (however he may then focus on the implications specifically for them), Gaston (1987: 57-62) and especially Johnson-Hodge (2007: 79-91) have perceptively argued that those ἐκ πίστεως in Rom. 4.16 and Gal. 3.7 indicate those who find their *origin* in Abraham via Christ (cf. Gal. 3.29), not, as respectively translated in the NRSV, "those who share the faith of Abraham" or "those who believe" as Abraham did. While "faith in God," as exhibited by Abraham towards the promise (cf. Rom. 4.18ff.), is indeed for Paul the central characteristic and fundamental marker of Abraham's family (cf. Rom. 4.11-12), the reality of this is presupposed by him as it now centers around God's act in Christ for the Jew and gentile alike (cf. Gal. 2.16b; 3.1-5; Jewett 2007: 329: "[F]aith has to do with participation in a new spiritual and social reality through acceptance of the gospel of God's righteousness made present in the Christ event"; see also Williams 1980: 276). Thus, righteous status is to be found "in Christ" rather than in the attainment and/or maintenance of Jewish identity (cf. Rom. 11.5-6). Ostensibly, Paul believed that prior to the coming of Christ and the inauguration of the new age proselyte conversion represented an appropriate, if not ideal, means by which gentiles could attain full covenant membership (cf. Gal. 5.11), even if he might have also granted the possibility of righteous gentiles (i.e., exceptions to the rule; cf. Gal. 2.15). As Johnson-Hodge (2007:43) succinctly points out, "For Paul, ethnic identity is inextricable from a people's standing before God." See further n. 47 below.

with Nanos that the problem as Paul sees it is the refusal of certain Jews to recognize that with the coming of the Christ and inauguration of the new covenant and new creation[33] former covenant stipulations have given way to Christ faith and concomitant reception of the Spirit,[34] the result of which is that gentiles qua gentiles are entering the community of the redeemed alongside Jews qua Jews, which was God's plan all along, as the scriptures bear testimony.

Yet, while I disagree that driving Paul's critique is any notion of Jewish "cultural imperialism," I do nevertheless understand, as the other side of the problem of Israel's unbelief, an implicit criticism of presumed privilege on the basis of special election (cf. 2.11; 3.27; see also 11.19–22; and pp. 158ff. below).[35] Again, the grounding for Paul's argument in 2.17–29 is this very issue, which is raised explicitly and at length in chapters 9–11. But before turning attention here, Paul's letter to the Galatians contains an equally critical passage addressing the question of the relationship of church and Israel.

GALATIANS 6.16: "THE ISRAEL OF GOD"

Wright (1991: 250; 2001a: 689–90) and Donaldson (1997: 237–38) have interpreted Gal. 6.16 such that Paul applies the title "Israel" to the church. This reading is disputed by Campbell (1993b: 441–42), and Nanos also disagrees that gentiles are to be included in this expression. Presumably

---

33. In my view, both Harink and Martyn draw a false antithesis between new creation/apocalyptic and covenant/salvation history conceptions in Paul; see further on this point below.

34. Of course, not all covenant stipulations are eclipsed, as there is for Paul a clear continuity of many of Torah's central behavioral demands placed upon covenant members in the ages before and after Christ (cf., e.g., Rom. 6.1ff. [compare with 1.26–32]; 13.8–14; Gal. 5.13–6.2; 1 Thess. 4.1–8; 1 Cor. 5.1ff.; 6.9–11; 7.19; see also Amos 5.21–25; Isa. 5.7; 42.1–9; Jer. 7.5–7; Matt. 23.23–24; Luke 11.42).

35. This is what Wright refers to as "automatic national privilege," though I do not draw the same connections between this and the "ethnocentric reading" characteristic of both his and Dunn's approach. As pointed out in n. 6 above, by advancing this sort of critique from within, *Paul stands squarely in the prophetic tradition of Israel*. See further here Jewett 2007: 219–37; on p. 221 he comments on 2.17: "In an elegant manner that Paul's audience would have enjoyed, Paul augments the previous depiction of the pretentious bigot with a series of boasts that exaggerate well-known Jewish claims. As in the previous half-pericope, Paul's target is ostensibly far from his audience. They are invited to join Paul's indictment of an insufferable arrogant bigot, not realizing that similar pretensions will later be exposed in their own behavior toward one another."

Gaston and Harink would similarly disapprove.[36] However, I will conclude that the "Israel of God" is indeed a reference to the church of Jews and gentiles.

Of the other possible interpretations for the phrase, the following should be noted: (a) "The Israel of God" refers to historical Israel as a whole (cf. Davies 1977: 10). In this reading Paul is perhaps qualifying his harsh polemic in the preceding portion of the letter against those (Jews) who would influence his gentile converts to be circumcised by calling for God's mercy upon the Jewish people as a whole. (b) "The Israel of God" refers exclusively to Jewish Christ followers (cf. Rom. 9.6). (c) The title refers to the total elect from historical Israel (cf. Mussner 1977: 417; Bruce 1982: 275; Burton 1921: 357; Richardson 1969: 82–83). That is, Paul is calling for God's mercy upon Jews who already have come to accept Jesus as Messiah and also those Jews who at some point will do likewise in accordance with divine election (cf. Rom. 11.26). As such, this reading is effectively similar to interpretation (a) (save perhaps in a two-covenant approach) but makes explicit the (eschatological) hope that lay behind this last clause of Paul's benediction. (d) "The Israel of God" refers to those (Christ-following) Jews who do not compel gentile Christ followers to be circumcised (cf. Schrenk 1949: 81–94; Robinson 1965: 29–44; Betz 1977: 323). Here, it is generally held that the "influencers" who are targeted in the letter's polemic are "Jewish Christian" missionary opponents of Paul. Outside of a possible two-covenant approach, then, the inference from this reading is that Paul is restricting the title "Israel" not merely to the body of Jewish Christ followers, but to those within this group who adhere to the implications of his gospel for the gentiles.

Additionally worth noting are readings in which "the Israel of God" includes gentile Christ followers but—so it is claimed—is not to be associated directly with the church. Dunn (1993: 345) is illustrative of such a position. He suggests that the phrase has as its primary reference the Jewish people as a whole, yet "in light of [Paul's] earlier argument, that would have to mean the Jewish people precisely in their covenant identity, 'Israel' rather than 'the Jews.'" As such, the title also includes gentile believers, as Israel consists "of all of Abraham's seed and heirs" (cf. Gal. 3.29).

---

36. This is a logical deduction based upon the views they have expressed, but neither to my knowledge have dealt explicitly with this passage.

Sam K. Williams (1997: 167) similarly proposes that the phrase refers to the "Israel of God's future," by which he means the "Israel made complete by the inclusion of *all* nations, in accordance with God's promise to Abraham (3.8)." Timothy George (1994: 440) likewise suggests, in supposed contrast to identifying the phrase with the church, a futurist-eschatological reading whereby "the Israel of God" includes gentile Christ followers along with all Jews who have and will come to trust in God's act in Christ. Still further, Frank J. Matera (1992: 232) comments,

> [I]t is clear from ch. 3 that Paul does not view the Church as the new Israel. . . . Rather, those who are "in Christ," Gentiles as well as Jews, are Abraham's descendants. Consequently, the Israel of God refers to those Gentile and Jewish believers who walk according to the new creation established by God's act in Christ. In this verse, then, "the Israel of God" includes the Galatians but goes beyond them. Paul extends a greeting of peace and mercy to the Galatians, and then to all of those who, like him, conduct themselves according to the rule of the new creation.

Yet it must be asked how different these "Jews plus gentiles" readings really are from the notion that "the Israel of God" is the church. While it may be argued that Dunn's understanding represents a significant distinction from a strictly ecclesiological interpretation of the phrase in that Jewish unbelievers are not excluded, he nevertheless asserts here, along the lines of interpretation (c) above, that what undergirds Paul's prayer in 6.16 is the hope that any such unbelief will in the end give way to acceptance of his Christ gospel.

Thus, despite the oft-accompanied special pleading to distinguish readings of this sort from an ecclesiological one, and the eschatological character notwithstanding, to claim that "the Israel of God" (a) is (ultimately) christologically conditioned, and (b) includes gentiles, is in effect to suggest that it is the equivalent of the church either (from, of course, Paul's perspective) in its present or prospective form.[37] And there are several arguments in favor of a reading that understands "the Israel

---

37. In addition to Wright and Donaldson, scholars who hold this position include Dahl (1950: 161–70), Ridderbos (1953: 226–27), Guthrie (1969: 162), Cousar (1982: 150), Fung (1988: 309–11), Barclay (1988: 98), Longenecker (1990: 298–99), Scroggs (1991: 223), Weima (1993: 105), Thielman (1994: 138), Martyn (1997a: 574–77), Hafemann (1997: 366–67), Witherington (1998: 452–53), Esler (1998: 37), Longenecker (1998: 87–88), Beale (1999: 204–23), Hays (2000: 346), and Silva (2001: 184).

of God" in Gal. 6.16 to represent the total elect among both Jews and gentiles, or the church prospectively.[38]

But before articulating these arguments it will be advantageous to explicate the several difficulties the text presents, and the way in which such difficulties are addressed by Peter Richardson (1969), as his reading is among the most frequently referenced for support by opponents of the ecclesiological interpretation of this passage.

Galatians 6.16: Textual Complexities

The formulation of this "peace" benediction is unusual among what is typically found in the Pauline letters in that it: (a) combines εἰρήνη with ἔλεος; (b) lacks explicit mention of the divine source; (c) is conditional rather than indicative; and (d) identifies the recipient as "those who follow this rule" (of 6.15) and "the Israel of God" rather than the typical "you" (cf. Rom. 15.33; 2 Cor. 13.11; Phil. 4.9; 1 Thess. 5.23; 2 Thess. 3.16; see also Eph. 6.23-24). Regarding (a), additional examples where one finds the coupling of "mercy" and "peace" are absent in the undisputed letters, and quite rare in the New Testament in general—only 1 Tim 1.2; 2 Tim. 1.2; 2 John 3 (preceded by χάρις in each of these instances); and Jude 2 (all four references contained in their respective letter introductions in contrast to here).[39]

Further, the word order in Gal. 6.16 is reversed from the general pattern otherwise followed. As particularly represented by the standard New Testament letter salutation, χάρις καὶ εἰρήνη, Richardson (1969: 77) points out that "in Pauline prayers, blessings, and liturgical formulae generally, where co-ordinate or consecutive words are used they are arranged logically [he notes for further example: Eph. 3.14-19; 6.23f.; 2 Cor. 13.13; 1 Cor. 13.13]. . . . [T]he order is based on the logic of God's activity among men: source then benefits."[40] Additionally unique is the

---

38. While Paul did not hold to a concept of a "universal church," as per Ephesians, it would seem that he nevertheless viewed the individual Christ assemblies as collectively representing the people of God (cf. Gal 1.13; 1 Cor. 10.32; 15.9), and this in total at the eschaton.

39. Beale (1999: 221) notes that the combination of "mercy" and "peace" does not at all "appear in either the introductions or conclusions of Hellenistic epistolary literature of the earlier or contemporary period with the NT. . . . This combination is unique to the OT, a very few early Jewish texts, and the NT."

40. The one exception noted by Richardson (p. 77) is Eph. 6.23f. This is explainable, he suggests, "on stylist grounds—that it is intended to build up to χάρις."

grammatical structure of 6.16, which contains two uses of both the preposition ἐπί and conjunction καί.

With respect to parallels found in the Old Testament, the Greek ἔλεος is the normal translation in the LXX of the familiar Hebrew term חסד, which denotes God's covenant love and faithfulness, and the theme of "mercy upon Israel" is a relatively standard one (cf., e.g., Ezek. 39.25; Amos 5.15; Ezra 3.11; Hos. 2.23; *Pss. Sol.* 4.29; 6.9; 8.33–34; 9.19; 11.9; 17.51). But the expression "peace upon Israel" appears only in Pss. 124.5 LXX (125.5 MT) and 127.6 LXX (128.6 MT). And, like the New Testament, rarely are the terms "mercy" and "peace" (in the LXX or the Hebrew equivalents in the MT) found together within a reasonably close proximity—only Ps. 84.8–9, 11 LXX (85.10 MT); Isa. 54.10; and Jer. 16.5 MT.[41] In every instance, both here and otherwise in the New Testament, "mercy" always precedes "peace."

A Parallel to Galatians 6.16 in the Nineteenth Benediction?

A close parallel to Gal. 6.16 is found in the added Nineteenth Benediction of the *Shemoneh Esreh*: "Bring peace, goodness, and blessing, and grace and favor and mercy over us and over all Israel, your people." Here is observed the same reverse order of "peace" then "mercy" found in Gal. 6.16. But as G. K. Beale (1999: 208) notes,

> [I]t would be hard to demonstrate the probability that the language in question in the Shemoneh Esreh existed in an earlier form as far back as the first century, since the Palestinian recension, which approximates the wording of the prayer around AD 70–100, omits about half of the wording of the later Babylonian recension's nineteenth benediction, including the crucial word "mercy."

Clearly, then, there is no real parallel to Gal. 6.16 in the New Testament, and potential sources informing Paul's thought in this benediction from the Old Testament are limited; none which supply the peculiar word order. Given this, and despite the dating issue that surrounds it, Richardson (1969: 78–83) understands the passage to be an allusion to the Nineteenth Benediction, where he notes two groups envisaged: the worshippers present and the Jewish community at large (cf. Betz 1979: 321–22). But in Galatians Paul gives this "an ironical twist" that turns

---

41. Outside of the Old Testament, cf. *2 Bar.* 78.2; *Jub.* 22.9; 1 QH 13.11.

the "'us' and 'them' (who are an extension of 'us')" of the Nineteenth Benediction "into 'us' and 'them,' where 'they' are people who should be connected to 'us' but are not" (p. 81).

In consideration of the double ἐπί and καί, the second καί given a slight ascensive force, Richardson translates 6.16: "May God give peace to all who will walk according to this criterion, and mercy also to his faithful people Israel." Though there is an ambiguity still present in this translation, he concludes, nevertheless, that Paul is referring to two groups: (1) present Christ followers upon whom Paul is calling for peace, and (2) mercy for "all those Israelites who are going to come to their senses and receive the good news of Christ" (p. 82)—that is, interpretation (c) noted above. As such, this reading suggests an "expanding" relationship between two groups like that found in the *Shemoneh Esreh*, rather than a "decreasing" one, as in interpretation (b) or (d) above, or merely a single group referred to in two distinct ways (p. 79).

Richardson (p. 82) offers the following three main arguments in support of his interpretation:

> [F]irst . . . ἔλεος is in the Pauline epistles usually associated with God's special mercy in bringing to salvation; it has expectant overtones that cannot be confined in a formula of blessing. Secondly, the future στοιχήσουσιν may carry, by analogy, a future element into the parallel prayer dependent upon "mercy": Israel is not yet the Christ-believing Jews, it is those who are still to believe. Thirdly, *tou theou* is not intended to be set over against *kata sarka*. The proper antithesis of *kata sarka* is only *kata pneuma*. . . . Paul, in Galatians 6.16, is not contrasting *Israēl tou theou* with *Israēl kata sarka*. The change from *kol yisrael* to *Israēl tou theou* can only be interpreted on the grounds that for Paul "all Israel" is too ambiguous (though he uses it in Romans after a long discussion of his meaning); he expects that only a part, *Israēl tou theou*, will be blessed in the way he prays. There is an Israel (of God) within (all) Israel.

Confirming this reading for Richardson, as also noted by Campbell (1993b: 441–42), is the absence of any explicit identification of the church with Israel until Justin Martyr in 160 CE.[42]

However, Richardson's interpretation is problematic for several reasons, and a more plausible alternative is available.

---

42. Cf. *Dial.* 123.7; 124.1ff.

Second Isaiah: The Background for Galatians 6.16

First, it is a highly tenuous conclusion that Paul was dependent (consciously or otherwise) on the Nineteenth Benediction, because of the unlikelihood that the necessary form existed as early as the first century. As persuasively argued by Beale (1999: 204-23), a more likely background for Gal. 6.16 is found in Isa. 54.10 LXX, perhaps in conjunction with Jer. 16.5 MT and Ps. 84 LXX (85 MT).[43] Paul directly quotes from Isa 54.1 in Gal. 4.27, and allusions to the greater context of Isa. 54 pervade much of the letter. Beale (p. 218) notes Isa. 53.1 in Gal. 3.2; Isa. 64.10 in Gal. 3.10; Isa. 44.1-3 and 59.21 in Gal. 4.4-6; Isa. 54.1 and 66.6-11 in Gal. 4.25-26; and the Spirit's fruits of Isa. 32.15-18 (as well as Isa. 27.6; 37.31-32; 45.8; 51.3; 58.11; cf. 55.10-13 with 56.3; 60.21; 65.8, 17-22) in Gal. 5.22-25.[44] He observes in summary, "Isaiah 40-66 contains the same major themes which Paul develops in Galatians: the Abrahamic covenant, Abraham's seed, the inheritance, the return of a sinful people to God, and the new creation" (p. 218; cf. Jobes 1993).[45]

Though Second Isaiah would thus seem to be paramount in Paul's thought, Beale (p. 210) also points to several affinities between Ps. 84 LXX and Galatians

> (1) "mercy" and "peace" are pronounced "upon" Israel (cf. εἰρήνην ἐπὶ τὸν λαόν in Ps 84,9 and εἰρήνη ἐπ' αὐτούς in Gal 6,16); (2) the notion of new "life" is associated with the salvific state of God's people (cf. Ps 84,7 . . . and Gal 5,25); (3) the pronouncement of "peace" in Ps 84,9 is made to three groups; however, these

---

43. The Jeremiah reference concerns the removal of "mercy" and "peace" due to Israel's covenant violations that lead them into exile, and Ps. 84 evokes "the return of these two aspects of divine favor when God restores the nation from exile" (Beale pp. 208-9).

44. Beale (p. 218) additionally points out that in the "other well-known reference to 'new creation' in 2 Cor. 5.17" Paul alludes to Isa. 43 and 65, "contexts which are not far from Isaiah 54 in location and pertain to the same theme of Israel's restoration pictured as a new cosmos."

45. It is important to note that the prophecy of Isaiah is fundamental not simply to Paul's letter to the Galatians, but to his entire gospel program. Both direct citations as well as allusions to Isaiah also permeate Paul's letter to the Romans; cf. Rom. 2.24 (Isa. 52.5); 3.15-17 (59.7-8); 9.27-28 (10.22-23; 28.22); 9.29 (1.9); 9.33 (28.16; 8.14); 10.11 (28.16); 10.15 (52.7); 10.20 (65.1); 10.21 (65.2); 11.8 (29.10); 11.26-27 (59.20-21; 27.9); 14.11 (45.23); 15.12 (11.10); 15.21 (52.15); and the following allusions: Rom. 2.9 (Isa. 8.22); 4.25 (53.6, 11-12); 8.32 (53.6, 12); 8.33-34 (50.8); 8.35 (8.22); 9.6 (40.7-8); 9.20 (29.16; 45.9); 9.30-31 (51.1); 10.18-19 (40.21, 28); 11.8 (6.9-10); 11.34 (40.13); 13.11 (56.1); 14.13, 21 (8.14) (Wagner 2002: 342).

are, in fact, different ways of referring to one group, Israel ("peace upon [ἐπὶ] his people and upon [ἐπὶ] his saints and upon [ἐπὶ] the ones who turn their heart to him"); likewise in Gal 6,16 peace is pronounced on multiple groups (with two ἐπὶ clauses), and, if this is any reflection of the Psalm, the two groups there are probably the same; (4) in both contexts "peace" is listed among other attributes which are part of eschatological fertility imagery (cf. Gal 5,22–25).[46]

While it may be argued that neither this proposed background from the Old Testament or the Nineteenth Benediction is itself sufficient to demonstrate one particular reading of Gal. 6.16 over against another, when one considers how aspects of the Isaiah text are interpreted throughout the letter to apply to the Christ community indivisibly—e.g., the seed of Abraham (3.16), the eschatological Jerusalem (4.26), the new creation (6.15)—the weight of evidence shifts considerably to an ecclesiological reading of the benediction.[47]

The "Israel of God" as the Church of Jews and Gentiles

It is clear that Paul recognized the ongoing distinction within the church between Jew and gentile, and developed this necessary distinction as an integral part of his theological program and pastoral counsel (as it was also to his missionary practice; cf. 1 Cor. 9.20–21). This comes to fullest expression in his letter to the Romans (cf. 3.30; 4.11–12, 16; 9–11; 14.1—15.13). But Paul's rhetorical purpose in Galatians is quite different than that of Romans, which had yet to be written.

---

46. Beale (p. 213) further notes the similarities shared with *Jub.* 22 and 1 QH 13, including: (a) creation renewal (cf. *Jub.* 22.14; 1 QH 13.15–18; see also *Jub.* 1.27–28; 4.26; 19.21–25; 1 QH 17.15); (b) covenant renewal (cf. *Jub.* 22.15, 30; 1 QH 13.23–25; see also *Jub.* 1.21–25); and (c) "a promise of blessing on believing (elect) Israel."

47. Cf. Jobes 1993: 315–16: "According to Paul in Galatians, the sign that Christians are united to Abraham as his heirs is not circumcision but the specific nature of their shared faith in God's power to raise the dead as demonstrated in Jesus Christ.... That is, Sarah's identity as the barren woman to whom God promised a miraculous birth merges with that of the barren one of Isa 54:1 at only one point in history—when Jesus, the seed of Abraham (and hence the son of Sarah) arose from the grave to be the firstborn son of the New Jerusalem. In Gal 3:16 Paul announces that Jesus is the son ("seed") promised to Abraham, and therefore Jesus is Sarah's son. ... Paul is arguing that the nation which God promised to bring from Sarah's dead womb and the population of the New Jerusalem prophesied by Isaiah are those people who are born through the resurrection of Jesus, not those who are circumcised."

Here, Paul must demonstrate the sufficiency of Christ as the basis of covenant membership in response to growing pressure upon Christ-following gentiles to submit to circumcision in order to obtain full acceptance as status equals within the covenant community.[48] While Paul held that Jewish Christ followers may continue to observe the ordinances of Torah, he is adamant that gentiles in Christ should not submit to it. To do so would imply that membership in the covenant, the family of God (cf. 3.26—4.7; 6.10), is dependent on such, and thus that the new age signaled by the ingathering of the nations (cf. 3.8a) has not yet arrived, the promise to Abraham has not yet been fulfilled (cf. 3.8b-18), and eschatological/Spirit life (cf. 2.19–20; 5.16ff.) is not a present reality. It is in effect to deny God's faithfulness (i.e., righteousness) realized through Christ's own faithfulness (cf. Rom. 1.16–17; 3.26).[49]

---

48. A notable exception to this widely held understanding of the context of letter is Elliot 2003, which attempts to demonstrate that Paul opposed circumcision because "it was too similar to the ritual castration of the *galli*, the self-castrated servants of the Mother of the Gods. He saw circumcision as a particular threat that would return them to their previous condition. He presented this danger to the Galatians in terms veiled just enough to keep from re-empowering the figure of the Mother of the Gods in their lives" (p. 14). While fascinating, I find Elliot's conjecture wholly unconvincing in contrast to the majority view. The language of "circumcision" as indicative of Jewish identity defined against the non-Jewish world is unquestionably present within the letter itself (cf. Gal. 2.3, 7, 9, 12; 5.3), others of Paul's letters (cf., e.g., Rom. 2.25f.; 1 Cor. 7.18f.; Phil. 3.3–6), the book of Acts (cf. 15.1), and is otherwise ubiquitous in much of the relevant literature, as Nanos 2002a: 88–90 has shown (cf., e.g., 1 Macc. 1.15, 44–48, 60–61; 2.45–46; 2 Macc. 6.10; *Jub.* 15.25–34; Josephus, *Ant.* 1.192; 13.318–19; 18.34–48; 20.38; *Ag. Ap.* 2.137, 140–42; Philo, *Spec. Laws* 1.1–11; *Migr.* 92; *y. Meg.* 3.2.74d; *b. Yebam.* 47b; *Exod. Rab.* 30.12; *m. ʿEd.* 5.2; *b. Pesaḥ.* 8.8; Strabo, *Geogr.* 16.2.37; Diodorus Siculus, *World History* 1.55; Horace, *Sat.* 1.9.60–72; Petronius, *Satyricon* 68.8; 102.13–14; Persius, *Sat.* 5.179–84; Martial, *Epigrams* 7.35.3–4, 82; 11.94; Tacitus, *Hist.* 5.5.2, 8–9; Juvenal, *Sat.* 14.96–106; Suetonius, *Dom.* 12; Paulus, *Sententiae* 5.22.3–4).

49. I favor this reading of *pistis christou*. In addition to Hays 1983, cf. the persuasive argument for the subjective genitive rendering in D. A. Campbell 2005: 178–232 and Johnson-Hodge 2007: 79–91. However, while I nevertheless believe Paul to have had a firm sense of Christ's own faithfulness in accordance with God's plan of redemption (cf., e.g., Phil. 2.5–8), I hold open the possibility that *pistis christou* may simply be employed by Paul as basically synonymous for his Christ gospel (the fulfillment of God's covenant faithfulness that calls for the response of human faithfulness) without the precise content suggested by either the objective or subjective genitive reading, though perhaps implying both. In any case, Williams (1980: 275) is surely correct in his assertion that the "'coming of faith' [Gal. 3.24] is indistinguishable from the coming of Christ" (cf. Rom. 3.21–22).

In order to stress, then, the equality in Christ of gentiles qua gentiles with Jews qua Jews, and the unity this must precipitate, Paul will only speak of God's people as an inseparable eschatological entity.[50] This is made abundantly clear in his christological interpretation of Abraham's offspring to whom the promises were made (in some contrast to his treatment in Rom. 4.16) and his metaphor of adoption into God's family in 4.1–7.[51] And the oneness of God's people is most explicitly demonstrated

50. Contra Donaldson (1997: 180), Wright (1991: 143), and Witherington (1998: 240), who understand the first-person plural "we" in 3.14 to refer specifically to Jewish Christ followers, as well as Stowers (1994), Gaston (1987), and Johnson-Hodge (2007: 71), who oppositely suggest Paul is simply identifying with his gentile audience. In regard to this latter notion, while Paul is undoubtedly referring strictly to the gentiles when he employs the term ἔθνη in 3.8, 14 (contra Dunn 1993: 179), it should not be inferred that the fulfillment of the promises to Abraham by virtue of Christ has no direct relevance to Jews. Rather, it has foremost value for them (cf. 2.15–16; Rom. 1.16; 3. 30; 4.16; 7; 9.24; 11.5, 13ff.; 1 Cor. 1.22–24), which is presumed by Paul, but his focus here is on the implications for the gentiles. The "we" in 3.14, then, naturally includes Jews (a given for Paul), and necessarily gentiles.

So too in 3.23, 25; 4.3, 5, the "we" simply refers to God's family "to be" (whether self-consciously so or not; cf. 1.15; see also p. 110 n. 46 below)—both Jews and gentiles. As pointed to in Davies 1948: 168–71; Donaldson 1997: 206–7; and Gaston 1987: 26–28, the association of Torah with Wisdom in Jewish tradition (cf. Sir. 24.8, 23; Bar. 3.37–4:1; *T. Lev.* 14.4; *Sib. Or.* 3.195; *Sipra* 86b; see similarly Paul's association of Christ with wisdom: 2 Cor. 4.4; Col. 1.15–16; Phil. 2.6 [cf. Wisd. 7.26] ; 1 Cor. 1.24; 8.6; 10.4 [cf. Philo, *Leg.* 2.86; Wisd. 10.17; 11.4]; Rom. 10.6 [cf. Bar. 3.29–30]) led to a view in which Torah was universally applicable to all nations (cf., e.g., 4 Ezra 3.28–36; 7.19–24, 37–38, 79–82; 8.55–58, 9.10–12; Pseudo-Philo 11.1–2; 2 Bar. 48.40–47; 13.1–12, esp. v. 8; *1 En.* 63.1–12, esp. v. 8; *Apoc. Ab.* 31.6). It would seem that in some sense Paul presupposes this view of Torah, notwithstanding his assertion in Rom. 2.14 that gentiles do not by birthright possess it. Of course, he concludes that the Torah has now found its fulfillment in Christ (cf. Rom. 7.1—8.4; 9.30—10.4).

51. Paul's use of this metaphor suggests here that both Jews and gentiles have only now in Christ been brought into the divine household (cf. Burke 2006: 68–70, 111–20; Martyn 1997a: 390–91; Dunn 1993: 216–18; Bruce 1982: 196–97; Betz 1979: 209–10), and thus there is no advantage to be had in becoming a proselyte. In the Roman legal process known as *adoptio* "one came under the authority of the *patria potestas* of the adopting father through a fictitious purchase. . . . This was carried out by the *paterfamilias* selling off his offspring into civil bondage (*in mancipio*), thereby making him a slave" (Burke 2006: 68). After three such sales the son was finally free from his father's *potestas*. "After the first two sales, however, the son could be manumitted . . . back to his father, who would receive him by a fresh act of *adoption*" (Dunn 1993: 217). Yet, "Principally, adoption constituted on the one hand a break with the old family and on the other a commitment to the new family, along with all its attending privileges and responsibilities" (Burke 2006: 69). This provides the proper background for Paul's assertion in Gal. 4.1–7.

Burke explains that "the 'redemption of a slave was prerequisite. . . . [and] actually a

in Gal. 3.28: "There is no longer Jew or Greek, there is no longer slave or free, there is no longer male and female; for all of you are one in Christ" (cf. 1 Cor. 12.12–13; Col. 3.11).

Certainly, Paul does *not* mean here that all such sociopolitical distinctions are erased in Christ (cf. esp. Johnson-Hodge 2007: 126–31), but rather that the inequality and divisiveness that traditionally accompanied them is a thing of the former age, which has been eclipsed by the apocalypse of Christ and dawn of the new age (cf. Rom. 3.28–30; 15.5–12; see also Eph. 2.11–22; 3.5–6; 4.1–6).[52] Nevertheless, Paul's ac-

---

step toward adoption' (Theron 1956: 10; Stibbe 1999: 162). . . . I. A. H. Combes asserts that 'adoption of a slave within one's household was in the Graeco-Roman world of the first century . . . not uncommon . . . and many did obtain freedom from (and even adoption by) their masters' (1998: 69; see also Rollins 1987: 108). . . . Paul links a triad of interconnected metaphors—slavery, redemption and adoption. He moves from one to the next in describing his readers as *slaves* (Gal. 4:3; cf. Rom. 8:15), their need of *freedom* (redemption, 4:5) and then receiving *adoption* (4:5; cf. Rom. 8:15). In all this the mediating role and function of Jesus Christ is fundamental, as Smail (1980: 146) concludes, it is 'only as a result of an event of son-making and adoption (*huiothesia*) whose objective basis is in the work of the Son [that] . . . we are now able to address God as *Abba* and to enter into the inheritance that belongs to those who are his children.' In sum, the goal of God's unique Son coming into the world was to secure the believer's adoption" (p. 120). Dunn similarly comments: "the purpose of Christ's death was to recover for the 'sons of Adam' the status of 'sons of God' (cf. Luke iii.38)" (2006: 218; cf. pp. 158ff. below).

It is additionally worth noting here that, despite his different emphases, Paul is quite consistent in his use of this salvific metaphor. Adoption is an eschatological phenomenon caught between the "already" and "not yet" (cf. Rom. 8.14–23; see also 1 Cor. 15.20–57; n. 52 below), and firstly the privilege of Israel (cf. Rom. 9.4; see also 1.16), though available to all who believe, both Jews and gentiles (cf. Rom. 10.11–13; Gal. 3.22ff.). Contra Johnson-Hodge (2007: 67–77), who holds that for Paul adoption is, irrespective of and prior to Christ, an existing reality for Israel, and a new phenomenon among gentiles now being realized through Christ.

52. Clearly, this was in Paul's understanding fully anticipated within the salvation-historical plan of God, beginning with the call of Abraham. I believe Martyn (1991, 1997b: 161–75) confuses Paul's emphasis in Galatians on fulfillment in Christ—and his way of arguing for that reality and its implications—with a repudiation of salvation history. It is not Paul's aim to overturn a "linear, redemptive-historical picture of a covenantal people" with a "punctiliar portrait of the covenantal person, Christ" (Martyn 1997b: 169). Rather, Paul is suggesting the fulfillment of the former by means of the latter, with the intent of demonstrating to his gentile converts that they are, in Christ, *already* "heirs, according to the promise" (Gal. 3.29; cf. Rom. 10.4). The apocalypse of Christ (which, in my understanding, is an "already/not yet" phenomenon—"already" as in Galatians [cf. 2 Cor. 5.17]; "not yet" as in 1 Cor. 15; 1 Thess. 4.13ff.; Phil. 3.20–21; 2 Cor. 4.14; Col. 3.4; Rom. 6.5; 8.23; cf. similarly Martyn 1997a: 105) dramatically and finally fulfills salvation history; it is not contrary to it (cf. n. 17 above).

tual language here must be taken seriously. Without denying the rightful place of Jews within the community (which is not in question here as it is in Rom. 9–11), Paul asserts "in the strongest possible terms that the Gentile members of his churches in Galatia are children of Abraham, heirs of God's promised blessing (3:6–9, 29), rightful heirs of the promise through Isaac (4:28, 31), Sarah's children. It is they who fulfill the Law (5:14; 6:2)" (Hays 2000: 346).

The same must also be true with respect to the title of God's covenant people, "Israel," which Paul indeed qualifies in 6.16 with the addition of τοῦ θεοῦ. J. Louis Martyn (1997a: 576) explains:

> Since the Teachers[53] are identified on the basis of Law observance, Paul will identify Israel on the basis of God, intending thereby to remind the Galatians that God has identified himself by his promise rather than by the Sinaitic Law. . . . Putting 3:15–29 together with 6.15–16, then, one can see Paul's intention. He is saying in effect that it is in the promise, rather than in the Law, that God has invested both the power to bring about the *new* creation and the power to provide the identity of his people Israel, the church. The God of Israel is first of all the God of Christ (3.16, 29), and it follows, for the author of Galatians, that the Israel of God is the people whom God is calling into existence in Christ (1: 6, 13), the community of those who know themselves to be in Christ.

Paul's focus on eschatological fulfillment means that historical Israel's status as nothing less than God's people in the era prior to Christ does not come into explicit view. However, in Rom. 9–11 he will continue to employ the title of "Israel" exclusively for the Jewish people, and irrespective of their acceptance of Jesus as Messiah (though in the context here of an eschatological tension; see chapter 4 below). Martyn therefore remarks, "It would be a great mistake to attribute to Paul the simplistic view that the church has replaced the Jewish people as God's own" (p. 576). But I would additionally point out that the Jewish people are part of the church, and are its founding members. That non-Jews also participate, even if in greater numbers, does not change this fact, and there is thus an absurdity to what amounts to a notion that Jews can replace themselves.

As Paul writes in 2.15–16,

---

53. "Teachers" is the title chosen by Martyn to refer to those influencing Paul's Galatian converts to be circumcised, as targeted in the letter's polemic.

> We ourselves are Jews by birth and not gentile sinners; yet we know that a person is deemed righteous not by the ordinances of Torah but through the faithfulness of Jesus Christ / the faith realized through Jesus Christ [cf. n. 49 above]. And we have come to trust in Christ Jesus, so that we might be deemed righteous by the faithfulness of Christ / the faith realized through Christ, and not by the ordinances of Torah, because no one will be deemed righteous by the ordinances of Torah. (author's translation)

In other words, with the advent of the new creation God's (new) covenant people are defined solely on the basis of Christ and *not* the traditional identity markers prescribed in Torah, "For neither circumcision nor uncircumcision is anything" (3.15; cf. 5.6; 1 Cor. 7.19).

Though disagreeing with the conclusion reached here, Campbell (1993b: 442) has noted that "Paul operates with a fluid concept of Israel." And it seems a virtually inescapable conclusion that the Ἰσραὴλ τοῦ θεοῦ in Gal. 6.16 is the (polemical) equivalence of the οἰκείους τῆς πίστεως (6.10) and the ἐκκλησίαν τοῦ θεοῦ (1.13),[54] as the majority of commentators have affirmed.

Objections to an Ecclesiological Reading

The objection that Paul would not wait until the end of the letter to make such an assertion fails to consider the letter's overall structure and the rhetorical strategy employed. Matera (1988: 79–91; cf. 1992: 179ff.) has aptly demonstrated that "Gal. 5.1–6.17 forms the culmination of Paul's argument to the Galatians, the point he has intended to make from the beginning of the letter. . . . [T]hese chapters . . . are the climax of Paul's deliberative argument aimed at persuading the Galatians not to be circumcised" (p. 80). In fact, though it lay behind the entire discourse of the letter beginning in chapter 2, it is not until chapter 5 that Paul deals explicitly with a prohibition of circumcision for his gentile converts (p. 82).

Richard N. Longenecker (1990: 221) rightly observes that in 5.2–12 all "that Paul has argued for and exhorted previously in Galatians comes to focus here" and parallels the *exordium* in 1.6–10 (compare 1.6 with 5.4, 8; 1.8–9 with 5.3, 10b, 12; cf. also Witherington 1998: 360). He further notes that, while often viewed as something of an excursus from the central concern of the letter up to this point, the paraenetic material of

---

54. Cf. 1 Cor. 3.16; 2 Cor. 6.16, where Paul refers to the church as the ναὸς θεοῦ.

5.13—6.10 serves to advance this same agenda by explicating the sort of intra-community dynamics that are inextricably connected with the Galatians' very identity as "Abraham's offspring, heirs according to the promise" (3.29), which has been called into question because of the "influencers" (cf. 3.1–5; see also Barclay 1988: 216–20).

In this regard, Esler's social psychological approach (1998: 216–17) is once more instructive. He explains "that there is a close relationship between the position of a group with respect to outsiders and its internal conditions." The "uneasy relationship" of a community with other competing groups, is often "reflected in tensions among the membership, such as those which Paul is concerned in Gal. 5.13–6.10." It is inappropriate, then, to draw a "sharp distinction between the outer and inner aspects of a community." Successful incorporation of community members is necessarily dependent upon "their developing a distinctive identity" rather than "simply acquiring a new status or a different set of ethical norms." And it is thus this need for identity transformation—or rather identity recognition—that lay behind Paul's exhortation in Gal 5.13–6.10.

This section is then followed in 6.11–18 by a second set of "forceful arguments against accepting circumcision," which parallels the first set of arguments (compare 5.3 with 6.13a; 5.6 with 6.15; 5.11 with 6.12) (Matera 1988: 83). Hans Dieter Betz (1979: 313) is surely correct in his assertion that found here is the hermeneutical key to the entire letter (cf. Weima 1993: 90–107; Witherington 1998: 445). Longenecker (1990: 287) concurs, remarking that more "directly than in any of his letters, Paul's subscription in Galatians brings to a head and highlights the central matters discussed within the body of his letter."

In all, Ben Witherington (1998: 364) accurately summarizes the significance of chapters 5–6, explaining that

> Paul has followed the indirect strategy known as *insinuatio*, reserving his direct comments about the problem in Galatia until near the end of his arguments. Pursuing such a strategy in a deliberative piece of oratory may be necessary if one is in a position of some disadvantage and if one's audience had in fact given serious consideration to doing the very thing one wishes them to avoid. Paul could not simply dismiss such considerations or ridicule them, he had first to provide solid arguments for his own views before he could exhort the audience to forgo circumcision.

But what is to be made of the reverse order of "peace" and "mercy"? Similar to what has been proposed by Ronald Y. K. Fung (1988: 311), I suggest that Paul first calls for peace upon his readers who follow the rule of the new creation, and then for mercy (God's חסד in bringing about the final, eschatological redemption of his people) also on the total elect from among the Jewish *and* gentile world, as consistent with the prophecy of Second Isaiah LXX (cf. esp. 54.5: "For it is the Lord who is making you; the Lord of hosts is his name; and the one redeeming you, he himself is the God of Israel, and *he will be called so by the whole earth*" [emphasis added]; also 54.15: "behold proselytes[55] will come to you through me and they will sojourn with you, and they will run to you for refuge").

As such, I can affirm Richardson's basic translation (though "faithful people Israel" is far too loose a rendering, obscuring rather than clarifying Paul's actual language), as well as his insistence that there are two groups envisaged here (though they are much more like the "multiple groups" of Ps. 84.9 LXX). And further, that the second group is an expansion of the first (but without, of course, Richardson's so-called "ironical twist"). I would also note that if indeed the Nineteenth Benediction is the background for 6.16 it does not alter the conclusion reached here, which is in any respect more probable than the one he offers.

Two final matters are the otherwise absent explicit identifications of the church as "Israel" in extant Christian literature until the period beginning with Justin Martyr in 160 CE, and a similar absence of such in the rest of the Pauline corpus. Regarding the first point, frankly, it is the weakest of all arguments opposing an ecclesiological reading. It

---

55. Though the context of Isa. 54 may be contrary to any idea of gentile inclusion in the covenant (the LXX translating גר with the usual προσήλυτος, despite the contextual difficulties), it would seem, nevertheless, that Paul equated the "proselytes" envisaged here and perhaps in other biblical texts (cf., e.g., Isa. 56.6–8; Amos 9.11–12 LXX) with his gentile converts, but simultaneously maintained on the basis of the Abrahamic promise, in conjunction with eschatological pilgrimage expectations, that gentiles in Christ should retain an ethnic identity distinct from Jews. That is, they are "proselytes" to the covenant community (cf. 1 Thess. 4.5; 1 Cor. 5.1, 9–13; 10.1ff.; 12.2) that was formerly comprised exclusively by historical Israel, but with the apocalypse of Christ has been fully realized and transformed into a multiethnic community in accordance with God's original promise to Abraham. Thus, his gentile converts must *not* become proselytes according to the traditional terms of the former age. They have already gained entrance into the covenant according to the terms of the new creation, namely, Christ (cf. Acts 15.12ff.).

really says nothing about the meaning of Gal. 6.16 in the context of that letter. As with any arguments from silence there are in reality a host of possible explanations for this, and to conclude on this basis that Paul did not himself make such an identification, or further that his original addressees would not have understood him to have here done so, is a leap of enormous incertitude.

The Christian literature that dates from this period is both variegated and limited. And thus great caution needs to be exercised in making generalized claims as to what early Christians believed, and how they interpreted the biblical texts or Paul's letters specifically.[56] It is, however, worth noting that both *1 Clement* and 1 Peter[57] suggest a strong association of the church with Israel (cf., e.g., 1 Pet. 2.9-12[58]; *1 Clem.* 29.2-30.1), but as distinguishable from the sort of replacement theology that was the agenda of Ignatius[59] or Justin Martyr, and corresponding

---

56. As Wright (1992: 341) points out, much more is known about Second Temple Judaism (however limited that may be) than about the church from 30-135 CE.

57. Welborn (1984) suggests a date of authorship of *1 Clement* between 80 and 140 CE; Lane (1998: 226-27) affirms the conventional date of 94-97 CE; Achtemeier (1996: 43-50) argues for a date of authorship of 1 Peter between 80 and 100 CE.

58. A very similar passage is found in Rev. 5.9-10, in which the vocation assigned to Israel in Exod. 19.6 (cf. Isa. 61.6) is here applied to the church of Christ: "[F]or you are worthy to take the scroll and to open its seals, for you were slaughtered and by your blood you ransomed for God saints from every tribe, and language and people and nation; *you have made them to be a kingdom and priests serving our God* and they will reign on earth" (emphasis added).

59. Cf. Zetterholm 2003: 178-224; he suggests both internal and external pressures led gentile Christ followers in Antioch to separate from the Jewish Christ-following community, and this forms the proper context from which to understand Ignatius. Internally, following the "Antioch incident" of Gal. 2.1-14, gentile Christ followers were relegated by the Jews in the Christ community to "God-fearer" status, and thus were no longer being viewed as full covenant partners with Jews. Externally, the consequences for refusing to participate in the official cult of the *polis* could be obviated only by passing as Jews to the civil authorities. And the close association with Jewish Christ followers made these gentiles vulnerable to general anti-Jewish sentiment and persecution by the populace of the region (which only increased after the Jewish revolt against Rome). Following the Jewish war and replacement of the voluntary temple tax with the poll tax *fiscus Judaicus*, the situation became even more precarious, as to pay the tax would affirm one as a Jew. Such ethnic identification would have been, moreover, contrary to the ideology these gentile believers had embraced, and as agreed upon by both James and Paul, whereby gentiles in Christ *remain* gentiles.

Zetterholm explains that it was these socio-political factors that motivated gentile Christ followers, frustrated "at being reduced to Gentile God-fearers and being trapped in the religious/political system without any possibility of expressing their true religious

anti-Jewish rhetoric of other Christian writers of the second century (cf. *Barnabas, Diognetus*) and thereafter.⁶⁰ One might conclude, then, that this identification was simply taken for granted in at least some quarters, and that there was no rhetorical necessity to make it explicit.

Moreover, to suggest that the church in the time of Paul's writing did not understand itself as "Israel" (or that Paul himself could not have drawn this association) because the eventual schism between what now represents two religious traditions, Judaism and Christianity, did not occur until a much later period of time, is a non sequitur.⁶¹ It falsely

---

identity" (p. 207), to sever their relationship with Jewish believers in order to establish themselves as a recognized *collegium* in their own right. It is from this context that Ignatius writes. The incompatibility of Judaism and Christianity assumed by Ignatius (cf. *Magn.* 10.2-3; *Phil.* 6.1) is "nothing but the ideological goal of the social movement that emanated from the need to create a religious movement separate from Judaism" (p. 203). See also Walters 1998: 183–88; Lieu 2002b: 24–25.

60. Notwithstanding the evident, if not entirely explicit, identification of the church with Israel, Richardson (1969: 24) affirms that *1 Clement* "nowhere suggests that Christianity is set over against Israel, or that Christianity is a *tertium genus.*" Walters (1998: 193) similarly notes: "Whereas the common approach to the Old Testament for early Christian writers was to claim the traditions while attacking the Jewish institutions, Clement used both and attacked neither."

Achtemeier (1996) points out that in 1 Peter, likely written to a mixed audience of both Jews and gentiles (cf. p. 51), the "language and hence the reality of Israel pass without remainder into the language and hence the reality of the new people of God. As a result the language is more than simply illustrative—it is foundational and constitutive for the Christian community" (p. 69). Yet, he also notes that "this is evidently not an instance of anti-Semitism. There is neither the kind of negative invective that characterized the anti-Semitism of the Hellenistic world at this time, nor any hint that Jews have been rejected by God. If anything the implication appears to be that Jews and Gentiles alike have now been taken up into the one chosen people. Nor can it be the case that Jews are simply absent from the regions to which the letter is addressed. There were large Jewish populations throughout the Mediterranean world, including the regions in Asia Minor to which this letter is sent. The reason is simply that for the author of 1 Peter, Israel has become the controlling metaphor for the new people of God, and as such its rhetoric has passed without remainder into the Christian community" (p. 72).

61. The so-called "parting of ways" of Christianity and Judaism is itself a problematic notion, if it refers to the rabbinic Judaism that developed into modern Judaism. Though it would be a clear overstatement to suggest a complete discontinuity between later and earlier forms of Judaism, it is nevertheless the case that rabbinic Judaism was never directly associated with the Christ movement, having come into being no earlier than the late first century, and becoming the dominant form of Judaism not until the fifth century. As illustrated in n. 59 above, if a "parting of ways" is to be envisaged (and I question whether this terminology accurately reflects the historical phenomenon it

presupposes that the church, in identifying itself with Israel, *necessarily* indicates the rejection of one socioreligious group and the establishment of another. But the association of the church with Israel could easily serve the purpose of a non-sectarian reformer like Paul. As such, the reform movement (properly conceived) is depicted as an ideal representation (in some way) of the larger group, but in no way suggesting the usurpation of that group.[62]

As is unquestionably the case with Pauline theology, textual constructs that originate in regard to one set of issues defining a community frequently result in unanticipated and unintended implications for other issues and circumstances that arise over time, which, indeed, can have a profound affect on the community's self-understanding. Thus, *because later generations of the church assumed the identity of "Israel" with the goal of "de-Judaizing" Christianity does not mean that Paul, in initially making this association, would have to have had the same goal in mind. I assert that he did not.*

With respect to the second point, the particular context and hortatory agenda of Paul's letters, the "contingency" of his teaching, must be appreciated. Campbell (1993b: 441–42) has suggested the impropriety of reading an ecclesiological interpretation of Gal. 6.16 into Romans. But to be equally noted is the similar impropriety of reading Rom. 9–11 into Gal. 6.16 (contra Davies 1977: 10).[63] In my view, and that of many scholars, Paul was a coherent thinker. But it should occasion no surprise to observe that he was also a contextual one and could think (with great

---

attempts to describe), it takes place at first between competing Jewish groups—those accepting Jesus as the Messiah and the implications this held for non-Jews seeking entrance into the covenant community (cf. p. 127 n. 10 below), and those that rejected this development—and here clearly beginning already in Paul's time. A *second* split would then need to be posited *within* the Christ movement itself—and here certainly not at any decisive point in time (cf. Lieu 2002b: 11–29, Runesson 2008: 78–92).

62. The premise of Paul's assertion to his gentile converts in Gal. 6.15–16 would seem to be quite clear: Israel should realize that God has through Christ redeemed all creation (in fulfillment of the prophecy of Isaiah), and therefore the gentiles are acceptable to God on this ground alone. Thus, to view the Pauline communities living in accordance with Paul's teaching, i.e., bearing the "fruit of the Spirit" (Gal. 5.22–26), is to see what God promised Israel would be in the new creation (cf., e.g., Isa. 30.18–26; 32.15–17; 44.1–4; 59.21; contrast Isa. 5.1–4; 30.1–17). Why, then, would these gentiles need to become Jews?

63. This is not to suggest that observations made in other of Paul's letters cannot assist in determining the meaning of any part of the one in question. But priority must always be given to the immediate context.

interpretive creativity; cf. n. 55 above[64]) along different "tracks" dependent upon the circumstances that required his pastoral attention.

64. Fishbane's comments on haggadic exegesis (1988: 283) are instructive here: "Aggadic exegesis is thus not content to supplement gaps in the *traditum*, but characteristically draws forth latent and unsuspected meanings from it. In this way, aggadic exegesis utilizes the potential fullness of received formulations and makes this potential actual. For if inner-biblical exegesis particularly serves to fill a felt lack in the *traditum*, and to clarify for all practical or theoretical purposes the plain sense of a Scriptural dictum, inner-biblical aggadic exegesis, by contrast, gives particular emphasis on its *sensus plenior*, its fullness of potential meanings and applications. Legal exegesis and aggadic exegesis thus illuminate different facets of a text's inherent possibilities: the one, legal exegesis, shows how a particular law can be clarified and reinterpreted *qua* law; while the other, aggadic exegesis, characteristically shows how a particular law (or topos, or *theologoumenon*) can transcend its original focus, and become the basis of a new configuration of meaning."

4

Exegetical Investigation, Part II

ROMANS 11.26: "AND SO ALL ISRAEL WILL BE SAVED"[1]

IT IS PERHAPS QUITE ironic that while Paul clearly intends here to remove a certain ambiguity for his audience in regard to God's redemptive plan for Jews and gentiles, this passage has, nevertheless, proven to be puzzling for Pauline scholars. There have in fact been several interpretations proposed for the statement, "And so all Israel will be saved," though I would suggest that most interpreters have in the end rejected what I believe to be the most plausible reading.

Five views of Rom. 11.26 that have been advanced in contemporary scholarship to date include what I have designated (a) "eschatological miracle,"[2] (b) ecclesiological, (c) Roman mission, (d) two-covenant, and (e) total national elect. I will conclude that (e) represents the most exegetically sound understanding of the passage in the context of both the larger argument of chapters 9–11 and the letter in its entirety. As such, the passage, while not demonstrating a direct equation of the church

---

1. An earlier form of this section was published as "'And So All Israel Will Be Saved': Competing Interpretations of Romans 11:26 in Pauline Scholarship," *JSNT* 30.3 (2008): 289–318.

2. I have borrowed this title from Nanos 1996: 257.

with Israel, as Wright holds, neither suggests that these entities are wholly distinct, as per the two-covenant interpretation of Gaston. Nor does it suggest, as in Harink's reading, that while ultimately accomplished through Christ, historical Israel's election is the guarantee of their salvation, irrespective of their acceptance of the gospel.

Additionally integral to the question of the relationship of church and Israel, it will be seen that, contra Donaldson and Campbell, the final restoration of "all Israel" is for Paul an *inaugurated* reality in Christ and does not await a future period of time.[3] Before attending directly to the arguments supporting interpretation (e) above, I will offer a brief survey and critique of the other four options.

Eschatological Miracle

First is the prevailing opinion among contemporary scholars, which I have called the "eschatological miracle" interpretation (a). Here, "all Israel" represents the historical nation, which will turn to Christ after the ingathering of the gentiles and, as also generally held, at the Parousia.[4] It is frequently noted that the idiom "all Israel" is well established in Scripture and the relevant Jewish literature as referring to the people as a corporate whole.[5] As Dunn (1988: 681) explains, its function here is to contrast with both the "remnant" referred to in 11.5 as well as those hardened in 11.25. This partial hardening of Israel recalls Paul's earlier

---

3. Cf. Witherington 2004: 92; in an attempt to refute Wright's interpretation of the church as Israel he asserts, "Paul will go on to insist in chs. 9–11 that non-Christian Israel still has its own story [distinct from the church] and that God intends to complete that story." But for Paul "non-Christian" Israel's story finds its conclusion in God's wrath, as does that of the entire "non-Christian" world (cf. Rom. 2.8-9; 4.14ff; 1 Thess. 1.10; 2.14-16; 5.1-11). Though for Paul Jewish identity (traditionally/non-christologically defined) is and will always be a living reality, there is no promise of blessing for the Jew or gentile outside of Christ, i.e., the church; see further below.

4. So Bruce 1966: 220-22, Munck 1967: 131-38, Mussner 1976: 241-55, Cranfield 1979: 572-79, Käsemann 1980: 311-15, Sanders 1983: 194, Dunn 1988: 677-84, Hofius 1990: 19-39, Barrett 1991: 204-7, Fitzmyer 1993: 618-25, Stuhlmacher 1994: 170-73, Bell 1994: 127-45, Moo 1996: 710-29, Byrne 1996: 348-55, Scott 2001: 489-528, Wagner 2002: 276-98, Esler 2003: 305-6, Witherington 2004: 273-76, Jewett 2007: 694-706, Das 2007: 235-60.

5. E.g., Josh. 7.25; 1 Sam. 7.5; 25.1; 2 Sam 16.22; 1 Kgs 12.1; 2 Chr. 12.1; Dan. 9.11; *Jub.* 50.9; *T. Lev.* 17.5; *T. Jos.* 20.5; *T. Ben.* 10.11; Pseudo-Philo 22.1; 23.1; *M. Sanh.* 10.1.

statement in 11.7 concerning the division of the nation between the "elect" and the "rest."[6]

According to this view Israel's hardening will terminate once the fullness of the gentiles has come in. The fullness of the gentiles is understood as either the completion of the gentile mission (Munck 1967: 135)[7] or the coming to faith of the total number of elect gentiles, as held by most scholars.[8] The phrase καὶ οὕτως in 11.26 is taken by some, notably Reidar Hvalvik (1990: 97), Otfried Hofius (1986: 315; 1990: 35), and Richard H. Bell (1994: 136), in a logical sense, such that it points to what precedes as "the factual and temporal presuppositions of what follows" (Hvalvik 1990: 97). Understood in this way, Paul is claiming that Israel's final salvation is predicated upon the prior salvation of the gentiles.

However, despite the difficulty it presents, Dunn, Douglas J. Moo, Brendan Byrne, Robert Jewett, and most commentators who hold this view read οὕτως in the usual modal sense, indicating the manner of Israel's salvation. Though a temporal sense to οὕτως scarcely occurs in the Greek of the period,[9] these same scholars still read a temporal reference behind Paul's usage of the term here that points to the eventual removal of Israel's partial hardening as the way in which all Israel

---

6. Cranfield (1979: 575), Fitzmyer (1993: 621), Dunn (1988: 679), and Moo (1996: 717) understand πώρωσις ἀπὸ μέρους τῷ Ἰσραὴλ γέγονεν to refer to a partial hardening experienced by all the people of Israel (so also Gaston 1987; see below). Others such as Barrett (1991: 206) and Käsemann (1980: 313) hold it to mean that a part of Israel has experienced a hardening. While ἀπὸ μέρους should probably be understood adverbially and taken with πώρωσις or γέγονεν rather than adjectivally and taken with Ἰσραὴλ (contra Käsemann), the latter meaning is still more plausible given the greater context. The reading "a hardening has partly come upon Israel" or "a partial hardening has come upon Israel" can in either case still bear this quantitative sense provided by the RSV and NRSV of something that affects a portion of the nation and thus reflect the division Paul refers to in v. 7. For this understanding cf. Nanos 1996: 263-64, Byrne 1996: 354, Wright 2001a: 688, Jewett 2007: 699-700.

7. While not exactly holding this position, Cranfield (1979: 575-76) notes its plausibility; cf. Wright 2001a: 688.

8. E.g., Käsemann 1980: 313; Dunn 1988: 680; Ftizmyer 1993: 622; Stuhlmacher 1994: 172; Moo 1996: 718-19, Jewett 2007: 700; and with some qualification Byrne 1996: 354: "Paul is thinking globally; he does not necessarily mean every individual Gentile."

9. It is frequently pointed out that LSJ, BAGD, and TDNT do not indicate a temporal meaning for οὕτως. However, as Van der Horst (2000) has demonstrated, Fitzmyer (1993: 622) and Wright (2001a: 691) may overstate the case in asserting the complete absence of this meaning in Greek.

is saved (Dunn 1988: 681; Moo 1996: 719-20; Byrne 1996: 349-50, 354; Jewett 2007: 701).[10]

In 11.26b-27 Paul quotes Isa. 59.20-21 and 27.9.[11] Most follow Käsemann (1980: 314) and Dunn (1988: 682) in understanding this as a reference to the Parousia, at which time Israel will experience its promised eschatological salvation (cf. Moo 1996: 727; Jewett 2007: 704).[12] While the Parousia is seen, then, as responsible for Israel's salvation, both Dunn (1988: 683) and Hofius (1990: 37) argue that this in no way indicates a so-called *Sonderweg* for Israel that bypasses the gospel and trust in God's act in Christ. It demonstrates only that Israel will come to such faith in the same manner as Paul himself, through a direct revelation of Christ.

It has been questioned here as to whether Paul has in mind the whole nation, but not every single member, as held by the great majority of commentators,[13] or if in fact he is positing the salvation of every Jew, as Bell (1994: 137-40) and Jewett (2007: 702) have suggested. Further, there is disagreement as to whether "all Israel" should be understood diachronically[14] or synchronically. In other words, does it refer only to the nation at one moment in time, such as the generation of Jews alive at the time of the Parousia (the majority position), or does it also include faithful Jews of all time, as Joseph A. Fitzmyer (1993: 623), Franz Mussner

---

10. Another possibility is to connect οὕτως, understood modally, with what follows, καθὼς γέγραπται, rather than the preceding. However, it is rare that Paul employs the order οὕτως . . . καθὼς (Phil. 3.17 being the only instance), and he never pairs οὕτως with the formulaic phrase "just as it is written," rendering this reading highly unlikely; contra Stuhlmacher 1971: 560.

11. Paul's quotation of Isa. 59.20 basically follows the LXX, but ἕνεκεν is replaced by ἐκ; for explanations of this modification see Hvalvik 1990: 91-95; Dunn 1988: 682; Moo 1996: 727; Jewett 2007: 703-4; Stanley 1993; Wagner 2002: 280-98.

12. Bryne (1996: 355) is an exception among those who hold to the eschatological miracle reading, noting that Paul understands this prophecy "as speaking out of its proper time reference, pointing to a 'coming' (of a 'deliverer') which for Isaiah lies in the future but which for Paul has already been realized in the original appearance and saving work of Christ."

13. E.g., every scholar listed in n. 4, with the exception of Bell and Jewett, though Sanders (1991: 126-28) seems to have modified his view from his earlier work, suggesting a universal image of salvation operative in 11.26-36 (i.e., everyone will inevitably be saved; cf. Dodd 1932: 184), despite the tension this presents with Paul's other statements denoting a contrary perspective.

14. See Mal. 3.22 LXX (4.4 MT) as the only instance in the Old Testament where "all Israel" bears this sense; also cf. *m. Sanh.* 10.1; *T. Ben.* 10.11.

(1976: 241–45), and Hofius (1990: 35–36) propose?[15] In either case, this view suggests that the content of Paul's mystery[16] is twofold: (a) Israel's hardening is temporally limited and (b) the salvation of all Israel will follow rather than precede that of the gentiles. Thus, Käsemann (1980: 313–14) has pointed out that Paul is here reversing the traditional Jewish apocalyptic expectation that the ingathering of the gentiles would follow the restoration of Israel—the very order of salvation history he affirms in Rom. 1.16 (cf. Cranfield 1979: 576; Dunn 1988: 682; Jewett 2007: 698).

Despite this view's current scholarly and lay popularity, I would suggest that there is a more plausible way to read Rom. 11.26. Furthermore, although it may not be the role of critical scholarship to allow such a matter to influence exegetical conclusions, it should be noted that if this is what Paul intends to say here, we must judge either his vision of the future and/or overall argument a failure. For after so many generations of Jews have come and gone without this miraculous redemptive event having taken place, one must ask how or why such a salvific plan would be the defining demonstration of God's ultimate faithfulness to historical Israel.[17]

Ecclesiological

A second view, which I have called the "ecclesiological" interpretation (b), holds that "all Israel" is the multiethnic Christ community. This position finds, in addition to Wright (1991: 249–51, 2001a: 687–93), notable proponents in John Calvin (1961: 254–56) and Karl Barth (1968:

---

15. See also Bell 1994: 141. Fitzmyer notes, "For Paul, *pas* Israël means Israel in the ethnic sense and diachronically, because of the eschatological sense of the future σωθήσεται: The Jewish people as a whole, both the 'remnant' (11:5) or 'chosen ones' (11:7) and 'the others' (11:7), will be saved."

16. The term μυστήριον is used by Paul to indicate a hidden aspect of God's redemptive plan that has now been revealed through the gospel of Jesus Christ (Rom. 16.25; 1 Cor. 2.1, 7; 4.1; 15.51–52; Col. 1.26–27; 2.2; 4.3; see also Eph. 1.9–10; 3.3–9; 6.19). For a discussion on Paul's use of this term, see Cranfield 1979: 573–74; Dunn 1988: 677–79; Moo 1996: 714–15.

17. Of course Paul could be wrong about the future, and the historical outcome of what may be predicated in this passage should not be the ruling criterion of the text's meaning or even its ultimate value. However, most seemingly overlook the fact that if indeed this is the way Rom. 11.26 should be read, Paul's entire premise falls apart in the absence of a Parousia within his own generation.

412–17).[18] According to Wright (1991: 248–49) Paul is not anticipating here a

> large-scale last-minute restoration of "all Jews," irrespective of Christ faith, but the chance that Jews, during the course of the present age, will come to Christian faith and so be grafted back in. . . . Paul is envisaging a steady flow of Jews into the church, by grace through faith. God wanted a family from all nations, saved without favoritism and hence by grace alone. Only such a family, of Jews and Gentiles, together, would fulfill all the aspects of the promises made to Abraham.

The "mystery" of 11.25–27 is precisely this, the process in which God is saving his whole people, both Jews and gentiles. Wright (1991: 250; 2001a: 690) argues that "Israel" can justifiably have two different meanings in vv. 25–26, as Paul has already drawn such a distinction between two "Israels" in 9.6 (contra Cranfield 1979: 576). Moreover, the quotation of Joel 2.32 in Rom. 10.13, there applied equally to both Jews and gentiles, already represents the functional equivalent of 11.26, as "those who call upon the name of the Yahweh" is a regular designation for Israel in Scripture (2001a: 665–66). He suggests, therefore, that it is "greatly preferable to take 'all Israel' in v.26 as a typical Pauline polemical redefinition, as in Galatians 6.16 . . . and in line also with Philippians 3.2 ff." (1991: 250; 2001a: 689–90).

Accordingly, Wright (1991: 251; 2001a: 691–93) asserts that the quotation from Isa. 27.9 and 59.20[19] in 11.26b–27 is not a reference to the Parousia, or any other particular future point in time at which the historical nation will be saved. It represents, rather, the inauguration of the new covenant, which has for Paul already taken place by virtue of Christ's resurrection and on the basis of which both Jews and gentiles receive salvation. That the "covenant" referred to here is for Paul the "Jeremianic new covenant," which he believes is fulfilled in his gospel, is widely agreed upon (cf. Fitzmyer 1993: 625; contra Gaston 1987 below; see further Jewett 2007: 705), but the implication of such in the present context is a point of departure. In Wright's understanding it is the covenant in which God has finally dealt with the sin of the entire world,

---

18. See also Ponsot 1982: 413–15; Jeremias 1977: 200.

19. Wright understands Isa. 2.3 (and/or Mic. 4.2) and Jer. 31.34 to be interwoven in Paul's citation here.

not the basis for a special provision to be made for "Jews and Jews alone" whereby "'national righteousness' is suddenly affirmed" (1991: 251).

As such, Paul affirms in v. 27 that "'whenever' God takes away their sins, i.e., whenever Jews come to believe in Christ and so enter the family of God, in that moment the promises made long ago to the patriarchs are reaffirmed" (1991: 251). Regarding vv. 28-29, Wright explains that God is remaining faithful to historical Israel, because there "will always be ethnic Jews among the 'true Jews' of 2:29; there will always be physically circumcised people among the 'true circumcision' of Phil 3:3; there will always be some from 'Israel according to the flesh' . . . among 'all Israel'" (2001a: 693-94).

While this view may be more plausible than most commentators are willing to admit, it nevertheless remains for me untenable. The main difficulty with this reading is that it is seemingly inconsistent with Paul's rhetorical purpose in this section of the letter, namely, to undercut a "gentile supersessionism" taking hold in the church at Rome and to demonstrate that God's redemptive activity continues among the Jews, irrespective of appearances. Further, as will be developed below, many of the exegetical reasons that lead to this interpretation over the prevailing "eschatological miracle" view may be accounted for without having to resort to a redefinition of Israel that does not suit the greater context. One should observe that throughout chapters 9-11, outside perhaps 9.6 and 11.26, "Israel" unquestionably refers to the historical nation as distinct from the gentiles (9.[4], 27, 31; 10.19, 21; 11.[1], 2, 7, 11, 23, 25; cf. 15.8-12).[20]

20. Staples (2008) has made the interesting suggestion that Paul associates gentile Christ followers with the ten northern tribes of Israel, and this comports with Paul's quotation from Hosea in 9.25-26, the larger context of which envisages the restoration of the Northern Kingdom that had been dispersed and intermingled among the nations (cf. 1.9-10; 2.23; 7.8; 8.8). Accordingly, Paul is arguing here that the coming together again of the house of Israel with the house of Judah envisaged by the prophets (cf. Jer. 3.18; 30.3; 31.31-34; Ezek. 37) is now taking place in Christ. Staples thus understands Rom. 11.25 to be a direct quotation of Gen. 48.19 LXX: "[Ephraim's] seed will become the fullness of the nations." He then interprets 11.26 along the lines of the ecclesiological reading.

In response to this proposal, I would suggest that to the extent this understanding informs Paul's theologizing in Rom. 9-11 it could only represent one layer of his thought among others. To restrict Paul's soteriology to the restoration of the "whole house of Israel" in this fashion, leaving no role for the nations except in terms of their identification with Israel, is to suggest that the host of other prophetic texts that envisage the eschatological pilgrimage of the nations *consequent* to Israel's final restoration

Roman Mission

The third view identified above, which I have called the "Roman mission" interpretation (c), is one proposed by Nanos (1996: 239–88). Here "all Israel" represents Jews in Rome who have initially responded to the gospel, as well as those who are at present hardened, but, upon the beginning of Paul's apostolic mission to the gentiles in Rome, will be moved to jealousy by his success and consequently believe (pp. 247–55, 259–61). Nanos first suggests that the context from which to properly read 11.25–26 is what Paul understands to be an anomaly taking place in Rome of the divine two-step pattern that is apparent in Luke's portrayal of Paul in the book of Acts (pp. 268–72). The pattern consists of the restoration of Israel in each new location, as Paul first preaches in the synagogue, before the gospel proclamation can then fully turn to the gentiles, incorporating them into the people of God. It is this anomaly that is responsible for the false assumption among gentile believers in Rome that they have replaced Israel in God's redemptive plan; a notion Paul sets out to correct (pp. 273–74).

There are two central and interconnected aspects to Nanos's thesis. First, the division of Israel between the Christ-following remnant and those who are at present hardened signals the beginning of Israel's restoration and thus the beginning of the gentile mission (pp. 259–60). Second, Nanos reads the phrase in v. 25 ἄχρις οὗ τὸ πλήρωμα τῶν ἐθνῶν εἰσέλθῃ as a reference to the commencement of Paul's gentile mission in Rome (pp. 264–67). He argues that the temporal sequence and future sense of time indicated by ἄχρις οὗ renders the sense of εἰσέλθῃ along the lines of an event that is coming or beginning. Additionally, Paul's employment of the term πληρόω in Rom. 15.19 to refer to the completion of his mission in the east, and his stated intention in 15.29 to eventually come to Rome in the "πληρώματι of the blessing of Christ," suggests that Paul's reference here to the πλήρωμα of the gentiles should similarly be understood in the context of Paul's missionary activity.

Thus, what may appear here to be a reversal of the order of salvation history affirmed in Rom. 1.16 is not the case. Nanos concludes that Paul's purpose is to demonstrate to the gentile Christ followers that Jews

---

ultimately had no influence on him. As I will argue below, I find it more likely that Rom. 11.26 denotes the final salvation of Israel as interdependent with—but not inclusive of—that of the gentiles.

are vicariously suffering a hardening in order that salvation can come to them. And this hardening upon a part of Israel will cease once the gentile mission begins. At this time some Jews formerly hardened will be made jealous by Paul's missionary success and believe (pp. 260, 285).

While intriguing, and in my mind superior to the "eschatological miracle" interpretation, this reading does, however, beg an important objection in that it relies on a very speculative notion that Paul understood an anomaly of sorts taking place in Rome. Could he really have thought that the gentile mission would only fully begin in Rome upon his arrival?[21] Despite the correlations to his reading that Nanos attempts to draw from Paul's travel plans in Rom. 15, I do not at all see there Paul suggesting such a thing.

In fact, his assertion that he has chosen not to preach "where Christ has already been named," so as not to "build on someone else's foundation" (15.20; cf. 2 Cor. 10.15–16), suggests that, though he expresses hope to come soon to Rome and preach the gospel (1.15), Paul would not think (or at least claim) his presence critical for the advent of a mission to the gentiles. Moreover, Nanos's proposal that this anomalous state of affairs for the church in Rome meant that "their faith lacked a proper foundation" and that Paul must set them right (p. 239) does not seem to be warranted. The remarks of Karl Paul Donfried (1991: 45) bear mentioning:

> Paul in no way indicates a weakness in the foundation [of the church in Rome]. Quite the contrary, in 15.14 we hear, "I myself am satisfied about you, my brethren, that you yourselves are full of goodness, filled with all knowledge, and able to instruct one

---

21. Though Nanos's overall reading of 11.25-26 is not necessarily dependent on such, the notion that the content of Israel's jealousy (παραζηλώσω) is to be found in Paul's missionary success among the gentiles is in my opinion doubtful. Esler (2003: 288–93) demonstrates that the concept of jealousy refers, rather, to "the emotional intensity and chagrin with which [Israel] should view the blessings bestowed on Christ followers and desire to regain her rightful position in God's favor." This is the "point of the expressions 'provoked to jealousy' and 'provoked to anger' in Deuteronomy 32," which Paul quotes in 10.19. It "is not that Israel responded in wrath against her enemies, for Israel took not a step against them, but rather her anger is closely aligned with her jealousy as a way of describing the passion with which Israel should regard the successes being achieved by her enemies as a stimulus impelling her to return to God" (p. 292). Esler further comments with respect to 11.13b–14: "Paul says he is glorifying his ministry, meaning making much of it and showing how good it is, to stir up the passions of the Israelites to reacquire what is really theirs when confronted with others who have laid hold on it instead" (p. 297).

another." Then in the next verse he explicitly indicates that what he has just written is "by way of reminder"—hardly a situation which would indicate "that for Paul, Christianity in Rome still needed an apostolic foundation. . . ." Further, one would hardly expect Paul to do such a rebuilding job simply "in passing" (15.24) as he goes to Spain [cf. Jewett 2007: 916].

For these reasons I am unconvinced by the "Roman mission" reading.[22]

Two-Covenant

A fourth view is the "two-covenant" interpretation (d) proposed by Gaston (1987; cf. pp. 49–53 above), and prominently shared by Stendahl (1976a: 1–5, 1976b: 48–53),[23] Stowers (1994: 285–316), and Gager (2000a: 128–42). Stendahl (1976a: 4) points out that once Paul has directed his attention to the future of Israel, beginning in Rom. 10.18, there is no mention of Jesus Christ through to the distinct doxology without a christological element that concludes the section in 11.33–36. He argues that this is consistent with the rhetorical purpose of the entire section—to check gentile arrogance directed towards Jews that may express itself in an impulse to evangelize them (1976b: 53).

As noted in pp. 51–52 above, in Gaston's analysis the partial hardening of Israel does not refer to a division within Israel between Christ followers and non-believers, but to Israel's failure to understand that a way of salvation for gentiles was made available through Christ (1987: 143). Yet that a faithful remnant of Jews like Paul have responded to this missionary task is grounds for God to act graciously in saving "all Israel" (p. 148).

However intertwined Israel's salvation may be with that of the gentiles, it is nevertheless on different terms. It is brought about by the "Deliverer," according to Paul's quotation of Isa. 59.20–21, who is in this

---

22. One could perhaps merge aspects of Nanos's interpretation with the eschatological miracle reading such that it would not be necessary to understand the "fullness of the gentiles" as indicating the commencement of Paul's mission in Rome. Instead, Paul could be predicating the salvation of "all Israel"—understood as Jews who received the gospel at the first, as well as some formerly hardened—upon the prior salvation of the gentiles. But, rather than a "worldwide" phenomenon as it were, this would have to do with events in Rome in particular, along the lines of Nanos's reading. This would seem to be a more plausible alternative to the eschatological miracle view, but it nevertheless suffers from many of the same exegetical difficulties raised below.

23. Stendahl (1995: x–xi) had since distanced himself from this reading.

reading God and not the returning Christ. Gaston concedes that while Paul may have had Christ in mind here, it is Christ precisely as an agent of a special way of salvation for Israel (pp. 147–48). The quotation of Isa. 27.9 affirms God's commitment to the Sinai Covenant that applies only to Israel and according to which God faithfully forgives Israel's sins (pp. 143–44). Gaston suggests that 11.28–29 makes this quite explicit. Israel's election is irrevocable and thus their final salvation is sure (p. 148).

It is my opinion that this is the least plausible of the five interpretations examined here. That Christ is not explicitly mentioned from 10.18 through to the end of the section fails to demonstrate that Paul has in mind a parallel means of salvation. Paul knows of only one people of God, one (covenant) community of salvation that is composed of both Jews and gentiles, as his olive tree analogy in 11.17–24 clearly illustrates.[24] As it is for gentiles to enter anew, Jews remain or are brought back into this community solely on the basis of Christ faith, a premise that Paul thoroughly establishes from the very beginning of the letter and explicitly asserts in 11.23: "And even those of Israel, if they do not persist in unbelief, will be grafted in."

Gaston makes several exegetical attempts throughout Romans to argue for a dual redemptive track, including: (a) reading πᾶς, ἄνθρωπος, and Paul's "Adam-Christ" typology as referring exclusively to the gentile world (p. 116; he implicitly holds [pp. 64–79] that the first-person plurals in Rom. 5–8 should be understood similarly; cf. p. 56 above); (b) understanding the condemning function of the law and its inability to justify as only applicable to gentiles who stand outside Israel's covenant; and (c) interpreting the "righteousness of God" as God's inclusion of gentiles in the people of God, but apart from God's covenant with Israel

---

24. Interestingly (and perhaps tellingly), Gaston (p. 147) finds this section to be inconsistent with the rest of ch. 11. Nanos (2005a: 32) holds the interpretation of the olive tree metaphor as the "family of God" to be misguided and suggests that it should be read exclusively as a vehicle by which Paul can elaborate upon his prohibition against gentile supersessionism—gentiles have been made acceptable to God only by God's grace, and there are no grounds then for boasting (vv. 17–21). He notes Paul's reference to Jews who have "fallen" and thus been "cut off" (v. 22), which subverts his earlier assertion regarding Israel's "anomalous state"—their present "stumbling" but not "so as to fall" (v. 11). However, unlike v. 22, Paul in v. 11 is referring to Israel as a whole. Further, ἵνα is better read here as purposive ("in order to"), indicating the divine intention behind Israel's stumbling, and not resultant ("so as to") (cf. Jewett 2004: 673). Wright (2001a: 686) affirms, "Paul does not ignore the fact that some have indeed fallen, nor does he rule out the possibility that some individuals may remain in that condition."

(pp. 119–22). Yet, his reading remains unpersuasive because it does not adequately explain Israel's failure (9.31; 11.7)/"stumbling"/"rejection" and its resulting benefit for gentiles in 11.11–15, nor the existence of Jewish Christ followers such as Paul himself. Both of these problems have been addressed by Donaldson (2006: 27–54).

With respect to the first problem, Gaston's attempt to correlate Israel's "stumbling" with a rejection of Paul's gospel of righteousness for gentiles (pp. 33, 146) makes little sense. How can Israel's rejection of Christ as a means of salvation for the gentiles be the very thing that allows such to be possible? (11.11; Donaldson 2006: 34–35, 41–42). A secondary notion in Gaston's reading (clearly made necessary by the logical difficulty inherent in the first), which is more directly proposed by Stowers (p. 286), is that Israel's "stumbling" lay in their failure to fulfill the missionary task.

But if it be assumed that Paul continued to hold to the Torah alone, and not Christ, for the Jew how does this explanation account for the possibility of proselytism?[25] In that the number of proselytes most certainly outnumbered gentile converts to his gospel, how could Paul, understood in terms of a two-covenant approach, reasonably suggest a systemic error on Israel's part to adequately address the gentile problem, which only in turn made necessary Christ?[26] As Donaldson (2006: 42) affirms, it is difficult to imagine Paul would argue as he did on such fundamentally flawed grounds. The analysis of 2.17–29 in the preceding chapter demonstrates that while Israel did indeed fail at being "a light to the nations," this was the result of their yet-to-be-redeemed (i.e.,

---

25. Outside the Christ movement Donaldson (2006: 37) notes the absence in Jewish literature of a categorical rejection of proselytism in favor of some other form of universalism. Paul's argument from the Shema that gentiles qua gentiles have an equal share with Jews qua Jews in salvation (Rom. 3.29–30) is a direct result of and subordinate to the notion that God has provided the single means of salvation for all through Christ (Gal. 2.15–16; cf. Hays 2005: 69–74; see further below). Independent of this conviction there is little justification for holding that Paul would have believed necessary a means of salvation for gentiles qua gentiles (cf. pp. 69–71 nn. 29 and 31 above).

26. Stowers (1994) ignores proselytism (cf. only the brief mention on p. 151), focusing instead on Paul's objection to the "righteous gentile" approach to gentile salvation over against his Christ gospel. Gaston (1987: 139) finds Paul's critique in 2.17–29 directed towards the attempt of Jewish teachers to proselytize gentiles. But he fails to explain why Paul would have found the approach illegitimate and thus the need for another means by which gentiles could be saved. In fact, proselytes could have been deemed full members of Israel's covenant and therefore removed from the law's condemnation in accordance with his reading.

sinful) state shared with the gentile world (cf. Rom. 3.19-20; 5.12-14; 7.7-13; 11.32; Gal. 3.21-22). It seems apparent, then, that Israel's failure in 11.11-15 possesses explanatory power only to the extent that Christ is seen as integral to both those historically outside Israel's covenant and to the very fulfillment of the covenant itself (cf. 2.25-29; 3.21-31; 5.18-21; 8.1-4; 9:30—10.4; 11.27).

Regarding the second problem, Gaston (p. 77) and Stowers (p. 156) understand Paul to be an anomalous figure who sought to identify fully with his gentile converts in Christ but who nevertheless did not advocate other Jews to follow this example. Yet Paul's (a) expression of sorrow and anguish for Israel in 9.1-5, (b) quotation in 9.27 of Isa. 10.22, which speaks of the remnant of Israel who will be saved, (c) prayer for Israel's salvation in 10.1, and (d) desire to make Israel jealous that they may be saved in 11.14 strongly suggest in light of 10.9 that he indeed expected other "Israelites" (9.4), according to which Paul describes himself (11.1), to trust in Christ for salvation as he did (cf. Gal. 2.15-16; Donaldson 2006: 47, 50).[27] Gaston's proposal (p. 142) that the remnant of which Paul claims to be representative in 11.1-5 should be understood not as Jewish Christ followers but as those who have engaged the gentile mission further begs the question as to why Paul would have believed it necessary for himself to submit to God's righteousness in Christ (3.21-22; 10.3-4), but not for other Jews of which he was thus an example to do the same (Donaldson 2006: 50).[28]

Moreover, it is unlikely that Paul in Romans, as Gaston (pp. 13, 135) asserts, could have simply ignored the contradiction posed by the actual existence of Jewish Christ followers if he did not hold this to be normative. Paul does make mention of the church in Jerusalem, and hopes to enlist the support of the Roman believers in the successful delivery of his collection to them (15.25-31). It must be asked, then, if Paul would

---

27. Jewett (2007: 680) comments on 11.14: "The verb σῴζειν ('to save') reflects early Christian missionary language as 1 Cor 7:16; 9:22; and 1 Thess 2:16, and takes up the theme of 'salvation' from 11:11. In the light of Rom 10:8-10, it is clear that Paul functions as an agency in this charismatic process, which involves proclamation of the gospel, a response of faith, a public confession, and becoming part of a house or tenement church."

28. If Israel's "stumbling" lay in their past failure to fulfill the gentile mission, would not Paul see it incumbent upon all Israel to now join him as he sought to fulfill it? Gaston fails to adequately address the implications here, resulting in this thoroughly idiosyncratic portrait of Paul.

not have been compelled to offer some explanation of this phenomenon to avoid what would seem to cause certain confusion among his non-Jewish audience given Gaston's thesis (Donaldson 2006: 48–49).

Total National Elect

A fifth view, which I have called the "total national elect" interpretation (e), holds that "all Israel" refers to the complete number of elect from the historical nation.[29] I am convinced that even though it has minority acceptance among contemporary scholars this represents the most plausible understanding of the passage. There are four key arguments in this reading's favor.

Argument 1: Coherence of Chapters 9–11

The first argument concerns the coherence of Paul's argument in chapters 9–11—the relationship between Paul's statement here and what he has affirmed in chapters 9 and 10.[30] In 9.6-8[31] he explains that God's promise

---

29. For this position see Lenski 1945: 723–28; Ridderbos 1975: 354–61; Horne 1978; Hendriksen 1981: 379–82; Refoulé 1984: 181; and esp. Merkle 2000, for the following similar arguments in favor of this reading and counter-arguments against common objections.

30. To be considered is Campbell's caution (2000: 189) that one not "seek anachronistically to judge Paul by our standards of logic and inconsistency," but "maintain an awareness that Paul was operating in a culture very different from ours, where somewhat different standards of consistency—perhaps even rationality—and methods of argument applied." Nevertheless, the perceived contradictions and inconsistencies between chs. 9–10 and 11, as suggested by Dodd (1932: 183), Watson (1986: 168–74), Räisänen (1988: 182, 192–96), Beker (1990: 48), Bell (1994: 140), and others, are in my view more apparent than real. Though interpreting Rom. 11 differently than proposed here, see on this matter Campbell 2000: 187–211; Fitzmyer 1993: 609–10. While Paul was not a systematic Western thinker, he was undoubtedly a coherent one, and such coherence can and should be expected in his argumentation; cf. Ehrensperger 2004: 43–120.

31. The reference to "children of promise" in v. 8 surely intends to include gentiles in Christ (cf. 4.11-17; 8.14-17) in anticipation of 9.24-26. Yet, the presence of what may best be described as a "true Israel" alluded to in 9.6, a phenomenon that Paul grounds in the fact that not all of Abraham's physical descendents were chosen, likely points to strictly the believing remnant of historical Israel described in 9.27-29 (though clearly inclusive of all Jews who may still come to Christ faith), as the majority of scholars affirm, contra Wright (cf. esp. Johnson-Hodge 2007: 101–2; see also Cranfield 1979: 473–74, Dunn 1988: 539–40, Campbell 1992: 44, 143; 1993b: 442–43, Fitzmyer 1993: 559–60; Moo 1996: 574; Esler 2003: 279; Witherington 2004: 252; Jewett 2007: 574–75). But that Paul in 9.6 does indeed have his Jewish contemporaries already in view is evident in light of vv. 1–5. This assertion can hardly be restricted to God's past operation, e.g.,

to Abraham never extended to all of Abraham's physical descendants and therefore God has been faithful to the promise irrespective of the rejection of Jesus Christ by many within Israel. This does not necessarily rule out that Paul could later advance a notion in which at some point in time the "elect" would encompass the nation in its near entirety.[32] However, it does suggest that Paul assumes the saved of historical Israel would comprise a smaller group from within the people as a whole.

Still further, in 10.12 Paul asserts that there is no distinction between Jew and Greek (cf. 3.22). As discussed in the preceding chapter, Paul's premise that he is at pains to demonstrate throughout both Romans and Galatians is *not* that ethnic distinctions are erased in Christ, but that (a) there is now equality between these two groups (with the intent of unity; cf. Rom. 15.3–12; Gal. 3.28) and (b) the Christ event represents the single means by which Jews and gentiles participate in God's redemptive activity—"Everyone who calls on the name of the Lord shall be saved" (10.13; cf. Eph. 2.11–22; 3.5–6; 4.1–6). On the basis, then, of both 9.6 and 10.12 it must be asked if Paul would nevertheless propose either an alternative means by which "all Israel" is saved or some sort of miraculous salvific event (e.g., a direct revelation of Christ at the Parousia) for Israel alone. It seems unlikely he would.

Additionally, there is the matter again of Paul's expression of sorrow and anguish for Israel in 9.1–5 and his prayer for their salvation in 10.1. There is little question that Paul believes the Parousia to be imminent (cf. Rom. 13.11–12; 16.20; 1 Thess. 4.15–17; 1 Cor. 15.51–52). If he is then envisaging in 11.26 either the salvation of all Jews or some sort of definitive large-scale salvific event for the nation prior to or at the Parousia, "9.1–5 is a sham and 10.1 a mere formality" (Wright 2001a: 689; cf. Hvalvik 1990: 100).

Argument 2: The Nature of Paul's Rhetorical Questions Regarding Israel's Salvation

A second argument is that the critical questions posed in 11.1 and 11.11 ask only whether Israel has completely forfeited their privilege as God's

---

as a reference merely to the figures of Ishmael and Esau in the Abraham story. Even less likely is Gaston's proposal (1987: 93), in which Paul is affirming that non-Jews in Christ, while equally Abraham's children (ἐξ' Ἰσραὴλ), are nevertheless not part of Israel.

32. It might be suggested that Paul's stress on God's freedom in election throughout ch. 9 anticipates this very thing in ch. 11 (but see n. 46 below).

people (Merkle 2000: 713). Paul's single concern is if God's redemptive activity will continue among the Jews. This would indeed be an important question to address for a gentile audience that had apparently begun to presume God's attention was wholly redirected from Israel to non-Jews, especially in light of both the historic tension between Jews and Greeks in the Greco-Roman world surrounding the turn of the era[33] and that between unbelieving Jews and the Christ movement (cf. 11.28a). But while often read as such, there is simply nothing here to indicate that Paul has in mind a special salvific plan for Israel as the necessary corollary to his insistence that God has not cast off his people.

Argument 3: The Timing of Paul's Expectations Concerning Israel's Salvation

Third, throughout chapter 11 the present outworking of Israel's salvation remains the focus and direction of Paul's thought (Merkle 2000: 713). The evidence that God has not rejected his people is according to v. 5 that "in the present time there is a remnant chosen by grace." In vv. 13–14, Paul's hope for Israel's eventual "fullness" is expressed in terms of his contribution in saving more Jews, however many this may be,[34] by provoking them to jealousy through his own mission to the gentiles (cf. 10.14–21).[35] Finally, v. 31 states that νῦν is the time in which Israel is the recipient of God's mercy.[36] The salvation of all Israel can hardly then be

33. See Stanley 1996 for an analysis of this interethnic conflict in the cities of the eastern Mediterranean basin during this period; cf. also Esler 2003: 357–59.

34. As Munck (1967: 124) points out, τινές need not necessarily imply a small number, but only less than πάντες. See my remarks above on Rom. 9.6–8.

35. Though Paul assuredly did not think that he alone would be the agent responsible for Israel's "fullness," there is no real contextual evidence to suggest he is deliberately contrasting the "limited" result of his own mission with a supposed future salvific event for the nation; contra Hafemann 1988: 51–52; Johnson 1984: 97–98; Moo 1996: 692.

36. This second νῦν in v. 31 is included in several MSS and followed by most commentators. Moo (1996: 711) notes that "the arguments in favor of its inclusion slightly outweigh those for omitting it." But that νῦν expresses here eschatological imminence, as suggested by Dunn (1988: 687), Moo (1996: 735), Käsemann (1980: 316), Bell (1994: 150–51), or that Paul understands the entire time between the Christ event and the Parousia (i.e., the present age) is the "eschatological now," as proposed by Cranfield (1979: 586), Barrett (1991: 209), Jewett (2007: 711), is unconvincing and unnecessary. Wright's comments on this verse (2001a: 694) are instructive: "Even if this 'now' were missing . . . the earlier occurrence of the same word in v. 31, together with the hint that this mercy comes about 'because of the mercy shown to you,' would be enough to tell us what Paul thinks is going on. The mercy that is shown to Israel according to the flesh is not something for which they will have to wait until some putative final day; it is

predicated upon some particular future point in time, whether a period after the ingathering of the gentiles or the Parousia.

Argument 4: The Substance of Paul's "Mystery" in 11.25b–26

A fourth argument for this view concerns the very content of vv. 25b–26. First is the stress that should be placed upon "until" in v. 25b (Merkle 2000: 715). Both the eschatological miracle and Roman mission readings understand ἄχρι οὗ to indicate a temporal sequence resulting in a change of circumstances. Yet it must be asked if this presumed change of circumstances to take place after the event in question has been completed is contextually relevant. For example, in 1 Cor. 11.26 Paul writes concerning the continual observance of the Lord's Supper ἄχρι οὗ the Lord comes. Clearly, Paul is not stressing to the church at Corinth that there will come a time when the Lord's Supper will lose its significance. Rather, the point is that this practice continues to function as such as Paul explains until the end of the age. In the same way, the point here is not that Israel's hardening will be reversed after the fullness of the gentiles has come in, but that at this time Israel's hardening will be eschatologically fulfilled (Merkle 2000: 716).

But moreover, a second matter is that the notion of hardening[37] itself seemingly belies the insistence that it will be at some point in

---

not, therefore, something that can get the church off the hook by postponing a serious reckoning with contemporary Judaism until a conveniently delayed eschaton—as the laissez-faire thought of the Enlightenment might urge. It is available 'now.'"

37. See the discussion of "hardening" (πώρωσις) in Nanos 1996: 261–64. Though Nanos (wrongly, in my view) holds that the hardening envisaged here is temporary, he rightly explains that hardening is "a strengthening in the course [unbelieving Israel has] chosen for themselves.... [W]hile God may 'strengthen' them in their chosen course to accomplish his purpose for his people, he does not choose their course for them. They have chosen not to believe; God has 'strengthened' them in this course so that 'salvation [can come] to the Gentiles, to make them jealous'" (cf. p. 65 n. 18 above). This is an important recognition, however inexplicable the question of the relationship between human responsibility and divine sovereignty—to the extent that Israel's unbelief is in the first place an integral part of God's redemptive plan—remains to be (cf. 11.33–36!). As with Pharaoh, God's imposition is not upon Israel as tabula rasa, but upon (like all humanity) a sinful and rebellious people through whom God will freely and unconditionally bring about the greatest good (cf. 9.14–16)—salvation not only for Israel but also the gentiles. It is according to which that Paul evokes in 11.20–21 the pottery imagery of Jer. 18.1–6; Isa. 29.16; 45.9 (cf. Wisd. 15.7; Sir. 33.13; 1QS 11.17–22); see Wright 2001a: 640, Wagner 2002: 62–68.

Coming to a similar conclusion, Wagner (2002: 240–54) holds that Isa. 6.9–10 "stands behind Paul's conflation of Deuteronomy 29.4 and Isaiah 29.10" in Rom. 11.8,

time reversed. Wright (2001a: 639, 677-78; 1992: 271) argues that in an apocalyptic context[38] hardening is understood as befalling those who do not accept God's forbearance as an opportunity to repent (cf. Rom. 2.1-11).[39] As a result, once judgment finally does come upon them it will be seen as just (cf. 1 Thess. 2.14-16; 2 Macc. 6.12-16; Wisd. 12.9-27; 19.4-5; Gen. 15.16). This period of hardening happens then "during a temporary suspension of God's judgment that would have otherwise fallen," allowing time for some to escape. This is further suggested by Paul's Pharaoh analogy in 9.17-18.[40] It is not something that occurs for

---

as (a) Isa. 6.9-10 and Deut. 29.4 are the only two texts in the LXX that "speak of the failure to perceive with the heart, eyes, and ears," and (b) Isa. 6.9-10 and 29.10 "explicitly attribute the blinding of Israel to God's judgment on the nation" (pp. 245-46). Asserting that "the wider theological and literary contexts shape Paul's appropriation of these texts," he comments, "Isaiah 6 stands as a pivotal passage within the book of Isaiah. It sets up a profound theological problem with which much of the rest of the book must deal, namely, that God himself has determined to judge his people for their rebellion against him. In order to ensure the inevitability of their punishment, God commissions Isaiah to make them yet more stubborn and unresponsive to his word.... Within LXX Isaiah as a whole, however, this dire pledge of inevitable and unrelenting destruction is not God's final verdict on Israel. Subsequent oracles continue to sound the dark notes of Isaiah 6, but running alongside this somber motif is a countermelody that grows in strength and eventually swells to become the dominant strain of Isaiah's prophecy. Israel's God, who has afflicted his wayward people with blindness and insensibility, promises in due time to heal and to comfort them" (pp. 252-53).

38. For the pervasiveness of apocalyptic material in Rom. 9-11, see Johnson 1989: 124-31.

39. Wagner (2002: 240-57), who follows Robinson (1902: 92) in understanding πώρωσις as denoting "insensibility," suggests that, as in Isa. 29, Israel's "spiritual stupor" is only temporary and will in fact be reversed at the eschaton, in accordance with the eschatological miracle interpretation. But this is to misunderstand Paul's eschatology. The "reversal" envisaged by Isaiah is in keeping with the "new covenant" theology (cf. Isa. 32.15; 44.3; 59.21; Deut. 30; Jer. 31; Ezek. 36) that informs Paul's view of the significance of the Christ event, *and is thus for him an inaugurated reality*. The restoration of Israel prophesied by Isaiah has begun and will come to its fullness as Jews beyond the present remnant continue to trust in God's act in Jesus Christ, being stirred to jealousy through the salvation of the gentiles. It is not that God removes Israel's πώρωσις that allows for them to accept Jesus as Messiah, but it is the acceptance of Jesus as Messiah that removes the πώρωσις, allowing for the prophesy of Isa. 29.18-19 LXX to be realized: "And in that day the deaf will hear the words of a book, and the darkened and befogged eyes of the blind will see; the poor will rejoice with gladness on account of the Lord, and those without hope will be filled with gladness" (cf. 2 Cor. 3.3-16; nn. 41 and 42 below).

40. According to Wright, God "raised up" Pharaoh "rather than cutting him off instantly," for the purpose of both "rescuing Israel" and "declaring God's name to the world." This is what Paul understands God to be now doing through Israel. Note Wright's

a period of time only then to be removed, "except in the context of a coming to faith" (Wright 2001a: 677; cf. 2 Cor. 3.16).[41] Paul's quotation of Ps. 69.22-23 in 11.9-10 makes this quite explicit.[42] Instead it is allowing time for gentiles to enter the covenant community (cf. 11.19-20),[43] as well as for Jews like Paul himself to recognize Jesus as the Messiah through whom the promises are confirmed (cf. 11.23; 9.4-5; see also 4.16; 15.8-9).[44] This is precisely what is proposed in 9.22-26,[45] the notion of which underlies the entire section—by the paradoxical means

---

understanding here of ἐξεγείρω, contra Fitzmyer (1993: 597), Moo (1996: 594-95), and Dunn (1988: 554) who, drawing parallels with Hab. 1.6; Zech. 11.16; Jer. 50.41 (27.41 LXX), understand the term in the sense of "introduce into (salvation) history."

41. Wright notes (1996: 681) that Moo "gets this exactly the wrong way around," as do seemingly all who hold to the eschatological miracle interpretation.

42. Of dispute here is the meaning of διὰ παντός. Following Wright (2001a: 678) I hold the RSV, NRSV, NASB, and NIV correct to translate the phrase "forever" and not "continually," as Fitzmyer (1993: 607) suggests. But the same basic point is made in either reading. Wright (2001a: 677) comments, "This judgment is simply the other side of the coin of ethnic Israel's rejection of the crucified Messiah. The judgment, moreover, will not be reversed; as long as ethnic Israel refuses to see the crucified one as Messiah and Lord, their eyes will be darkened (v. 10) and their backs bent (cf. 2 Cor. 3:14-15)."

43. Donaldson (1997: 222-23) similarly points out this purpose that lay behind Israel's unbelief. Contrary to the two-covenant reading, it is only in this way that Israel's "stumbling means riches for the world" and "their defeat . . . riches for the gentiles" (11.12). He notes the similarity here with a strand of Jewish tradition, whereby gentiles who do not submit to the law will perish in the final judgment (cf. 2 Bar. 30.4-5; 44.15; 51.6; 82.3-9 with 41.1-6; 4 Ezra 7.37-38 with 7.72; 8.56-58; Apoc. Ab. 31.1-8; also represented at Qumran: CD 14.4-5 with 4.7-12; and the Tannaitic literature: b. ʿAbod. Zar. 3b; b. Yebam. 24b.; Pesiq. Rab. 161a; pp. 224-25).

44. It is apparent that Paul did not view the hardening of unbelieving Israel as insurmountable, otherwise he could not hold out the hope that some from this group (the "rest" of v. 7) would be saved (and thereby numbered among the "elect") by means of his own gentile mission (11.13-14; cf. 10.19-20; see also n. 21 above) (except in the case of the Roman mission reading that is otherwise problematic). But while the logic of Paul's premise might require as much, Wright (2001a: 678) is likely correct when he remarks, "Paul does not suppose that any particular ethnic Jews are subject to this condemnation; there is always room for them to come to faith. The perpetual condemnation, as far as this passage is concerned, lies upon the rejection of the crucified Messiah, not upon this or that person who acquiesced in that rejection."

45. With respect to vv. 25-26, in contrast to Campbell (cf. p. 47 above) I understand Paul's quotation from Hosea to point to the creation of God's "new covenant" people that includes both Jews and gentiles in Christ. That the original context is consistent with such a reading seems to once more (as in 2.24) escape Stanley (2004: 157-59). For this view, see further Wagner 2002: 78-92.

of Israel's hardening God is effectually calling[46] both Jews and gentiles through the gospel of Christ (cf. 10.14–21; 11.11–15).[47]

46. The notion of "call" (καλέω) (cf. 1.7; 8.28–30; Gal. 1.6; 5.8, 13; 1 Cor. 1.2, 24, 26; 7.18; Phil 3.14; 1 Thess. 2.12; 4.7; 5.24; 2 Thess. 1.11–12; 2.13–14; Col. 3.15; see also Rom. 1.1; Gal. 1.15), as Wright (2001a: 642) explains, "is one of the regular ways of describing the process whereby the gospel's sovereign summons evokes the obedience of faith." It seems that for Paul, as probably consistent with Pharisaic thought (cf. Josephus, *J.W.* 2.162–63; *Ant.* 13.172; 18.13; but also note in the Qumran literature: 1QH 6.5–10; 15.13–19; 16.1ff.; 1Q14 frg. 10, 7; see Sanders 1977: 261–70; 1992: 373–74, 418–19), divine and human action work together, representing two sides of this same salvific process; cf. Witherington 2004: 246–49. Inextricably connected are thus God's freedom, initiative, and sovereign purpose and "human freedom, responsibility [and] obedience" (Wright 2001a: 603). And he perhaps presupposed the former in light of the latter (cf. 1 Thess. 1.4–10).

Paul has established in ch. 9 that the basis for membership in God's people has always been preeminently the free exercise of God's grace and mercy rather than the observance of the ordinances of Torah (9.12), which, according to "the regular rabbinic exegesis ... the patriarchs were already obeying ... even before it was given to Moses" (Wright 2001a: 637; cf., e.g., *m. Kid.* 4.14; *2 Bar.* 57.1–2; *Jub.* 24.11; Sir. 44.20). And there is therefore no natural right to such (cf. 4.1–8), for either the Jew or gentile (cf. 11.21–22). In the culmination of God's sovereign redemptive plan that began with the promise to Abraham (cf. 4.13–22) and worked its way through the story of Israel (cf. 9.4–13), God's grace and mercy has been manifested in the gospel of Christ (cf. 3.21–26), trust in which being then the evidence of membership in God's called/elect people (9.25–26; cf. 11.5–6; 3.28–30). Barrett (1991: 171) explains, "It is important to recall here that the seed of Abraham ... became ultimately Christ (Gal. iii. 16), and was subsequently expanded to include those who were in Christ.... This means that election does not take place (as might first appear from Paul's examples) arbitrarily or fortuitously; it takes place always and only *in Christ*. They are elect who are in him; they who are elect are in him (cf. Gal. iii. 29)."

47. To be especially noted is the ambiguity in 9.22–23 concerning the agent responsible for the σκεύη ὀργῆς, as compared with the σκεύη ἐλέους of whom God is the express agent. Concerning such, Bryan (2000: 163) suggests, "There is, of course, no implication that [the vessels of wrath] need to remain so. Indeed, the divine patience that has endured them is by its nature a constant sign they need *not* remain as they are, and an invitation to repent.... Similarly with ripe for destruction—it is significant that Paul does not say *prokatērtismena* ('prepared in advance')—a word he certainly knows, for he uses it at 2 Corinthians 9.5—but merely *katērtismena* ('prepare,' 'ready,' or, as I suggest, ripe): the whole point being, again, that those of whom Paul speaks are in a state where they are begging for destruction *at this point in the story*. By whom, then, have they been thus made ripe? Even in *Koinē* Greek written by a Jew, we should not simply assume that all passives are 'divine.' In this case Chrysostom was surely on the mark when he suggested that Paul's meaning is that the vessels have prepared themselves—that Pharaoh, for example, was 'fully ripe indeed, but to be sure, from his own resources and by himself' (*Homilies on Romans* 16.8). What matters, in any case, is that the divine patience surrounds Pharaoh and all those others of whom Paul speaks. Thus the entire phraseology with which he describes their sin is really only a foil whereby he may make

A third aspect of vv. 25b–26 is the proper sense of οὕτως. Paul consistently uses this term in a modal sense (e.g., Rom. 1.15; 4.18; 5.12, 15, 18–19, 21; 6.4, 11, 19; 9.20; 10.6; 11.5, 31; 12.5; 15.20) and, as the majority of scholars confirm, it should be understood in this way here.[48] But, contrary to Dunn, Moo, and Jewett, there is no real contextual support for understanding any temporal weight behind οὕτως. Thus, the mystery that Paul reveals is not the limited nature of Israel's partial hardening after which time all Israel will be saved. If Paul really wanted to say this one would suspect he would have written καὶ τότε (as many of the Greek church fathers apparently wished he had; cf. Scott 2001: 491–92), not καὶ οὕτως. The mystery is rather how Israel's salvation is interdependent with that of the gentiles, as 11.11–24 establishes and vv. 30–32 confirms.[49]

In addition to the arguments in support of this interpretation, I believe it firmly holds up against the four common objections to it.

Objection 1: The Role of the "Remnant" and the Anticipation of Israel's "Fullness"

Scholars such as C. E. B. Cranfield (1979: 576–77) have criticized this reading as rendering 11.26 anti-climactic.[50] But perhaps this is merely a case of anticipating a certain conclusion Paul himself never reached. And so, for example, many rightly note that the remnant motif in 11.1–5

---

clear the miracle of that patience, and the grace that follows it." See also Wright 2001a: 641–42; Cranfield 1979: 495–97; Barrett 1991: 177–78; Witherington 2004: 257–59; Jewett 2007: 596–97; contra Moo 1996: 597–600, 607; Byrne 1996: 302.

48. Contra Käsemann 1980: 313; Van der Horst 2000; Witherington 2004: 274. Though Rom. 1.15; 6.11; 1 Cor. 14.25; and 1 Thess. 4.17 have been claimed to demonstrate the so-called logical meaning, they arguably bear the same sense of manner as every other occurrence of οὕτως in Paul.

49. This reading corresponds quite well with Paul's hortatory purpose in the section to quell ethnic pride and arrogance over Jews. Further, it is worth pointing out that this is the only understanding of Israel's salvation presented here, save perhaps the ecclesiological reading, that could be reasonably arrived at if vv. 25–27 were absent from the section. The omission of these verses has no prima facie affect on the larger argument; the logic of Paul's thought flows seamlessly from v.24 directly to v. 28. This begs the question as to whether it is hermeneutically appropriate to interpret Paul's clearer and more extensive discourse through the lens of three enigmatic verses, or if the reverse would be more advisable.

50. See also Nanos 1996: 256. Moo (1996: 722) notes the faulty notion behind the criticism that this reading turns 11.26 into a "purposeless truism": "Paul's focus is not so much on the *fact* that all Israel will be saved as on the *manner* in which it will be saved."

functions as a sign of hope for the future of Israel and not as a substitute for the whole nation (Johnson 1984: 96; Hafemann 1988: 49; Wagner 2002: 108-17, 273, 353; cf. Wright 2001a: 676).[51] But this only suggests that Paul expects more, perhaps many more, Jews to be saved.

As mentioned above, the same can be said for Paul's reference to Israel's "fullness" in 11.12. It need not at all imply a future mass salvific event. It seems far more likely that it simply denotes all those of Israel who will eventually believe (cf. Jewett 2007: 677-78).[52] It is thus roughly parallel to Paul's reference to the fullness of the gentiles, which, against Nanos, most scholars understand along these same lines. It should not be taken as incidental to the point that Paul explicates in vv. 11-15 a process through which God is saving both Jews and gentiles.

Objection 2: The Eschatological Character of 11.15

Another objection is that Paul's association of Israel's acceptance with resurrection in 11.15 indicates that all Israel's salvation awaits the Parousia when the final events of the age will ensue.[53] But such an understanding, if it is accepted, does not suggest anything other than the time when all of the elect from Israel will have come in (cf. 4 Ezra 4.35-37; 2 Bar. 23.4-5; Rev. 6.11; 7.4; 14.1). And this would be consistent with the apparent widespread belief in Second Temple Judaism that the eschaton would follow Israel's repentance (Allison 1985: 23-30; Donaldson 1997: 223-24; see further pp. 168-70 below).[54]

---

51. As Sanders (1985: 95) has noted, "remnant" language evokes the hope of national restoration in the Second Temple period (cf. p. 168 n. 52 below).

52. Wright (2001a: 680-81) comments on 11.12, "This is the first moment that Paul has suggested an increase in the number of Jews who come to be not merely Abraham's physical descendents but his 'seed' in the full sense of 9:7-8. Up until 10:21 the number seemed to be diminishing, whittled down to a remnant. Even in 11:1-10 this 'remnant' seemed to consist simply of the small number who, like Paul, had through God's electing grace abandoned the status based on 'works' and embraced the messianic faith focused on Jesus. Now for the first time he begins to say something further may yet happen. Israel according to the flesh has been 'diminished' [ἥττημα]; now it will be brought to fullness."

53. So Cranfield 1979: 563; Käsemann 1980: 307; Dunn 1988: 658; Moo 1996: 694-96; Barrett 1991: 199-200; Stuhlmacher 1994: 167; Byrne 1996: 339-40; Witherington 2004: 269; Jewett 2007: 681. For an opposing viewpoint see Fitzmyer 1993: 613; Wright 2001a: 682-83.

54. Cf. Bar. 2.27ff.; 4.1ff.; Jub. 1.14-23; 23.26; T. Dan 5.4-13; 6.4; T. Sim. 6.2-7; T. Jud. 23.5; T. Iss. 6.4; T. Zeb. 9.7-8; T. Mos. 1.18; 2 Bar. 78.6-7; Tob. 13.5ff.; 14.4-7; 4

However, it is also likely that Paul, intending to humble his gentile audience and inspire in them a desire to see more Jews saved, interprets here Israel's role christologically (Hays 1989: 61–62; see also Wright 2001a: 682–83; Donaldson 1997: 223). He is saying that because Israel's rejection functioned like the death of the Messiah in bringing salvation to the gentiles, whenever a Jew is saved it carries the significance of resurrection. It should be celebrated, then, in the words of Wright, as a "little Easter."[55]

Objection 3: The Language of Paul's Quotation of Isa. 59.20 and 27.9

A third objection concerns Paul's quotation from Isaiah, but, as explained in p. 96 above, there is no reason to understand 11.26–27 as a reference to the Parousia.[56] The purpose of the citations from Isaiah would seem to simply underscore Paul's assertion throughout the entire section: God *is* fulfilling through Christ his promise to save Israel.

As Wright (2001a: 693) notes, "God said that Abraham's family would be the bearers, as well as the recipients, of salvation, and this is what will happen" (cf. 3.1–4). The word of God has not failed (9.6a). In spite of the resistance to the gospel on the part of many within Israel (11.28a), Jews have been and will continue to be saved (cf. 11.24; see also 5.6–11), because "they are beloved, for the sake of the ancestors; for the

---

Ezra 4.38–39; 4QMMT C 12–32; see also *b. Sanh.* 97b, 98a; *b Šabb.* 118b; *Sipre Deut.* 41; Acts 3.19–20.

55. Cf. Wright 1991: 248. That 11.15 connotes both a christological and eschatological meaning is probable, particularly given the eschatological framework in which Paul views his own apostolic mission—this mission being the context of vv. 11–15.

56. Cf. Hvalvik 1990: 93: "Another argument in favour of an eschatological interpretation is the more or less clear eschatological ring of the quotation and the context (cf. v. 25). This is, however, seldom spelled out.... It is, of course, a prophetic future within the framework of Isaiah, but does Paul understand it as future? Probably not. As in the case of Isa. 11.10 quoted in Rom. 15.12 the future tense in 11.26 should be regarded 'als schon realisierte Prophetie'. For Paul the Deliverer has already come from Zion (cf. 9.33). This is clearly seen if one compares Rom. 11.28 with 15.8. In 11.26–28 the salvation of 'all Israel' is linked with the promises to the fathers (cf. also 9.5), and in 15.8 Paul tells how these promises have been confirmed when 'Christ became a servant to the circumcised'. This means that God's truthfulness toward his promises is seen in Christ's first coming." I would qualify Hvalvik's remarks by suggesting that "God's truthfulness toward his promises" is seen by Paul as being *inaugurated* by Christ's "first coming."

gifts and calling of God are irrevocable"[57] (11.28b-29; cf. 9.7-13; 10.21[58]; see also argument 2 above). It is thus fully consistent with this reading.

Objection 4: "All Israel" Must Mean the Whole Nation and Not Merely the Elect

A final objection is that interpreting "all Israel" in such a qualified way does not do justice to the phrase. Can πᾶς Ἰσραὴλ truly indicate anything other than the great majority of Jews or even every Jew? First, as noted above, in the Old Testament and in Jewish sources the phrase is overwhelmingly used in a corporate sense without referring to every single member (see n. 5 above). This understanding, especially given what Paul has already claimed in 9.6-8, is also consistent with the often-cited parallel rabbinic expression in *m. Sanh.* 10.1, "all Israel has a share in the age to come," which is then followed with a list of exceptions (cf. Käsemann 1980: 313; Barrett 1991: 206; Wright 2001a: 689-90; see Sanders 1977: 147-82 for a full discussion surrounding this text).[59]

---

57. The adjective ἀμεταμέλητος means literally "without regret"; cf. 2 Cor. 7.10, which is the only other instance of this term in the Old or New Testament. Jewett (2007: 708-9) explains, "The formulation thus relates to the rhetorical question in 11.1, whether God has 'rejected his people,' and reaffirms the continued status of 'beloved [by God] on account of the fathers' in 11.28. That the God of biblical faith was in fact frequently depicted as changing his mind [Jewett notes: Gen. 6.6-7; Exod. 32.14; Deut. 32.26; 1 Sam. 15.11, 35; Jer. 18.8, 10; 26.13; Jonah 3.10] provides the background for this denial that she had done so with regard to Israel's distinctive gifts and calling. Although God was free to withdraw such privileges, while humans often come to regret and then to renege on their commitments, God's faithfulness remains firm."

58. Cf. Jewett 2007: 648-49: "The final citation in the chain is drawn verbatim from Isa 65:2, with a transposition of the expression 'all day long' to the point of emphasis at the beginning of the sentence.... The transposition seems to resonate with the poignant question that opens the next pericope, whether God has rejected Israel. The entire argument [of Rom. 9-11] aims at denying this prejudicial possibility. The transposition reinforces the idea that God's patient mercy remains 'continually' in force with regard to his beloved Israel. The expression of reaching out hands also points in this direction: the NT hapax legomenon ἐκπετάννυμι τὰς χεῖράς μου ... is a 'gesture of appealing welcome and fellowship' [Cranfield 1979: 541]. The expression ὅλην τὴν ἡμέραν ... is a semiticism meaning 'uninterruptedly' or 'without pause,' thus accentuating the extraordinary steadfastness of God's mercy.... The function of the citation is to draw the final consequence from [10.14-21], namely, that while they remain a 'disobedient and disputatious people,' God continues to reach out his hands imploringly to Israel.... [A]s the subsequent pericopes will go on to show, divine mercy will in the end rule the day (11:32)."

59. As pointed out above, Jewett (2007: 702) holds 11.26 to mean every member of "the house of Israel, who, without exception, would be saved." He notes πᾶς "does

Second, Moo's contention (Moo 1996: 722), developed apparently from Cranfield's objection to the ecclesiological interpretation (1979: 576), that "Israel" in v. 26a must have the same referent as in v. 25b (where the nation collectively is in view), and therefore should not be understood in terms of the elect alone, is simply illogical. Strictly speaking, it is an unavoidable conclusion that "all Israel" is the elect from the nation.[60] By definition, those who are ultimately saved must be the elect, even if this would mean the nation of Israel in its near entirety (after the partial hardening is supposedly removed) at the Parousia, as per his reading.

That the "elect" and "rest" of v. 7 represent for Paul fixed memberships, as seemingly presupposed by the eschatological miracle interpretation, cannot be maintained in the scope of chapter 11 (see nn. 44, 46, and 47 above). Again, there is at the time of Paul's writing a remnant of Jewish believers, and he firmly believes more Jews will be saved via the paradoxical means of hardening that has come upon a part of the nation. This is "all Israel"—the "elect" as distinguished from the "rest" who remain in unbelief. Thus, while Paul's hope is for the elect to eventually include a large number from the historical nation, he makes no definitive predictions here, or in any of his other letters, that such will actually be the case. There is every reason to believe Paul understood a number of individual Jews would in the end be disqualified from the future age (as would also be clearly the case among the gentiles).

On the basis of the overall integrity of this view in contrast to the others that have been offered, it would seem that the salvation of "all Israel" in Rom. 11.26 should indeed be interpreted as the total elect from the historical nation. It not only makes sense of the immediate context,

---

not lend itself to expression of exceptions," and suggests that nothing in the immediate context suggests any exceptions, "because v. 27 goes on to argue that 'all' of Israel's sins will be taken away and v. 32 concludes that God will show mercy 'to all.'" However, this is to ignore Paul's premise regarding the true identity of Israel. *All* who truly are Israel will be saved, having *all* their sins forgiven (cf. n. 50 above). With respect to v. 32, "all" is not a reference to every individual, but to people groups. God has shown mercy to both the Jew and gentile, and thus to all humanity, by means of the Christ event (cf. p. 62 n. 9 above).

60. Except in the case of the ecclesiological interpretation, whereby "all Israel" would constitute not just those from historical Israel but gentiles as well.

but also stands in agreement with Paul's teaching throughout the entire letter and elsewhere.[61]

SUMMARY OF FINDINGS

The exegetical analyses of Rom. 2.29; Gal. 6.16; and Rom. 11.26 have yielded a complex picture as to the relationship of church and Israel. Romans 2.29 demonstrates that Paul could apply the title "Jew" to Christ followers, irrespective of traditional ethnic markers. Galatians 6.16 similarly demonstrates that even the covenant title "Israel" could be applied to the church, the total elect from both the Jewish and gentile world. However, Rom. 11.26 reveals that Paul still conceived of Israel exclusively in traditional ethnic terms, as distinct from the other nations. But at the same time the passage suggests that only those of historical Israel who accept Jesus as Messiah would ultimately have right to this identity. Jews who have yet to submit to the gospel, while still in the present time part of Israel, must turn to belief before the impending judgment in order to participate in the promised covenantal blessings, which are realized only through Christ.

There seems to be in Paul's perspective, therefore, a certain crisis of identity within Israel; though it is a crisis that he understands to be ultimately integral to God's redemptive program. And one might preliminarily conclude on the basis of Rom. 2.29 and Gal. 6.16 that Paul would indeed make the polemical claim that Christ-following gentiles are more truly "Israel" than Jews who fail to believe (cf. Phil. 3.3). Yet, *Paul explicitly warns in Rom. 11 against any such triumphalism and supersessionism among his gentile converts* (cf. 1 Cor. 4); this is not befitting God's people who must earnestly seek the salvation of all Jews, to whom

---

61. Of particular interest here is 1 Thess. 2.14–16. Much has been made of its apparent theological disparity with Rom. 11, leading some to postulate that it is an interpolation; e.g., Pearson 1971 (note that Pearson articulates several other objections to authenticity as well). However, as the above analysis has demonstrated, the passages are in fact quite consistent with one another. Concerning the contemporary theological and ethical implications that arise, then, from this reading, I would suggest any understanding that holds Israel's partial hardening as a phenomenon extending beyond the first century to be wholly inappropriate. In terms of a canonical reading of Paul, I believe the divine hardening and judgment proposed here can be viewed as proleptically fulfilled in the events of 70 CE (cf. Matt. 8.11–13; 10.16–23; 11.21–23; 21.42–43; 23.29–24.51; 26.64; 27.25; Mark 13; 14.62; Luke 10.13–15; 13.34–35; 17.22–37; 19.41–44; 21; 23.27–31; Rev. 6–19; see also 2 Thess. 2.1–4).

these gentiles are indebted.⁶² *They have become part of Israel's story* (cf. 1 Cor. 10.1ff.; Rom. 1.1–4, 16; 9.4–5; 11.16–18; 15.8–12; see also Johnson-Hodge 2007: 131).⁶³

In the following two chapters I will return to the various viewpoints surveyed in chapter 2 and offer a critical review of their respective strengths and weaknesses in light of the exegetical findings of this and the preceding chapter. And, in dialogue with these scholars, I will also engage other relevant Pauline texts, as they help to further clarify the question at hand.

The main focus of chapter 5 will be the matter of whether or not Paul should be read as a sectarian. As already suggested in chapter 3, I hold that Paul was a Jewish reformist who remained personally connected to the synagogue, and understood the church to be a natural extension of the greater Jewish community, not as its replacement. As has been broached in both chapter 3 and here, chapter 6 will concern the universality and yet Israel-centeredness of Paul's Christ gospel—how Christ is the fulfillment of the prophetic promises of both Israel's restoration and that of all creation. Accordingly, I will confront the charges of anti-Judaism and supersessionism, as per the views of Gaston and Harink. With respect to Harink's view in particular, the relationship between apocalyptic and salvation history readings will also be addressed. Finally, I will discuss the fundamental issue of divine election, as it brings to light the way in which Paul could properly conceive of the church as standing in continuity with Israel.

---

62. I would note here the rather obvious, but nonetheless important, point that Paul possessed a sense of moral authority in his criticism of the Jewish people, as expressed in Phil. 3.5–6; Rom. 11.1; and Gal. 1.13–14, which would not be shared by his gentile converts. And this makes all the more precarious an undertaking to interpret Paul faithfully, yet with sensitivity, as one who along with Paul's historical gentile converts neither shares this ethnic background.

63. The brilliance of Israel is that their story in Scripture is really the story of the whole world. The origin of the Jewish nation is not grounded in creation, but is a historical innovation in response to a universal plight, requiring in turn a universal salvation. As Brueggemann (1997: 431–32) notes, "The call of Israel is juxtaposed to the crisis of the world, a crisis that arises because the nations have not accepted their role in a world where Yahweh is sovereign. One reason for Israel's existence is that creation is under curse for disobedience, and Yahweh insistently wills that the world should be brought to blessing. Israel's life is for the well-being of the world." See further on this point in ch. 6 below.

5

Negotiating Perspectives, Part I

SEVERAL IMPORTANT ASPECTS TO the question of the relationship of church and Israel are brought to the fore by C. H. Dodd and Ernst Käsemann, despite the absence (and, largely, antithesis) in their respective work of much of what would eventually come to form the New Perspective on Paul. Crucial to Dodd's perspective is the notion of salvation history: the continuity between Israel's history, the coming of Christ, and the subsequent formation of the church. The emphasis here is on realized eschatology—promise and fulfillment via the transformation of God's people in Christ. However, for Käsemann the crux of the matter lay in his apocalyptic interpretation of the Christ event that stresses, rather, the discontinuity between the periods before and after. Though he does admit to some degree of continuity (and warns against the "profaning" of Israel's sacred history; cf. 1971: 87), in this reading the church preeminently represents a new people of the new age in contrast to Israel, the people of the former age that has been superseded by Christ.

What is particularly pertinent in these respective viewpoints is that they reflect on a certain fundamental level the point of departure for later scholarship addressing this question. However, most concede that there is some measure of truth to be found in each, and the question is then how to properly correlate these elements in such a way as to accurately reflect the full picture presented in the Pauline corpus. The resulting combinations of continuous and discontinuous elements, both in terms of Paul's theology as well as his social context, have produced a spectrum of competing interpretations.

In any case, the above has demonstrated that a good deal of what Dodd and Käsemann have specifically proposed on the question has in fact been incorporated by various scholars since the advent of the New Perspective. But there is as well a good deal that has rightfully been rejected and need not be revisited; a full defense of New Perspective insight is beyond the scope of this study. The advances made in Pauline scholarship as a result of this movement have been largely presupposed throughout. Though Paul's doctrine of justification pervades both Dodd and Käsemann's understanding of the relationship of church and Israel, it will not be attempted here to refute the Reformation model of this doctrine, or overt misconceptions of first-century Judaism characteristic of "old perspective" scholarship. The following negotiation will focus, therefore, on the other seven scholars represented in chapter 2.

THE CHURCH IS ISRAEL

In agreement with Dunn, Wright, and Donaldson, I understand Paul to conceive of the church of Jews and gentiles as, in a precise sense, "Israel"; in continuity with the covenant community from its inception, but dramatically transformed—expanded—into a multiethnic community as a result of the Christ event, in fulfillment of the promise to Abraham. *The central point here is that "Israel" and "covenant community" are in one respect synonymous for Paul.* Their social identity having been reconstructed within the Jewish symbolic universe, gentile Christ followers have thus become in a very real way part of God's historical people, who are now affirmed so by virtue of Christ faith.

Though necessarily maintaining a subordinate identity distinct from Jews (see below), gentiles in Christ have nevertheless come to share with them a common heritage. Though not arriving at the same conclusions here, the main assertion of Caroline Johnson-Hodge in her recent study of kinship and ethnicity in Paul's letters (2007) is most relevant: "For Paul, kinship and ethnicity cannot be merely metaphorical, for lineage, paternity, and peoplehood are the salient categories for describing one's status before the God of Israel" (p. 4). Indeed, as Williams suggests (1997: 167), Galatians demonstrates that Paul can think of "Israel" as only fully realized after the advent of Christ and consequent inclusion of the gentiles.

All considered, this understanding provides the best explanation for (a) the several passages in which Paul draws a sharp distinction between his gentile converts and the gentile world (cf. 1 Cor. 5.1, 9–13; 10.20; 12.2; 1 Thess. 4.5), while claiming Israel's history as their own (cf. 1 Cor. 10.1ff.); and (b) the status he affords to both Jews and gentiles in Christ as "the circumcised" (Phil. 3.3; cf. Col. 2.11–15), "holy ones" (compare Dan. 7.18, 27 with Rom. 1.7; 1 Cor. 1.2; 2 Cor. 1.1; Phil. 1.1; Col. 1.2; 1 Thess. 3.13; 2 Thess. 1.10; see pp. 158ff. below), "Jews" (Rom. 2.29), "Abraham's offspring, heirs according to the promise" (Gal. 3.29), "the Israel of God" (Gal. 6.16), and participants in the promised covenant renewal (cf. 2 Cor. 3.3ff.; 1 Cor. 11.23ff.).

While for Paul the status of "Israel" is seemingly both affirmed and conferred on the basis of Christ, Dunn and Donaldson have correctly observed that he does not deny to the unbelieving portion of the nation the identity of "Israel" in the full covenantal sense, though they are presently disobedient to God's purposes.[1] The resulting tension in demarcating God's people is rightly interpreted, then, by both scholars as a product of the overlap of the ages: the eschatological tension between the "already" and the "not yet" in which Paul situated his apostolic mission. Ultimately only the believing part of historical Israel—those who accept Jesus as the Messiah—will retain the covenant title "Israel."

However, a point of disagreement with Dunn and Donaldson (as well as Campbell) concerns Paul's understanding as to how this will come about. The notion that Israel's final restoration will occur in conjunction with or just prior to the Parousia and will entail a mass salvific event for the nation has been shown to be a largely implausible reading of Rom. 11. Closer to the mark is Wright, yet his equation of "Israel" with the church in v. 26 is equally unlikely. It is best to understand the passage as describing the eschatological process initiated by the resurrection of Christ, with which Paul was actively engaged, whereby God is both restoring historical Israel and calling those from the gentile world who are to be included among God's people.

This is in particular where Donaldson's approach is flawed. Because he reads Rom. 11 along the lines of the "eschatological miracle" interpretation, and notes the emphasis on historical Israel's present failure that makes possible the mission to the gentiles, he discounts any sense

---

1. However, it seems that Paul refers to Israel when they are not exhibiting covenant fidelity in a qualified way, as *merely* Ἰσραὴλ κατὰ σάρκα (1 Cor. 10.18; cf. Rom. 9.8).

in which Paul may be drawing from "eschatological pilgrimage" conceptions as the basis of his apostolic mission. According to this notion the ingathering of the gentiles is *necessarily* dependent upon Israel's prior restoration; the order of salvation cannot, then, be reversed, lest the logic on which the notion itself stands is completely destroyed.

Although Paul does indeed point to Israel's collective "stumbling" as instrumental to the gentile mission, as Nanos has observed (though I also disagree with his overall reading), this is not antithetical but actually integral to their own restoration, which is from Paul's perspective a present, process-orientated reality. It is part of Israel's eschatological "pruning" (cf. Nanos 1996: 260), which will both bring about and reveal the identity of the "true Israel," the elect from within the historical nation.

In relation to this, what is further problematic in Donaldson's analysis is the limitation he places upon Paul's creative use of the existing traditions found in first-century Judaism. Why must Paul's apostolic self-understanding be located within a single track of thought? Donaldson concedes the plausibility of combining "righteous gentile" and "eschatological pilgrimage" patterns of universalism (so Nanos, Campbell; cf. also Fredriksen 1991), but asserts the impossibility of combining "righteous gentile" and "proselyte" notions. But this remains impossible only if one excludes a priori the possibility that Paul thought multilaterally. There is every reason to believe that Paul utilized all categories of universalism available to him in first-century Judaism as a conceptual grounding for his gentile mission, depending upon the particular contexts with which he was confronted and to which he responded in his letters.

THE CHURCH IS NOT ISRAEL

And it is precisely "righteous gentile" and "eschatological pilgrimage" categories that allow Paul to continue to observe an ongoing distinction between Jew and gentile in Christ. Thus, equally significant to the notion that "Israel" has become the equivalent of the church, is the parallel conviction that as a result of the Christ event the nations are now joining a restored Israel in worship of the one creator God, the God of Israel.[2] As such, Israel remains ever distinct from the nations, yet both

---

2. In Paul's understanding the ingathering of the gentiles that follows Israel's restoration means that they are brought into Israel's covenant on equal terms. This is a concept seemingly foreign to the majority of relevant prophetic texts (outside perhaps Isa. 54.15 LXX; 56.6–8; 66.18–21; Amos 9.11–12 LXX), as well the postbiblical literature outside

groups are united as one in Christ.³ *In this respect, "Israel" and "covenant community" are not the same entities. It is only the latter that has been transformed to the extent that it is no longer occupied exclusively by the former, but now by representatives from all nations in accordance with the promise to Abraham.*

Much of Paul's letter to the Romans is consumed with the dynamic of this new social reality, as Esler (2003) has observed in terms of recatagorization theory (cf. p. 61 above). Nanos (2000: 221–22) likewise asserts that Israel and the gentiles remain distinguishable groups but are given through Christ a superordinate identity (i.e., children of Abraham), which is the basis for these separate groups to be united as one. Campbell (2006: 138) similarly points to the importance Paul places upon the preservation of ethnic diversity within the Christ community: "'In Christ' Jews and gentiles do form one real association in which they are indissolubly connected because they all belong to him. Their unity emerges not from ethnic transfer on either part but from their being reconciled to one another in their abiding difference to form one new body in him."

I would suggest, moreover, that Paul in Romans nuances this notion relative to specific rhetorical motives in different sections of the letter. On one hand, Israel's covenant privileges are now extended equally to gentiles (cf. Campbell 1992: 47–48, 88; 1993a: 513; 2000: 196; 2005: 305–7; 2006: 100–101, 129–31; Dunn [1998: 523, 525–26] also proposes this line of thought, though drawing other implications from it). This

---

the New Testament, which suggest either (a) the subordination of the gentiles by virtue of such pilgrimages (cf., e.g., Isa. 14.1–2; 18.7; 45.14; 60; Hag. 2.6–7, 21–22; *Pss. Sol.* 17.29–35; *Jub.* 32.19; Sir. 36.11–17; *Tg. Isa.* 25.6–10; *1 En.* 90.30; *2 Bar.* 72.2–6) or (b) the gentiles' salvation independent from Israel's covenant, in which their status in relation to Israel is ambiguous (cf., e.g., Isa. 2.2–4; 25.6–10; 42.1–9; 49.6; 51.4–6; Jer. 3.17; Mic. 4.1–3; Zeph. 3.9; Zech. 2.11; 8.20–21; Tob. 13.11–14; 14.5–7; *1 En.* 10.21–11.2; 48.4–5; *Sib. Or.* 3.556–72, 710–23, 757–75; *T. Levi* 18.2–9; *T. Naph.* 8.3–4; *T. Jud.* 24.4–6; 25.5; *T. Zeb.* 9.8; *T. Ben.* 10.3–11; also possibly 4 Ezra 6.25–28). However, we must reasonably allow for some creative and innovative use of existing traditions on Paul's part, which would not have to indicate a departure from Judaism; see further pp. 158ff. below.

3. Despite the totalizing, polarized worldview that Paul largely assumes, whereby "the nations" constitute a monolithic group in opposition to the Jewish people (cf. Johnson-Hodge 2007: 48–58), it is important to note here that the implications of his theologizing suggests that, however transformed, each of the many people groups who have turned in worship of the God of Israel maintain their own unique identity in addition to the superordinate identity found in Christ.

seems to inform Paul's argument in chapters 9–11, in which he is attempting to dissuade gentile arrogance (cf. esp. 9.4–5; 11.16–24). On the other hand, though by necessity given first to Israel in service of the other nations, the privileges afforded to Israel in the covenant were originally intended for and are now available to all nations (cf. Nanos 2000: 222). This seems to be Paul's basic premise in chapter 4, where he stresses the legitimacy of gentiles qua gentiles as members of Abraham's family alongside Jews qua Jews (cf. esp. vv. 9–17).

By disqualifying this aspect of Paul's theologizing, Donaldson is forced to conclude that Paul exhibits "category confusion" in assenting to an "Israel" according to traditional ethnic norms, while also claiming that it has been redefined around Christ. However, it is quite possible that with full clarity and intent Paul expresses the realities brought into being by the advent of Christ and dawn of the new age within multiple, and sometimes overlapping, conceptual frameworks.

Both Gal. 3 and Rom. 4 exemplify these overlapping frames through which Paul argues for the inclusivity of covenant identity on the basis of Christ. Donaldson (1997: 126–27) correctly observes that Paul does not explicitly argue here for the righteous status of gentile Christ followers independent from a shared kinship with Abraham's family; that is, on the basis of either eschatological pilgrimage texts (such as Isa. 2.2–4; 25.6–10; Mic. 4.1–4; or Zech. 8.20–23) or righteous gentile conceptions. Indeed, Paul is engaged in identity construction along *ethnic* lines. But it would be a mistake to assume that Paul's identification of gentile Christ followers as descendents of Abraham is simply a radical reworking of the proselyte notion, in which Christ replaces Torah-based boundary markers—i.e., circumcision—as the means by which gentiles can thereby gain entrance into God's people.

As Johnson-Hodge (2007) has aptly demonstrated, it should occasion little surprise that an argument concerned with identity, status, and power relationships in the context of an ancient Mediterranean culture would be grounded upon patrilineal descent. This is a strategy common among ancient authors, according to which desirable characteristics ascribed to an ancestor are thought to be necessarily conferred upon descendents.[4] In employing this very strategy Paul imagines a point of

---

4. As Johnson-Hodge (2007: 28) explains, the efficacy of this strategy relies on the "dual nature of kinship and ethnic claims." While "open to human intervention," such ties are nevertheless "perceived to be natural and inevitable."

entrance into Abraham's family for non-Jews in that they are "in Christ." She explains,

> With this "in" language, Paul invokes familiar and authoritative patterns of descent and inheritance to authorize and reinforce a new kinship for Gentiles. . . . [In Gal. 3] Having already claimed that gentiles are "in" Abraham, Paul goes on to explain how this is possible. Christ, as a genuine descendent of Abraham, serves as the crucial link between the gentiles and Abraham. Being "in" Christ enables them to be "in" Abraham. (2007: 103)[5]

Yet, apart from Johnson-Hodge, I find it overwhelmingly the case that Paul believes gentiles *and* Jews must be found in Christ to gain access to the inheritance promised to Abraham (cf. Gal. 2.15–16; 3.28–29; Rom. 3.30; 4.11–16; 9.8; 10.9–13; 1 Cor. 1.22–24), and, further, that he understands Jews to most naturally occupy this place (cf. Rom. 1.16; 4.16; 9.24; 11.24). Still, Paul does clearly argue in both Rom. 4 and Gal. 3 for the inclusion of gentiles qua gentiles among Abraham's heirs, the people of God, on the basis of the original promise(s) to Abraham, which he finds to be fulfilled in his Christ gospel (cf. Rom. 4.17–18; Gal. 3.8).

However, given all else he claims in each of these letters, it seems unlikely that Paul's understanding of Gen. 12.3 and 17.5 was not governed by a broader (salvation history) theological matrix (cf. p. 69 n. 29) in which the eschatological pilgrimage motif was central. In other words, the multiethnic family originally promised to Abraham (cf. n. 5 above) has been fulfilled precisely because God has *now* made possible the restoration of Israel and *consequential* ingathering of the nations (cf. p. 70 n. 32 above)—these righteous gentiles being fully anticipated by the reality of the uncircumcised Abraham who initially received the covenant blessing (cf. Rom. 4.9-10). *Both* groups—on the sole ground of God's sovereign grace and mercy (cf. Rom. 3.27; 4.1–8, 13–15; Gal. 6.14–16; p. 110 n. 46 above)—are found in Christ, which, as asserted above, secures their place in Abraham. Thus, while on the surface Rom. 4 and Gal. 3 may suggest that proselyte patterns of universalism singularly

---

5. In keeping with this line of thought, Johnson-Hodge (2007: 106, 131) rightly suggests that for Paul gentiles have become a part of Israel while nevertheless remaining non-Jews. In this regard, the phenomenon of multiple or nested identities offers clarity in understanding Paul's perspective.

inform Paul's argument, his thinking on the matter is in actuality much more complex.⁶

On the other end, a similar problem is demonstrated in the assertion of both Campbell (cf. 2006: 56) and Nanos (cf. 2002a: 99–100) that Paul did not conceive of gentile Christ followers as in any way proselytes. Unquestionably, he did not view them as proselytes according to the traditional norms of the synagogue community. Notwithstanding, the simple fact that there are some instances where Paul assumes his gentile converts cease to properly belong entirely in the category of ἔθνη (cf. 1 Cor. 5.1, 9–13; 10.1ff.; 12.2; 1 Thess. 4.5) suggests he did view them along the lines of what Donaldson has proposed. They are proselytes to the covenant community—a community demarcated no longer by circumcision and other central markers of Jewish identity, but by trusting in God's act in Christ and concomitant reception of the Spirit (cf. Rom. 3.30; 4.14–16; 10.4; Gal. 2.15–16; 3.1–5; p. 85 n. 55 above).

A NON-SECTARIAN CHURCH

But with Campbell (cf. 2006: 47–48, 66) and Nanos I do not recognize Paul primarily as a sectarian who perceived the Christ communities he founded as the replacement for the synagogue. Rather, I understand Paul to be a Jewish reformer who remained personally connected with the synagogue and presumed an open relationship, at least in potential, between the Christ movement and greater Jewish community.

While there were clear social boundaries established for the church (e.g., an entrance requirement of Christ belief, initiation rite of baptism, followed by particular demands upon lifestyle), and that this set the church apart from the greater Greco-Roman world (though even here not the complete separation typical of introversionist groups such as the Qumran community; cf. Esler 1994: 79–84; 1 Cor. 5.9–10; 10.27),⁷ Campbell (1992: 122–31; 2005: 309–14) has convincingly argued that

---

6. It is frequently observed that Paul's attempt to demonstrate the validity of his gospel on the basis of Scripture betrays a form of circular reasoning, as it already assumes a particular reading of it that is necessarily informed by his gospel (cf. Donaldson 1997: 101). While there is undoubtedly truth to this claim, it is generally accompanied by a failure to appreciate the integrity and coherence of Paul's scriptural reasoning, which creatively draws upon multiple biblical traditions, though not all of which are made explicit within any one rhetorical discourse.

7. Cf. also here the critique of sectarian-focused views of Christian and Jewish groups in Harland 2003: 182–200.

Paul sought no such separation from Judaism (contra Meeks 1983: 186; 1985: 106; Watson 1986, 2007a; Sanders 1983: 176-79; Witherington 1998: 98-99), and the communities he established may best be described as the resulting social reality of a movement from *within* existing Jewish tradition and society.[8]

Jewish Identity in Christ

Though Paul in Gal. 1.13-14 seemingly contrasts Judaism "with living a life in accord with the Gospel and within the assembly of God" (Witherington 1998: 98), it is probable that he means here a Pharisaic Judaism (cf. Acts 22.3-5; 26.4-5) marked in particular by violent zeal in the tradition of Phinehas, Elijah, and the Maccabees[9] (cf. esp. Acts 8.1-3; see also Giorgio 2006: 95).[10] Paul is not suggesting, then, that he left "Judaism"—a Jewish way of life—for something else—i.e., "Christianity"—but only from one interpretation of Judaism to another (cf. Nanos 2005a: 16-19; 2005b: 14-15).

But what of Paul's claims in both Phil. 3 and Rom. 7? Do not these texts suggest that Paul ultimately abandoned his ethnic heritage for Christ, indicating moreover (at least implicitly) that he believed other Jews should do the same?[11] Does being in Christ for Paul necessarily

---

8. It seems clear that Paul viewed the Christ community as itself a "Jewish" entity even when predominately composed of non-Jews; cf. esp. Rom. 11.13ff.

9. Cf. Num. 25.6-18; 1 Kgs. 18.40; 19.10; Sir. 45.23-24; 48.2; 1 Macc. 2.15-28, 54, 58; 4 Macc. 18.12; see further here Hays 2000: 213-14.

10. This zealotry was ostensibly directed at Jews within the Christ communities throughout the Diaspora for a perceived laxity of the Torah-based boundary markers, and thus the equal participation of gentiles among them. These mixed assemblies would naturally have been viewed by many Jews as a serious threat to the Jewish community at large (cf. 1 Thess. 2.16). However, Giorgio (2006: 80-89) notes that the original persecution reported by Luke (cf. Acts 8:1ff.) preceded the mission to non-Jews, and thus it could not have yet been motivated by their acceptance into the community. He suggests that at its core this persecution against specifically the Hellenistic Jews was motivated at the first by their high Christology, which saw Jesus—instead of Torah—as the means of reconciliation. I find this observation to be essentially correct, though I have difficulty with Giorgio's view that this was not also the understanding of the "Hebrew" Christ followers led by the apostles, and that they were not as well objects of persecution, even prior to the execution of James in 62 CE. Nor do I agree that this conviction meant a decisive break with Judaism; see further below.

11. Of course, Paul affirms his Israelite identity in Rom. 11.1-2, but 11.5-6 might nevertheless indicate for some an effective negation of this identity in favor of a "Christian" one.

mean being outside of Judaism? I find such a notion difficult to reconcile with Paul's insistence in 1 Cor. 7.17–20 that members of the Christ community are to retain the ethnicity in which they were "called" (cf. 1 Cor. 1.22–24), and thus that Jews should remain Jews—a rule, so Paul claims, for all the churches. I hold that Paul's rhetorical motivation in Phil. 3 and Rom. 7[12] is, similarly, not to reject Jewish identity[13] but to *reevaluate* and

---

12. As made quite explicit in 8.2, the κατειχόμεθα to which Paul refers in Rom. 7.6 does not refer foremost to the Torah (contra Käsemann 1980: 189–91; Stuhlmacher 1994: 104; Moo 1996: 420–21; Jewett 2007: 438–39). Rather, it refers to sin and death, which, while made manifest by the Torah (cf. Rom. 3.20; 5.20; 7.13; Gal. 3.19; 1 Cor. 15.56), could not be overcome by it (despite his critics, Cranfield [1975: 338] is almost certainly correct to restrict the meaning of ὁ νόμος to the law's condemnation; cf. Rom. 3.19–20; 4.15; 7.10; Gal. 3.22). The defeat of these forces, anticipated for Paul by the Torah, has once and for all been accomplished through Christ, the fulfillment of Torah (cf. Rom. 3.21–26; 5.12–21; 6.1–11, 17–18; 7.24; 8.1–4; 9.30—10.4; 1 Cor. 15.54–57; 2 Cor. 5.14–21). It is the "dispensation of Torah"—the era of the old covenant and creation ruled by sin and death (cf. 2 Cor. 3.7–11; 1 Cor. 15.56)—from which one is "discharged" (cf. Gal. 3.21–23), *not* the practice of Torah in the renewed covenant and creation inaugurated by Christ.

This is evident in two ways. First, those who are in Christ, both Jews and non-Jews, are able to keep Torah from the heart via the Spirit, according to the promise (cf. Rom. 2.14ff.). While this means for Paul that non-Jews already fulfill Torah without having to first become Jews, it does *not* indicate for him that Christ followers are then "lawless." As Hafemann (1996: 35) points out, "In the new covenant, like the old, what 'counts' is . . . 'keeping the commandments of God' as a result of knowing him. And at the heart of this covenant structure stands the Spirit. From Paul's perspective, given God's justifying and sanctifying work in the lives of his people *as guaranteed and brought about by the presence and power of the Spirit*, there is no excuse for the continuing, habitual disobedience that results from failing to trust God's gracious provisions and promises in Christ." This is Paul's premise in Gal. 5.13ff.; Rom. 6.1ff.; 8.1–17; 13.8–14; 1 Thess. 4.1–8; 1 Cor. 7.19; 9.21. Second, Paul is otherwise clear that Jews can continue to observe the ordinances of Torah specific to their own ethnic identity, namely, circumcision and food laws (cf. Rom. 2.25; 4.11ff.; 14.13ff.; 1 Cor. 7.18).

13. Esler (2003: 222) argues that, given Paul's overarching goal to reorient members of Jewish and gentile subgroups towards a common ingroup identity derived from Christ (such being fully explicated in Rom. 8), it was necessary for him to pay careful attention in the letter to both subgroups. In ch. 7, then, Paul turns his attention from gentile Christ followers, with whom he was occupied in ch. 6, to primarily Jewish Christ followers (cf. 7.1). I agree that Paul does have Jewish Christ followers in view here; though (former) gentile synagogue associates (i.e., God-fearers)—who likely represented greater numbers than Jews among the Roman churches—are similarly targeted. However, I assert that Paul in any case believed the Torah to have been in some way universally binding in the era from "Moses to Christ" (cf. p. 80 n. 50 above).

In other words, while Paul does divide humanity into those who possess Torah (Jews) and those who do not (gentiles) (cf. Rom. 2.14) he nevertheless understands all humanity liable to God via the demands of Torah (cf. Gal. 2.15; 5.11). Though frequently under-

relativize it in light of Christ and the eschatological framework I have proposed in my analysis above of Rom. 2.29, Gal. 6.16, and Rom. 11.26 (cf. 1 Cor. 7.19[14]).

Paul's consistent premise throughout his letters is that God is through Christ fulfilling the interconnected promises of covenant and creation renewal (cf. the next chapter). Both Jews and non-Jews are by virtue of this fulfillment now joining together into a single, and necessarily unified,[15] community of the redeemed, just as the scriptures had foretold (cf. Rom. 15.4–12; see also Gal. 3.28; 1 Cor. 12.12–13; Col. 3.11; Eph. 2.11–22; 3.5–6; 4.1–6). Thus, in comparison to the transformative power to be found in knowing Christ (cf. 2 Cor. 3.18; Phil. 3.21; 1 Cor. 15.42–57) *everything else pales in significance* (cf. 2 Cor. 3.7–11). In Gal. 2.16–21 Paul articulates this very understanding, which I have attempted to clarify here in my own expanded rendering:

> [W]e know that a person is deemed righteous by God, *which means membership in God's family/the covenant where life is inherited*, not by the ordinances of Torah but through the faithful-

---

stood as such, his point in Rom. 2.12 is *not* to suggest that the Torah plays no role in the condemnation of non-Jews (outside of Christ) (compare Rom. 4.15 with 1.18ff.; 2.8–9; 1 Thess. 1.10; 5.9; see also 1 Cor. 15.56). He states only that they will perish in the same state they lived—without possession of Torah. His point is, rather, that mere possession of Torah, as per Jewish identity, is no guarantee of God's favor. The Torah itself deems the Jewish world as equally guilty as the gentile world as far as sin is concerned (cf. Rom. 3.20–21; Gal. 3.22). Thus, all that Paul has to say in Rom. 7 would ultimately apply to both Jews and gentiles in his audience, though, again, it would have special significance to Jewish Christ followers and those gentiles who possess(ed) some level of attachment to the synagogue. While I further agree that behind the "I" of Rom. 7 is Israel under Torah, it must be considered here that Israel possesses "representational" significance for Paul (cf. pp. 158ff. below). What was made explicit for Israel is, therefore, implicitly true for humanity in general.

14. Paul is clear here that not only Jewish identity but *all* ethnic identities are secondary to being in Christ and experiencing the fulfillment of the new covenant and new creation, according to which one is enabled via the Spirit (cf. 1 Cor. 2.10ff.) to "obey the commandments of God" (cf. n. 12 above). Thiselton (2000: 50–51) remarks, "To remain Jewish or non-Jewish does not spring forth from general indifference, but from its salvific irrelevance. As in the case of gender, such distinctions are not abrogated wholesale.... The new creation *transforms* and *relativizes* such distinctions, but they have a place."

15. The attainment of unity within the Christ community is the fundamental objective of Paul's letter to the Corinthians (cf. 1 Cor. 1.10), and a significant factor in Romans, Galatians, and Philippians. It lay at the heart of Paul's entire missionary program, as evidenced especially by his collection project for the Jerusalem church (cf. 1 Cor. 16.1–3; 2 Cor. 9; Rom. 15.14–33).

ness of Jesus Christ / the faith realized through Jesus Christ [cf. p. 79 n. 49 above]. And we have come to trust in Christ Jesus, so that we might be deemed righteous by the faithfulness of Christ / the faith realized through Christ, and not by the ordinances of Torah, because, *as it has now been revealed*, no one will be deemed righteous by the ordinances of Torah.

But if, in our effort to be deemed righteous in Christ, we ourselves have been found to be sinners (*because we have accepted that membership in God's family/the covenant is obtained through trusting in the Christ event rather than our observance of the ordinances of Torah*), is Christ then a servant of sin? *In other words, since Christ has fulfilled the Torah—ushering in the new covenant and new creation—and in so doing has become the basis of membership in God's family/the covenant, and therefore the means to life, does this then imply the sanctioning of lawlessness, i.e., Godless behavior?* Certainly not! But if I build up again the very things that I once tore down—*that is, the "wall" created by the ordinances of Torah that separates Jews as heirs of the promise from the other nations*, then I demonstrate that I am a transgressor—*that is, I am behaving contrary to the ultimate goal of Torah*.

Because on the basis of Torah, *as the Torah declares the curse of death for failure to observe it—which was our former state of affairs—but also promises that God will, God's self, provide the means to life*, I died to Torah, *as the basis of membership in God's family/the covenant, and thus the means to life*, so that I might live to God. I have been crucified with Christ—*that is, I participate in Christ's death that exhausted the curse of death*, and it is no longer I who live, but it is Christ who lives in me—*that is, I participate not only in his death but also in his resurrection, and thus gain life in accordance with the promise of God in Torah*.

And the life I now live in the flesh I live by the faithfulness of the Son of God/the faith realized through the Son of God, who loved me and gave himself for me. I do not nullify the grace of God; for if righteousness comes through Torah, then Christ died for nothing. *In other words, if the Torah was in and of itself the means to life, then the Christ event is superfluous—which, we all agree, it is not!*

Even if one were to concede that these claims do not easily correlate with central tenets of first-century Judaism, it must still be asked whether Jews (either Palestinian or Diaspora) who participated in the Christ movement really perceived their own participation as a default departure from what is properly Jewish. I would find this to be an anachronistic—

even absurd—conclusion. It is in my view, therefore, improper to speak, as Donaldson does (1997: 77), of Paul moving *from* a "Jewish pattern of thought" to a "Pauline pattern," however different Paul's views were from those typical of first-century Judaism in all its various orientations.

That a relatively early split did begin to occur *within* the Jewish community over the Messiahship of Jesus of Nazareth and its implications seems quite evident to me (cf. p. 87 n. 61 above).[16] And this had the eventual consequence of marginalizing the Christ movement, and thus the ultimate failure for this (reform) movement to take a dominant hold in the Jewish world. But it simply does not follow that these Christ-following Jews thought of themselves as any less Jewish (cf. Rom. 9.1–5; 11.1–2). Moreover, the evidence from much of the Pauline corpus (cf. Gal.; Rom. 14; Phil. 3; 2 Cor. 11) strongly suggests that at least during the time of Paul there existed an inclination among not only Diaspora Jews, as Paul himself, but even many gentile Christ followers to remain connected with the greater Jewish community, however their theology and praxis may have ultimately been rejected by the majority of Jews.[17]

A largely contrary view is advanced in Jossa Giorgio's important study of Christian identity (2006: 89–102). Giorgio argues that Paul's letters reflect an early and decisive split between Judaism and Christianity, especially throughout the Diaspora. And this occurred largely because the Hellenistic Jews within the Christ movement drew "a more radical way of understanding the Lordship of the risen Christ . . . the practical consequences [of which] placed them in contrast with the Jews of Jerusalem."

Although Paul was not himself a Hellenized Jew, he nevertheless "took this position (which is precisely the one that he had earlier fought against) to its extreme consequences" (p. 97). Paul's conviction that entrance into God's people was on the basis of Christ alone and not Torah, and his concomitant redefinition of what it meant to be a Jew (cf. Rom. 2.28–29) and a member of God's people (cf. Gal. 6.16), suggests that he inevitably understood himself as ceasing to belong to the synagogue

---

16. However, I suggest that this did not occur in any sort of decisive and/or monolithic fashion. And there was certainly a great deal of ambiguity surrounding the Christ movement within the early Jewish community (cf. Gal. 2.4; Acts 15.1ff.), especially throughout the Diaspora (cf. Acts 28.21).

17. Further, the harsh polemic directed against Judaism by later Christian writers of the second century points to the continuing reality that "Christians [were] adopting Jewish beliefs and practices" (Lieu 2002b: 127; cf. pp. 117–34).

community. He was now part of a wholly new social entity that was neither Jewish nor gentile.

I believe Giorgio's thesis, which is similarly reflected in much contemporary scholarship on the matter, is flawed on several counts. First, as I have argued above, Paul construes Israelite/Jewish identity on two different levels. That he may understand the multiethnic Christ community as "Israel" (and gentile Christ followers as in some sense "Jews") does *not* mean that he then abandons the Israel defined by traditional ethnic markers. Second, Giorgio seems to go well beyond the evidence in the sort of dissidence he proposes between the Hellenistic Jews, along with their champion Paul, and the Jerusalem church. In contrast, I would assert the following: (a) According to the accounts given by both Paul (Gal. 2.15) and Luke (Acts 15.11), the Jerusalem church equally viewed Christ as the single means of reconciliation. (b) The early debate within the Christ movement as to the role of the Torah concerned its relationship to non-Jews seeking entrance into the Christ community, and not whether Jews should remain submitted to it, upon which there was no dispute (cf. Gal. 2.7-10; Acts 21.17-26[18]). (c) The agreement that was reached (irrespective of whether the implications of it were not entirely followed through upon, as per Paul's testimony in Gal. 2.11-14) that entrance into the community did not necessitate Torah submission on the part of gentiles in no way indicated for *any* of the parties involved a departure from Judaism or the synagogue.[19]

---

18. According to Luke's report (as also possibly indicated by Paul himself; cf. Rom. 3.8), there was a misperception among some Palestinian Jews that Paul was indeed teaching Jews throughout the Diaspora to forsake the Torah. But it is clear from both the testimony of Luke and Paul that the leadership in the Jerusalem church understood and affirmed the actual content of Paul's gospel, which did not dissuade full Torah obedience on the part of Jews.

19. The conflict as Paul describes it was the failure of Peter, ostensibly influenced by the party of James, to follow through on the implications of the Christ event with respect to the relationship between Jews and gentiles. It had absolutely nothing to do with the continued practice of the Torah on the part of Jews, i.e., Peter's own observance of food laws. (It is important to note here that Luke's report of Peter's visionary experience in Acts 10.9-16, in which he violated kashrut, is interpreted in Acts 10.28-29 to mean that God is now including non-Jews in the covenant community. Food laws are thus relativized [cf. Mark 7.19b], as Paul similarly asserts in Rom. 14.14, 20, but they are not considered anathema.) Rather, at stake was whether gentile Christ followers, whom all parties involved agreed need not submit to Torah (that is, become Jewish) are *truly full members of the community alongside Jews*, which Peter denied by breaking table fellowship with them (cf. Nanos 1996: 337-71; Tomson 1990: 228; Howard 1990:

Paul's Rhetoric to the Philippians: A Closer Look

Expanding upon (c) above, I find unconvincing Giorgio's appeal to Phil. 3.20 (pp. 100–102), according to which Paul likens the Christ community in Philippi to an independent "urban community" governed singularly by Christ and no other law, which in turn "creates a clear separation from the synagogue" (p. 101). As with Giorgio, scholars have persistently read an anti-Jewish polemic in Phil. 3,[20] asserting, along the lines of Francis Watson (2007a: 86–99; 136–50), that it is characteristic of the sociological process through which sectarian groups develop from reform movements.

It should initially be observed that Paul's very warning regarding the κατατομή in 3.2[21] and the discourse concerning his own Jewish identity in. 3.4ff. makes little sense in a context in which there were not existing

---

xix-xx; Sanders 1990: 187). As Nanos (1996: 354) remarks, Paul's criticism of Peter was not apostasy but hypocrisy, as he as well as Paul had accepted that the Jew no less than the non-Jew receives "life" through Christ and not Torah (cf. Gal. 2.14; see also Acts 10.34–48).

That there were other Jewish missionaries, as per 2 Cor. 10–13, who may have opposed Paul's mission hardly points to a major fracture between him and the Jerusalem church over matters of Torah obedience. This hypothesis is clearly contradicted by Paul's collection efforts for the Jerusalem church, and otherwise possesses no real evidence to support it. In any case, the mere existence of Christ-following Jewish groups that disapproved of Paul and his mission does not itself indicate that Paul had in some way departed from Judaism.

20. I find it an almost unavoidable conclusion that Paul is directing this polemic towards certain Jewish groups (even if only in anticipatory fashion and not reflecting a present reality in Philippi) and not pagan influence, as Nanos (2008) argues. However, Nanos has importantly demonstrated here that while scholars have almost uniformly understood Paul's pejorative epithet "dogs" to be a reversal of a common Jewish invective towards gentiles, such is in actuality unfounded in the relevant Jewish literature. Further, he makes the compelling suggestion that Paul has drawn the three epithets, "dogs," "evil workers," and "the mutilation," from 1 Kgs. 18–22.40, where all three terms appear in the context of Elijah's battle with the prophets of Baal and the condemnation of the house of Ahab and Jezebel. Strengthening this conclusion is the fact that Paul explicitly refers to the same text in Rom. 11.2–4, in which he seemingly aligns himself with Elijah, and the body of Jewish Christ followers with the faithful Israelites of Elijah's time.

21. Paul's seems to be making a play on words, contrasting the κατατομή—Jews who have failed to recognize Jesus as the Messiah and the implications, and have thus kept themselves from participating in the new covenant and creation—and the περιτομή—the members of the Philippian church, and by extension all Christ followers, *both* Jewish and gentile (cf. Rom. 2.25-29), who have placed their trust in God's act in Christ.

ties between the church and the synagogue.²² It is only as such that one could imagine gentile Christ followers giving thought to Judaizing. But is Paul entreating his addressees to sever any such relationships? I do not believe so.

The persecution to which Paul refers in the letter (cf. 1.27–30) likely finds its source in the civil authorities (cf. 2.15; 3.20; see also Acts 16.20), and was initiated by the church's unwillingness to participate in certain activities of the polis. As Gordon Fee has suggested (1995: 31), Philippi's status as a Roman colony "would have meant that every public event . . . and much else within its boundaries would have taken place in the context of giving honor to the emperor, with the acknowledgment that (in this case) Nero was 'Lord and savior.'" And it is here "where believers in Christ could no longer join as 'citizens of Rome in Philippi.'"

It is in this context that one can begin to understand Paul's assertions in Phil. 3.1–16. In order to alleviate the prospect of suffering from the hands of Roman authorities, some in the church may have been entertaining the thought of obtaining proselyte status (see further on this point below). Yet, the absence of any direct rebuke in the letter concerning this matter, as found for example in Galatians, suggests that Paul only feared the potential for this occurrence and is attempting to deal with it preemptively.²³

In this light the text need not be read as denigrating a Jewish way of life or attempting to subvert attachments to the greater Jewish community. Contrary to the majority view, I hold that Paul's rhetoric reflects only, as in Galatians, an internal—albeit intense—Jewish debate. It is the product of his determined effort to see his gentile converts retain their ethnic identity, as it has *already* been transformed in Christ. They are to remain steadfast in the gospel that they have received (cf. 1.27–28; 2.12, 16; 4.1) even in the face of opposition, in the pattern that both he himself has demonstrated (cf. 1.3–13; 2.17; 3.17),²⁴ as well as did Christ (cf. 2.8).

---

22. I am not suggesting here that there was necessarily a synagogue in Philippi (as Luke seems to suggest otherwise; cf. Acts 16.13), but that collectively the network of churches Paul established were an extension of the greater Jewish community throughout the Diaspora. Indeed, according to Acts 16.13–15, the first converts in Philippi were God-fearers.

23. The absence of a local synagogue in Philippi may have forestalled the sort of exigency that is exhibited in the letter to the Galatians.

24. Cf. Esler 2003: 223–24: "[F]or a person to exert most influence over other group members, to be an effective leader, he or she needs to be an in-group exemplar or pro-

The central hope motivating the Philippian church to "stand firm" (4.1) was the return of Christ to fully establish his kingdom—of which they were already citizens—on earth. All things would then be made subject to him, not least the Roman Empire persecuting them (3.20-21).

THE RELATIONSHIP OF CHURCH AND SYNAGOGUE IN ROME AND GALATIA

I would not go so far, however, to suggest that Paul thought of the churches addressed in his letters as being *necessarily* dependent upon the greater Jewish community. But a reasonable case can be made that in certain instances a context in which there was some measure of dependency is presupposed by him as an entirely natural state of affairs.[25] On this point, Nanos has forcefully argued that the churches in Rome as well as Galatia were at the time Paul wrote his respective letters[26] within the purview of the larger synagogue community.

---

totype, that is, the person who is most representative of the shared social identity and consensual position of the group as a whole. In congregations that he founded, Paul based his claim to exemplify the group on his behavior among them. In particular, he went so far as to portray himself as the model of life in Christ that other Christ-believers should imitate.... Paul's position is that he epitomizes the social category of Christ-follower (that is, he both defines and is defined by it) and that other believers with personal knowledge of him should copy him; thus he exercises leadership."

25. Similar to what I have suggested above concerning Paul's letter to the Philippians, his harsh rhetoric in Galatians seeking to persuade his gentile converts to remain uncircumcised presupposes that a continuing relationship between them and the greater Jewish community will persist. Nowhere in the letter does Paul demand that any such ties be severed or that such an arrangement was *intrinsically* problematic. Though it might be argued that 4.30-31 points precisely in this direction, Paul's purpose here is strictly to identify the Galatian influencers with the persecuting "slave child" who fails to receive the promised inheritance over against the Galatians believers who have, like the "free child," already obtained it. It can hardly intend a course of action to be carried out by Paul's converts (contra Betz 1979: 251; Longenecker 1990: 217; Matera 1992: 177-78; Dunn 1993: 258; George: 1994: 347; Martyn 1997: 446; Witherington 1998: 338-39). Rather, Paul exhorts in light of this relationship that his converts remain steadfast in the teaching they have received from him, *accepting any consequential marginality—even persecution, as he himself has* (cf. 4.12; 6.12; see also 2 Cor. 11.24); see further below.

26. That the church in Rome originally developed from within the synagogue, at least in large part, is virtually unanimously affirmed by scholars, however different the implications they draw from it; cf., e.g., Schmithals 1975: 83-91; Meeks 1983: 26-28; Dunn 1988: xlv-li; Lampe 1989: 53-63; Walters 1993: 5-6; Brändle and Stegemann 1998: 117-18; Zetterholm 2003: 91-96; Watson 2007a: 163-91; Das 2007.

The Churches in Rome

Yet with respect to the churches in Rome, I find the evidence to be inconclusive. First, while the existence of certain prominent Jewish leaders in Rome (ca. late 50s or early 60s CE) is suggested in Acts 28, it is nevertheless likely that a centralized authority representing the entire Jewish community of the city was lacking. Rather, a diversity of Jewish groups each functioning with relative autonomy seems to be the case, as Wiefel (1991: 89–92) has pointed out on the basis of the extant synagogue inscriptional evidence. This would immediately suggest that questions of synagogue authority over Christ followers in Rome cannot be addressed in any sort of monolithic fashion. Further, no real clarity is offered by Luke's description in Acts 28 as to the general state of the larger Jewish community's relationship with the Christ movement. The text is sufficiently ambiguous, where opposing conclusions can reasonably be drawn (compare Nanos 1996: 378 with Witherington 2004: 13).

Additionally ambiguous, in my opinion, is what is to be made of the edict of Claudius in 49 CE expelling Jews from Rome and the effect this had on the Roman church (cf. Acts 18.2).[27] According to Suetonius (*Claud*. 25.4) the expulsion was due to disturbances instigated by a "Chrestus."[28] The traditional view understands this reference as reflecting an intra-Jewish dispute over Jesus Christ, and the edict has been integral to many reconstructions of the *Sitz im Leben* of Paul's letter to the Romans (cf., e.g., Wiefel 1991: 85–101; Walters 1993: 56–66; 1998: 176–83; Brändle and Stegemann 1998; Witherington 2004: 11–16; Das 2007: 149–202). As such, following the expulsion of Jews, the church in Rome became predominately gentile in composition, and fully independent of the synagogue. The re-entrance of Jews into the community in 54 CE resulted in the ethnic tensions alluded to in Rom. 11 and 14.[29]

---

27. The date of 49 CE for this edict of Claudius is asserted by the fifth-century historian Orosius (*Hist. contra Pag*. 7.6.15–16) who bases it on a statement by Josephus of which there is no extant record. Though Slingerland (1997: 123–29) suggests that Orosius fabricated this date, it is nevertheless accepted by many scholars.

28. The reference by Dio Cassius (*Hist. Rom*. 60.6.6) to Claudius's ban on Jewish assemblies is generally recognized to be a distinct episode from the later expulsion of Jews from the city; cf., e.g., Barclay 1996: 305; Slingerland 1997: 123–29; Esler 2003: 100; Gruen 2004: 36–38; Giorgio 2006: 128; Watson 2007a: 171.

29. According to Das (2007) the church in Rome at the time of Paul's letter (meeting perhaps as a *collegium domestica*, and thus falling outside of the laws governing associations; cf. pp. 181–82; Esler 2003: 105–7; see also n. 39 below) consisted *entirely*

Nanos (1996: 372–87) questions this historical reconstruction (as have many others; cf. Baur 1876: 329; Mason 1994: 263–68; Barclay 1996: 303–6; Murphy-O'Connor 1996: 333; Achtemeier 1997: 5–7; Slingerland 1997: 111–29; Wagner 2002: 34; Gruen 2004: 39), disputing that the "Chrestus" to which Suetonius refers had anything to do with the Christ movement, and that there was a significant enough departure of Jews from Rome to have any real affect on the Roman church.[30] He contests, moreover, that there is any support in Acts or Paul's letter for the sort of "irreconcilable animosity of the Jewish community(s) toward the Christian message" (p. 375) assumed in this reconstruction.[31]

The understanding that by the mid first century the Jewish community in Rome worshipped in *proseuchai*, while the Christ movement met in private homes (cf. Esler 2003: 88–107), also does not provide

---

of gentiles, but tensions developed between the former gentile synagogue associates and the new gentile converts with no previous connection to the synagogue, who likely harbored disdain for Jews/Judaism in general. As pointed out in p. 57 above, I am not convinced by Das's thesis, which does not adequately account for the possible return of Christ-following Jews (even if only a small number) generally assumed in this reconstruction; see n. 30 below.

30. Das (2007: 162–81) argues to the contrary that a quite limited expulsion of Christ-following Jews could have indeed created a disruption sufficient to cause a separation between the greater synagogue community and gentile Christ followers associated with it, and thus to the creation of two distinct assemblies. He comments, "God-fearers and sympathizers, provided they ceased from attending the synagogues, would pose no threat to the Jewish communities. Faced with the threat of imperial intervention, God-fearers could leave the synagogues and blend into other communities. Jewish and proselyte troublemakers, on the other hand, were identified primarily by their membership in the synagogue and, as full members of the community, would more likely be singled out for Roman attention. The Romans wanted the disturbance to the peace in Rome quieted. In carrying out the decree of expulsion, the Romans would have had to rely on information from the Jewish community in order to isolate the troublemakers, and less integrated God-fearers would not have been at the top of the list" (pp. 180–81).

31. Though proposing, contrary to Nanos and the majority of contemporary scholars, that Romans is addressed to a primarily Jewish audience (as per Baur 1876), Mason (1994: 262) similarly suggests that Roman Christianity possessed a "Jewish ambience long after Paul's time." His arguments for this view include: (a) the Jewish character of *1 Clement* and *Hebrews*, both written in perhaps the late first-century; the first a pastoral letter from Rome, and the second (at least arguably) addressed to a congregation in Rome; (b) "Christian borrowing of Judean burial customs"; (c) the statement by Tacitus (*Annals* 15.44) that Christianity spread "not merely in Judea, the source of the disease, but in the capital itself," and his charge against Christians of "hatred of the human race," "which is the same accusation that he makes against the Judeans in general (*Histories* 5.5)" (p. 267; cf. Zetterholm 2003: 95–96).

sufficient insight into the nature of the relationship between the two congregations at the time Paul wrote his letter. Even if it be conceded that Jewish groups did not as a rule meet in private homes, it would not be difficult to envisage the earliest Christ followers in Rome beginning immediately to hold additional meetings in members' homes, while viewing such gatherings as under the general auspices of the synagogues in which they participated and to whose authority they were submitted.

Thus, in the absence of more certain evidence, I am reluctant to claim that a decisive split had occurred between the synagogues and house churches in Rome by this time. In any case, it would seem likely that there were at least some instances of common worship between non-Christ-following Jews and the Christ followers addressed in the letter. As Esler (2003: 106) remarks,

> The critical issue is the probability that some Christ-followers, Judeans or even Greek God-fearers, also continued to attend the *proseuchai,* while others, Greeks (whether former God-fearers or one-time idol worshippers) more likely than Judeans (whose original socialization in the Judean ethnic group gave them more reason to do so), did not.

But though I do not dismiss Nanos's view outright, I still find no support for his reading of Rom. 14 (1996: 131), in which the "weak"[32] refer to Jews who have not (yet) embraced the gospel.[33] For Paul, Jesus Christ is Lord, and acknowledgement of his lordship is the non-negotiable basis for the community fellowship envisaged here (cf. 14.9, 14, 18; 10.9, 13; 15.3, 5–6; also compare 14.10–11 with Phil. 2.10–11; 2 Cor. 5.10). A more plausible interpretation is advanced by Campbell, in

---

32. Nanos (1996: 121–44) argues that the term ἀσθενέω, normally rendered "weak," can be better translated here "stumbling" (cf. Rom. 9.32; 11.11) and would have been understood as a "highly nuanced and respectful" way in which to refer to Jews who had yet to believe the gospel.

33. Nanos (pp. 91–94) refers to the traditional reading of this passage, which points to an "intra-Christian" debate concerning the continued observance of the law on the part of Jewish Christ followers, as "Luther's trap." This is because it is regularly concluded that while Paul instructs gentile Christ followers not to judge their Jewish brethren, he nevertheless held such Jewish practices to represent a deficiency of faith. The comments of Dunn (1988: 798) in this respect are exemplary: "[T]he weakness is trust in God plus dietary and festival laws, trust in God dependent on observance of such practices, a trust which leans on the crutches of particular customs and not God alone, as though they were an integral part of that trust." Nanos argues that readings such as this subvert the very intent of Paul's instructions here.

which the "weak" refer to non-Jewish or proselyte members of the Christ community who had maintained an attachment with the law and synagogue, and who were now being pressured to adopt a "separatist Gentile Christianity," perhaps by the leaders of the house groups in Rome (1995: 275–76; 2004: 77).

Campbell's reading stresses the orientation of these groups rather than their ethnic origins. Here, the "weakness" in question refers not to a Jewish conscience, but a "dilemma caused mainly by changing and transferring . . . allegiance" among former synagogue associates (2004: 77).[34] Sharing similar concerns with that of Nanos's perspective, this reading is equally sensitive to the notion thoroughly attested throughout the section that Jewish practices are not irreconcilable with membership in the Christ community (cf. 14.5–6, 14b) and do not in themselves constitute a deficiency in the Christ follower's trust in God.[35]

I suggest similarly that to the extent Paul acknowledges a deficiency among this group, which likely consisted of a majority of gentiles with

---

34. Campbell (2006: 161) alternatively suggests the possibility (as proposed by Tomson 1990: 64, 236–45; Ehrensperger 2004: 182–83) that τῇ πίστει refers to the way in which the "strong" are to welcome the "weak" "rather than assessing the quality of his/her faith." In this reading, the labels "strong" and "weak" can be understood in the context of the "hierarchical value system of Roman Society," and denote social class. They are thus indicative here of "the divisive influence which Roman imperial values are effecting within the Christ-communities." However, the close parallel between 14.1 with the assertion concerning Abraham in 4.19 that "he did not weaken in faith" seems to suggest that ἀσθενέω characterizes the faith and not the social class of the individuals in question. Nevertheless, it is clearly the case that these individuals have been stereotyped as such by the "strong," which is reflective of "the status obsessed society that was first-century Rome" (Esler 2003: 341). Jewett (2007: 836) observes, "From the opening words of this pericope . . . it must have been apparent to Paul's audience that he intended to reverse the shameful status of the 'weak.' Such a reversal required Paul to employ the discriminatory epithet evidently created and employed by groups opposing the 'weak in faith.'"

35. Moreover, given the likelihood that the "weak" encompass not merely Jews but gentiles as well (who probably represented the majority of the group), this suggests that, unlike the attempt to become a proselyte in the dispensation of Christ (as per the context of Galatians), Jewish practices as freely observed by non-Jews is not an affront to Paul's gospel, and should not therefore be cause for contention within the Christ community, of which Paul warns in Rom. 16.17–20. Jewett's comments on 14.1 (2007: 836) bear mentioning here: "In the context of welcoming fellow believers to love feasts, he flatly repudiates the ulterior motive of doing so to induce the weak to adopt the opinions of the strong. . . . in a cultural setting where intellectual competition was the order of the day, this was an extraordinary prohibition. It legitimates a 'certain diversity of opinion and practice' and does not seek 'to erase subgroup identities.'"

some level of attachment to the synagogue as well as Jews by birth and/or proselytism, it is predicated upon their lack of clarity in regard to the *required* praxis entailed in right covenant standing. That is, they are unsure as to what is now demanded of them in light of perceived inconsistencies between the normative behavior of the synagogue communities in which they participated/belong(ed) and that of certain of the house churches in Rome. They may be deemed "weak" by the "strong" because of their regard for Jewish practices. But for Paul any real "weakness" stems only from doubting that those who choose not to engage in such practices are still acceptable before God (cf. 15.1).

Beyond his reading of Rom. 14, I find further difficulty with Nanos's understanding of Paul's programmatic phrase "the obedience of faith" (Rom. 1.5; 16.26), as the incumbency upon gentiles in Christ to submit to the apostolic decree (cf. Acts 15.20) or, more generally, to observe the appropriate halakhah befitting gentile guests of the synagogue. Halakhic issues are of great import to Paul's gospel (cf., e.g., Gal. 5.13-26; 1 Thess. 4.3-8; 1 Cor. 8-10; Rom. 13.8-14; 14[36]; see also Tomson 1990).[37] And it cannot be discounted that Paul actually taught some version of the apostolic decree as recorded in Acts 15 to his gentile converts (cf. Zetterholm 2003: 143-49; Tomson 1990: 271-74).

However, given the context in which this phrase appears (cf. esp. 1.16-17), "obedience of faith" is best understood, rather, as "the human faithfulness that answers to God's faithfulness" (Wright 2001a: 420). Jewett (2007: 110) similarly notes, "The expression has a straightforward, missionary relevance: 'the obedience of faith means acceptance of the message of salvation' [Käsemann 1980: 15] that Paul intends to advance in this letter" (cf. 2 Cor. 9.13).

---

36. It is worth noting here that Rom. 14 concerns the observance of Jewish food laws within the Christ community, while 1 Cor. 8-10 concerns food offered to idols and the import of this matter for both new gentile converts within the Christ community, as well as gentile Christ followers in relation to those outside the community (cf. Tomson 1990: 189-220). Yet despite this difference of subject matter, Paul teaches similarly in both texts that one's "rights" should be set aside out of love and concern for the well-being of others (cf. Rom. 14.15-23; 1 Cor. 8.9-13; 10.23-24, 32—11.1). This "self-sacrificial" disposition is integral to the success of Paul's gospel (cf. 1 Cor. 9.19-23), to the character of and unity within God's people (cf. pp. 165-66 below).

37. I do agree with Nanos (1996) that Paul knows nothing of a "Torah-free" gospel in an absolute sense. Paul's gospel is Torah-fulfilled (cf. Rom. 3.31), and does not preclude continued submission to the Torah by Jews, or a limited submission for gentiles.

The Churches in Galatia

But with respect to the churches in Galatia, I find that there is a better case to be made for a much closer relationship between the synagogue and Christ communities when Paul wrote his letter. The widely held interpretation that the exigency of the letter is indicative of an intramural "Christian" debate over the necessity of circumcision, and that the "influencers" were themselves "Jewish Christian" missionary opponents of Paul, is not at all clear from the situational discourse of chapters 3–6, but unjustifiably assumed on the basis of the narrative discourse of chapter 2, as Nanos (2002a) has effectively argued.[38]

It is surely the case that the "influencers" were Jews by birth or proselytism. It must be asked, then, who would have a stake in and could exact this kind of pressure upon the largely gentile Galatian church other than members of the local synagogue community. This would seem to be the necessary conclusion, if only to consider in pragmatic terms (a) the prospect for political persecution these gentiles might experience outside of the umbrella of Judaism if they were to remain faithful to the full implications of Paul's gospel (i.e., renouncing idolatry[39]); and (b) the

---

38. I am not entirely discounting the presence of such Jewish missionaries. But if indeed individuals as these were involved, I find it almost impossible that they were operating independently of the larger synagogue community, and thus that this community was not integrally involved in the crisis as Paul sees it.

39. The assertion that first-century Judaism possessed the privileged status of a *religio licita* is perhaps not entirely accurate (cf., e.g., Rajak 1984; Harland 2003: 221–22; Das 2007: 181–90), and it would seem that the decrees issued by Julius and Augustus Caesar disbanding *collegia*, save those of long standing (cf. Suetonius, *Jul.* 42.3; *Aug.* 32.1–2; Josephus, *Ant.* 14.213–16; 16.162–66; 18.83–84), along with similar policies of subsequent rulers, point to more limited actions attempting to quell political unrest rather than to control religious associations throughout the empire, to which Rome was largely indifferent (cf. Walters 1993: 16). Das notes two key points: (a) "Official policy did not exist that would deter Christ-followers from meeting in their own homes apart from the synagogues" (p. 188); and (b) "Relations between Jews and their neighbors were often well-disposed. The same positive dynamic would likely have applied to fledgling Christian communities. As long as they did not draw excessive negative attention to themselves by provoking unrest, they would have enjoyed calm and peace" (p. 190).

Yet, due consideration must be given to the actual content of the gospel message upon which the Christ communities were founded. The proclamation of Jesus as Lord and its concomitant monotheism would have surely been perceived as a highly subversive socio-politico-religious ideology. That this would have induced a desire among gentile converts to seek the cover of the Jewish community is not surprising—at least until newly developing socio-political pressures would lead many of them to move in a different direction (cf. p. 86 n. 59 above).

consequences the Jewish community could face if their non-Jewish neighbors observed Jewish socioreligious boundaries compromised by the equal admission of gentiles qua gentiles and perceived this as an attempt to undermine the interests of the local polis,[40] as expressed in various (pagan) cultic activities among its citizens (cf. Nanos 2002a: 257–71).[41]

Additionally, Nanos (2002b: 405) points out that proselytes would "have a vested interest in guarding and facilitating the ritual process that negotiates hierarchical distinctions between righteous Gentiles and proselytes. Ritual circumcision defines their sense of self- and group-identity; it governs their social interaction; it defines their social reality and political worldview." Further, such proselyte influencers would themselves be subject to negative repercussions from the synagogue authorities if failing to uphold the social boundaries of the larger Jewish community (cf. Gal. 6.12[42]; see also Nanos 2002a: 219–24).

Given these factors, and with attention to the delicate honor and shame social values of the first-century Greco-Roman world (cf. Malina

---

40. In keeping with the observation of Das (cf. n. 39 above), I am not suggesting here that Jewish groups stood *wholly* outside the activities of the polis and did not in several ways relate positively to it, nor that there were not varying degrees of assimilation among Jews throughout the Diaspora (cf. also Rajak 1985, Barclay 1996, Harland 2003: 200–12). However, that there were certain activities from which Jewish groups, as a general rule, refrained is unquestionably the case. Harland (2003: 243) notes, "Failure to participate fully in appropriately honoring the gods (imperial deities included) in cultic contexts was one of the sources of negative attitudes towards both Jews and Christians among some civic inhabitants. Jewish and Christian 'atheism' could then be perceived by some as lack of concern for others ('misanthropy') and, potentially, as a cause of those natural disasters and other circumstances by which the gods punished individuals, groups, and communities that failed to give them their due (cf. Tertullian, *Apology* 40.1–5)."

41. Of course, there were very real theological commitments that demanded Torah submission for full acceptance in the community as a status equal. One must avoid a mirror reading that assumes the influencers who are the target of Paul's rhetoric have a nefarious or less than honorable agenda in seeking to encourage his gentile converts to be circumcised (compare 6.13 and 5.14), as Nanos has argued. In any case, it should be observed that the rights afforded Jews (even if not in the form of a unified policy throughout the Empire) to continue in their traditions provides an additional rationale for Jewish groups to actively seek the proselytizing of Paul's converts, given the potential for these gentiles to continue to publicly identify with the greater Jewish community, irrespective of the assent of the synagogue authorities.

42. As suggested above, the "persecution" of 6.12 may also very well reflect the prospect of this from Roman authorities, which could be exacted upon non-Jews refusing to participate in certain civil obligations thought to conflict with the implications of the gospel.

1993: 28–60; see also Burke 2006: 152–59), I find that Nanos's reconstruction of the letter's exigency makes good sense (Nanos 2002b; 2002a: 96–100). His illuminating description of the scenario warrants extended quotation:

> Imagine that these Gentiles, as relative newcomers to the Jewish communities, originally had gathered around the teaching of a visitor, Paul, with no reason to regard him as anything but a representative Jew working within representative Jewish groups. As time passed, however, they began to be aware that within the larger Jewish communities Paul's followers were regarded by other Jews as something of a subgroup. . . . Although they went to the larger assembly on the Sabbath for the reading of the scriptures, these Gentiles were more attuned to the members of their own little group than to others around them; there was an emerging "us" in the midst of a larger "them." . . . [W]e may suppose that during these months they internalized Paul's proclamation of their identity as righteous ones, entitled to full and equal membership within the people of God, though remaining non-Jews. . . . But then Paul left. The Gentiles ventured into larger meetings of the Jewish communities, perhaps for a holiday celebration or to hear the scripture reading or in search of jobs, since their pagan kinship and patron relations were deteriorating. There they were welcomed by some proselytes, formerly non-Jewish townspeople, perhaps old friends or neighbors. We may assume that these proselytes, as representatives of the larger communities, did not share Paul's views of the status of those Gentiles apart from proselyte conversion. When Paul's Gentile converts boldly announced their new standing among the righteous, claiming for themselves the "righteousing" power of their faith in a Judean martyr of the Roman regime, they might have been treated as confused, but sincere. They might have been gently put in their place and extended a helping hand. Imagine this "good" message [cf. Gal. 1.6ff.]: They could indeed gain the identity among the righteous that they sought, but they had not yet completed the course by which this identity was to be won. . . . Of course, this Gentile group is disappointed, shamed really, for their claim to honor had not been publicly recognized by those who knew and represented the communal norms. (2002b: 397)

In contrast, could Jewish missionaries or Zealot party representatives from Jerusalem (cf. Jewett 1970–71: 198–212) really convince these gentile converts, contrary to the teaching they had already received from

Paul,[43] to undergo such a dramatic procedure as entailed in becoming a proselyte on only theological grounds, without the dominant group pressure of and potential support from the local synagogue? This seems improbable,[44] and thus I conclude it highly likely that the churches Paul founded in Galatia were functioning in close contact with, and at least partially dependent upon, the local synagogue authority at the time his letter was written.

43. In contrast to Nanos, I read Gal. 4.1–11 to equate Torah observance by Paul's gentile converts—specifically in the context of proselyte conversion—with enslavement to the "elemental spirits" of the old creation. What Paul has argued throughout the letter is that for gentiles to now submit to Torah, as per proselytism, is to live as though the new creation has not yet dawned, and thus that both Jews and gentiles are necessarily enslaved by sin and death (cf. 2.21—3.5, 13–14, 22–25). It is important to emphasize here that while Jewish Christ followers may of course continue to fully observe Torah, for a gentile to attempt to do so—that is, to seek traditional proselyte status—is irreconcilable with the reality of Christ's coming. Notwithstanding, for Paul, not only gentiles but also Jews are, outside of Christ faith, still in slavery (cf. 4.25).

44. Cf., e.g., the critique of Jewett's view that understands the influencers (or "agitators," as Jewett refers to them) to represent the interests of Judean Zealotry in Nanos 2002a: 211–15 and Barclay 1988: 64–65.

6

Negotiating Perspectives, Part II

THE UNIVERSAL APPLICABILITY OF THE GOSPEL OF CHRIST

WHILE I FIND THAT there is much with which to agree in the viewpoints of the New Perspective scholars represented in chapter 2, I find far less agreement with the readings I have categorized as "beyond the New Perspective." Insightful at many points, Gaston does locate the error of "old perspective" scholarship in its faith/works dichotomy, misrepresentation of first-century Judaism as a "religion" of legalism and merit-based righteousness, and thus the inherent difficulty of readings such as found in Dodd and Käsemann. But fundamentally problematic in Gaston's reading is his quest to deny the centrality of Christ as God's means of salvation for all humanity, the Jew and gentile alike, which is at the very heart of Paul's theologizing and missionary practice (cf. Rom. 3.21–26; 8.1–4; 15.8–9; Gal. 2.15–16; 3.26–29; 1 Cor. 1.18–25; 2 Cor. 5.17–21; Phil. 2.9–11; Col. 1.15–20; see also Eph. 2.11–22; 3.5–6; 4.1–6).

Further, I understand Gaston's main thesis (cf. 1987: 57–58), that the "righteousness of God" refers specifically to God's inclusion of the gentiles in accordance with the promise made to Abraham but apart from God's covenant with Israel, to be exegetically implausible. Nowhere in Paul is the salvation of the gentiles, *as an independent phenomenon from that of the Jews*, seen as the manifestation of the "righteousness of God." Rather, as made abundantly clear in 2 Cor. 5.19-21 (cf. 2 Cor. 3.3ff.; 1 Cor. 9.19-23), the outworking of God's righteousness that is Paul's apostolic new covenant ministry is universal in scope, encompassing both the Jewish and gentile world.

Paul's premise is quite similar in Rom. 15.8-9, where he again evokes God's righteousness (cf. Rom. 3.3-7[1]). As routinely noted, the Greek syntax of these verses is somewhat ambiguous. But in my rendering the δέ in v. 9a introduces a consequence of the purpose clause in v. 8b. Verse 8b is, in turn, dependent upon the initial clause in v. 8a.[2] As such, the passage reads, "For I tell you that Christ has become a servant of the circumcised for the truthfulness of God in order to confirm the promises to the fathers, and as a result the gentiles may glorify God for (his) mercy."[3]

---

1. Paul refers here to the "truthfulness of God" synonymously with the "righteousness of God" (cf. Williams 1980: 268) and, I conclude, similarly in 15.8-9 (cf. Donaldson 1997: 96).

2. This rendering would be consistent with Paul's explicit (though metaphorical) assertion in Rom. 11.18 that the presence of gentiles among God's people is made possible in the first place through the promises to Israel's patriarchs, and thus gentiles have no basis for any supersessionist notions. And this admonition against judgmentalism and that seeks unity and mutual dependence among God's people underlies the entire section of 14.1—15.13, if not the entire letter. Alternatively, the δέ may function as explicative: "For I tell you that Christ has become a servant of the circumcised for the truthfulness of God in order to confirm the promises to the fathers, that is, that the gentiles would glorify God for (his) mercy" (see similarly Rom. 3.22; 9.30; 1 Cor. 10.11; Phil. 2.8; Eph. 5.32). Either reading would accord with the conclusions I have drawn below, and, in my view, are equally more favorable than understanding v. 8b and v. 9a as strictly parallel purposes statements, according to which the infinitive δοξάσαι is dependent along with βεβαιῶσαι upon εἰς τό, as per the NRSV translation (in question here is the relationship between ὑπὲρ ἀληθείας θεοῦ and ὑπὲρ ἐλέους; cf. n. 3 below). It should be noted, however, that the NRSV rendering can still be read such that the two clauses in vv. 8b-9a are not merely parallel but also consequential, and so if accepted would neither alter my conclusions here. I am similarly unconvinced by Wagner's translation (1997: 481-82; cf. 2002: 310) that presumes an ellipsis in v. 9a, which then requires one to read an explicit servant role for Christ with respect to the gentiles in parallel to the assertion regarding Christ's relationship to Israel in v. 8a: "For I say that the Christ has become a servant of the circumcised on behalf of the truthfulness of God, in order to confirm the promises made to the patriarchs, and [a servant] with respect to the gentiles on behalf of the mercy [of God] in order to glorify God."

3. According to Donaldson (1997: 99), ὑπὲρ ἀληθείας θεοῦ stands independent of v. 9 and, in light of the δέ, is set in contrast to ὑπὲρ ἐλέους. This suggests "that Christ's ministry represents both a demonstration of God's truthfulness (faithfulness to prom-

While this reading could support Gaston's contention, and while, moreover, the inclusion of the gentiles among God's people clearly occupies the thrust of the scriptural catena in vv. 9b–12, I still find it highly unwarranted to restrict τὰς ἐπαγγελίας τῶν πατέρων (v. 8b) to this idea as found in v. 9a (cf. Rom. 11.28–32; contra Gaston 1987: 133–34). If Rom. 4 offers any clarity to the present passage, though Paul there likewise emphasizes the inclusion of the "nations" as being integral to the promise made to Abraham, he nevertheless presumes that the promise includes the salvation of the Jews (cf. 3.30; 4.12–13, 16; see also Gal. 2.15–16; 3.28–29), as he also unambiguously asserts in Rom. 1.16–17 (cf. Rom. 11.13ff.). Thus, when Paul speaks here of the inclusion of the gentiles as the ultimate fulfillment of the promises made to Israel's patriarchs, this necessarily presupposes for him that the restoration of Israel has begun. That is, only by *both* effecting the redemption of Israel and then, *by virtue of this*, the redemption of the other nations, could the Christ event be rightly identified as the manifestation of God's righteousness/faithfulness (cf. Rom. 3.26; see further below).[4]

---

ises already made to Israel) and God's mercy (unexpected inclusion of the Gentiles in Christ on equal terms with the Jews)." He rightly observes that given the "tight connection in the Old Testament" between "truthfulness" and "mercy" these terms should not "be set over against each other in any absolute way." Yet, he holds that in the context of Paul's argument in Romans, where "mercy" is associated with God's sovereign activity in hardening Israel in order to save the gentiles (cf. 9.15–18), it would seem that "a contrast is to be probably inferred." However, I understand God's act of hardening as the means through which the gentiles *and* Israel will ultimately be saved (cf. ch. 4 above). On such contextual grounds I do not observe here any "contrast" (and do not, then, read the δέ as adversative), but rather an interdependent relationship between God's activity with respect to Israel and the other nations (cf. Rom. 11.30–32; Williams 1980: 285–89; n. 4 below).

4. Cf. the comments of Hays (1989: 73) on Rom. 15.12: "The full force of Paul's citation of Isa. 11.10 LXX becomes apparent only when the reader recollects Isa. 11.11–12: 'And it shall be in that day that the Lord will purpose to show his hand to be zealous for the remnant of the people that is left.... And he will lift up a sign for the Gentiles, and he will gather the lost ones of Israel, and he will gather the dispersed ones of Judah from the four corners of the earth.' Paul quotes only an excerpt that prophesies Gentiles placing their hope in the 'root of Jesse,' but the quotation also works as an allusion to Isaiah's vision of God's eschatological kingdom in which the lost ones of Israel rejoin these Gentiles in being gathered at the feet of the one whom God has raised up. This allusion in turn forges an intertextual link back to the remnant theme of Romans 11." Wagner (2002:318) has further proposed that Paul's citation here evokes the even wider context of Isa. 10–12 that as well concerns the restoration of Israel, which, *in turn*, brings about "blessing for Gentiles and for the entire created order." As Wright (2000a:747) remarks, for Paul, the "promises were both *to* Israel and *through* Israel to the world."

Beyond the exegetical and historical difficulties of his reading (cf. pp. 100–104 above), I find the sort of "religious pluralism" that informs Gaston's reading (cf. 1987: 33)—in addition to being anachronistically applied to the first-century—to amount to little more than "cheap grace," and thus a gross mischaracterization of what is found in both the Hebrew Bible and the New Testament. While he correctly points to the history of both latent and explicit anti-Judaism in the church and New Testament scholarship, his creative but ultimately unsuccessful two-covenant interpretation of Paul's letters is surely not the answer to this problem.[5]

Though critical awareness of and sensitivity to the ethical implications of one's interpretation is essential (cf. Schüssler Fiorenza 2000: 40–45; Kinzer 2005: 33–38), it is unquestionably the case that any reading can be used for negative ends, and so it has been with the Bible generally and Paul in particular. To suggest that the prospect for misapplication/misappropriation in itself disqualifies the validity of such a reading is false and, if followed to its logical end, invariably nihilistic.[6]

5. Highly indicative of Gaston's agenda is his imaginative reading of 2 Cor. 3 (1987: 156–64). Here he strives to present a Paul that is not in any way critical of Judaism independent of Christ. But while agreeing that the overall theme of the passage is a defense of the character of Paul's apostolic ministry (one of persecution and suffering) against that of rival Jewish Christ-following missionaries (cf. 2 Cor. 2.17; 4.7–12), in my view Paul is, nevertheless, undoubtedly suggesting in this section of the letter that which he explicitly asserts in Rom. 10.4, "Christ is the τέλος of the Torah." That is, God has through Christ renewed the covenant, which was God's plan all along; cf. Hays 1989: 125–49.

6. Illustrative is Schüssler Fiorenza 2001 that, pointing to the subjectivity and relativity of all "Jesus constructs," dismisses traditional/orthodox understandings, and asserts that one "cannot simply adopt the theological frameworks of the canonical gospels, because to do so would reinscribe not only their anti-Jewish reframing of the memory of Jesus but also their kyriocentric perspective, which focuses both on Jesus the divine man, who is seen no longer as a member of an egalitarian community but as 'G*d striding over the earth' (Käsemann), and on Jesus the charismatic leader, who as an integrated member of his Mediterranean society gathered around him a fellowship of male itinerants. *To acknowledge this kyriocentric perspective of the gospels as normative would mean to endorse Christian anti-Judaism and the marginalization of wo/men*" (p. 72; emphasis added).

The irony here is that Schüssler Fiorenza then defends her own work against charges of latent anti-Judaism (cf. pp. 115–44). She writes: "the accusation of anti-Judaism persists among some Christian feminists.... [M]y critics... *seem to be bent on reading my text against my clearly expressed intentions*" (p. 119; emphasis added). Schüssler Fiorenza's attempt to uncover the ideological agenda that lurks behind such, so-claimed, obvious mischaracterizations of her work notwithstanding, one must ask: given the fact that she has been so understood, does not this alone de-legitimize the conclusions she has reached in her work? Of course, the answer is "no," but the question precisely demonstrates the

And thus Gaston's reading, which he intends to replace what he deems an inherently anti-Judaic interpretation of Paul, in so separating Christ and the church from the Jewish people, can very easily be construed as simply another form of anti-Judaism, irrespective of his intention otherwise. In contrast to Gaston, I suggest again that for Paul *the Christ event belongs to Israel first* (cf. Rom. 1.1–4, 16; 9.4–5; 11.1–5, 16–18, 26–29; 15.8–12; see similarly Matt. 10.5–6; 15.21–28). Christ is Israel's promise, hope, and ultimate (covenant) blessing, according to which the gentiles also then take part. Here is found the central difficulty with the various two-covenant approaches as also suggested by Gager 2000a, 2000b and Johnson-Hodge 2007. They have understood the significance of Christ exactly the wrong way around.

SUPERSESSIONISM AND ANTI-JUDAISM

The same must be said with respect to Harink's view, as particularly expounded in chapter 4 of his *Paul among the Postliberals* (2003). While there are some legitimate observations made throughout, I must conclude with the 2004 review of Richard B. Hays that this is clearly the weakest chapter of the book. What is particularly troubling here is the uncritical use of labels such as "anti-Semitic" and "anti-Jewish" in regard to Wright's interpretation of Paul. Along with these labels comes, largely, a portrayal of Wright's views that ignores certain aspects of his reading in favor of other parts (see below), which in isolation from the former provide the grounds for Harink's negative exposition.

However, as pointed out in pp. 68–71 above, I do find some agreement with Harink in that Wright places too great an emphasis on "ethnocentrism" as the basis of Paul's critique of historical Israel (as likewise Dunn). As Donaldson has similarly asserted, Torah's role in demarcating Israel from the nations is not an intrinsic problem for Paul, but only so when it is still used as an entrance requirement for God's people now that the Christ has come, the covenant is being fulfilled, and the new creation has been inaugurated.[7] Wright's view in this respect, as well as

---

inevitable inconsistency and futility of all such attempts to completely do away with particular readings based singularly on how they may be or have been appropriated.

7. However, Donaldson's assertion (1997: 244) that the Christ event ushers in an unexpected interim period, in which the Torah is temporarily abrogated to allow for the salvation of the gentiles—only to be reaffirmed in the future and final salvation of historical Israel—is based upon a misreading of Rom. 11 and otherwise finds no support in the Pauline corpus.

his choice of language to articulate it, has no doubt hindered for some a full hearing and/or understanding of his position on the question of the relationship of church and Israel, Harink's assessment being indicative.

It should be noted that Wright quite explicitly asserts that Israel, though transformed in Christ, *cannot* and *does not* fail to include members from the historical nation in accordance with the promise.[8] The difficulty is that Wright does not discuss how Jewish identity could remain intact if the chief means through which Jews demarcated themselves from other ethnic groups must, in an absolute sense, come to its end. Yet, as additionally noted by Donaldson (1997: 306), given Paul's own historical context, with the expectation of an imminent Parousia, the continuation of Torah observance in subsequent generations would likely not have been a primary concern for him.

But while there is, in any case, room for legitimate critique here, there is much more in Harink's analysis that is suspect; the hallmark of which is his assertion that equating the church with Israel is inherently supersessionist. I would contend that the notion of supersessionism, as employed by Harink and others, would have been completely lost on Paul. Paul *is* keenly aware of the danger that lay behind any (false) assumption that gentiles have superseded or replaced historical Israel. Given the correct observation that Paul assumes Jews are and will always be part of the church, and that they have the right to continue in Jewish practices (contra esp. Dodd and Käsemann), any charge of ecclesiastical supersessionism directed towards readings that understand the church to be in some way Israel is thoroughly undermined. In short, such charges strike me as uncritically influenced by later historical developments and concerns largely foreign to Paul's worldview.

CHRIST AND THE RESTORATION OF ISRAEL

It is in my view unfortunate how some scholars, particularly those sympathetic to Gaston's reading, have failed to appreciate how thoroughly informed Paul's theologizing is by a promise-and-fulfillment schema[9];

---

8. Cf. Wright 1998: 54: "Paul is careful not to say, or imply, that the privileges of Israel are simply 'transferred to the church,' even though for him, the church means Jews-and-Gentiles-together-in-Christ. Rather, the destiny of Israel has devolved, entirely appropriately within the Jewish scheme, upon the Messiah. All that the new family inherit, they inherit in him."

9. As I have noted at several points throughout the above, this is certainly not to deny the crucial "not yet" dimension of Paul's gospel, as per the reading of Dodd. My

an understanding that his Christ gospel and apostolic mission represents the continuation—even culmination—of God's purposes relating directly to Israel.[10] Of course, the rejection of the hypothesis that Paul thinks in terms of such a continuing storyline for Israel, grounded in Scripture, and in which Christ and the church are an indispensable part (cf. 1 Cor. 15.3–4), is certainly not limited to those holding a two-covenant view. Harink (2003: 165ff.), for example, proposes that even if Paul does believe that Christ is ultimately responsible for Israel's salvation, he does not arrive at this conclusion on the basis of any continuity between Israel's history, the Christ event, and consequent formation of the church. If this were the case, Paul's appeals to scripture—not least in Rom. 9–11—rather than evoking this very "story," would amount to little more than abstract prooftexting for his gospel program.

Clearly at stake is whether the intertexual echoes of Paul's scriptural quotations and allusions should be taken seriously. I agree with Hays, Wright, J. Ross Wagner and others that "Paul's citations and allusions . . . are not plunder from random raids on Israel's sacred texts," nor is Paul interpreting "Isaiah and other scriptural texts in Romans in a detached and disinterested manner" (Wagner 2002: 356). Everything suggests, rather, that he was thoroughly entrenched in the scriptural drama of God's enduring relationship with his covenant people—a living and dynamic reality through which he attempted to interpret the new realities brought into being by the Christ event.

Accordingly, I argue that an implied premise of Rom. 9–11 is that Israel—prior to the advent of Christ—had yet to experience the fulfillment of the Scriptural promises of national restoration. Wagner (2002: 47) asserts,

> By concentrating on two of Israel's foundational narratives—the Abraham saga and the exodus—Paul frames his discussion of Israel's present plight in terms of God's covenant faithfulness to Israel in the past. . . . Paul's argument here consists of a highly selective and abbreviated retelling of Israel's history, beginning

---

use of the notion of "fulfillment" via the Christ event here necessarily implies the future return of Jesus and concomitant eschatological events (e.g., the general resurrection, final judgment).

10. Cf. Gaston 1987: 7: "Jesus is . . . for Paul not the Messiah. He is neither the climax of the history of Israel nor the fulfillment of the covenant." As pointed out above, though not necessarily following through with all the same implications, Gaston's overall position has been followed in many important respects in Stowers 1994, Gager 2000a, 2000b, Johnson-Hodge 2007.

with the promise of descendants to Abraham and reaching to Israel's rebellion, exile, and beyond.

Of much importance is that this story of redemption, as told in Isaiah, and which forms the narrative substructure of Deut. 27–32, is clearly occupied with the pivotal event of "exile."[11] As Paul quotes from and alludes to both these texts in extent throughout the section (cf. Hays 1989: 162–64), there is every reason to suspect that he reflected deeply on its present significance (cf. Hafemann 1997: 367–68; Wagner 1998: 215).[12] In both Isaiah and Deuteronomy's

> larger three-act "plot line" of rebellion, punishment and restoration, Paul locates himself and his fellow believers (Jew and Gentile) in the final act of the story. . . . Surprisingly, however, most of Israel remains mired in acts one and two, still rebellious and estranged from God, still blinded to the reality of the redemption God has wrought for Israel and for the world in Christ. (Wagner 2002: 354)[13]

---

11. While over generalizations regarding the significance of the Babylonian exile within early Judaism must be avoided, that at least some Jews believed the "exile" (in one form or another) still continued long after the return to the land in the sixth-century BCE should not be cause for serious debate. This is the claim made in Dan. 9.15–27 (cf. Ackroyd 1968: 242; Knibb 1976: 255), and the basic notion is likewise reflected in much of the relevant literature; cf., e.g., *1 En.* 85–90; 91.11–17; 93.1–10; Sir. 36; 48.10; 2 Macc. 1–2; *Jub.* 1.9–18; Tob. 13.5ff.; 14.4–7; Bar. 3.8; 4.5—5.9; *Pss. Sol.* 8.34; 11; 17; CD 1.3–11; 3.10–14; 1QM 1.2–3; 4Q504 5.7–21; *T. Lev.* 10, 14–18; *T. Jud.* 23; *T. Iss.* 6; *T. Zeb.* 9.5–9; *T. Dan.* 5.4–13; *T. Naph.* 4.1–5.; *T. Asher* 7.2–7; *2 Bar.* 68.5–7; 78.7; 4 Ezra 13.39–50; *Tg. Isa.* 28; *Tg. Hos.* 14.7–8; *Tg. Mic.* 5.1–3. See further here Steck 1967, 1968; Carroll 1992: 575; Knibb 1976, 1987: 19–22; Gowan 1977, 1986: 28; Thielman 1989: 28–45; 1994: 48–68; Elliot 1994: 134–38; Fuller 2006: 23–24; Vanderkam 1997; Scott 1993, 1997: 186–88, 192–93; Chilton 1997; Evans 1999.

12. With respect to Deuteronomy, quotations include: 29.4 (11.8); 30.12–14 (10.6–8); 32.21 (10.19); there are also allusions to Deut. 32.31 (11.11–14) and Deut. 32.4 (9.14). From Isaiah, Paul cites 10.22–23; 28.22 (9.27–28); 1.9 (9.29); 28.16; 8.14 (9.33; 10.11); 52.7 (10.15); 53.1 (10.16); 65.1–2 (10.20–21); 29.10 (11.8); 59.20–21; 27.9 (11.26–27); and he alludes to 40.7–8 (9.6); 29.16; 45.9 (9.20); 40.21, 28 (10.18–19); 6.9–10 (11.8); 40.13 (11.34) (Wagner 2002: 342, 354–55). Wagner notes, "Of particular significance is the fact that three times Paul links a citation from the last chapters of Deuteronomy to a passage from Isaiah" (p. 355); cf. Deut. 32.21 and Isa. 65.1–2 (10.19–21); Deut. 29.4 and Isa. 29.10 (11.8); Deut. 32.43 and Isa. 11.10 (15.10–12). "This interpretive strategy suggests that Paul understands Isaiah and Deuteronomy to be telling the same epic story of the triumph of God's faithfulness over Israel's unfaithfulness" (p. 355). To this can be added Paul's reference in 9.25–26 to Hos. 2.23 and 1.10, the larger context of Hos. 1–2 being the same as that of the Isaiah and Deuteronomy passages (cf. Wagner 2002: 89).

13. Of course, as suggested in n. 12 above, Paul also finds in these same scriptures

But the precise way Paul would have conceived of the "exile" as a continuing reality is in this respect really quite beside the point.[14] Even if he possessed a more positive assessment of the Diaspora (cf. Kraabel 1987),[15] and/or the sixth-century return, as per Ezra-Nehemiah, he had nevertheless come to view the Christ event as the single means through which Israel's *final* restoration was being accomplished. And if Paul is to be read within a Jewish context, and not rendered an idiosyncratic thinker who merely fabricated a Jewish predicament in light of his new-found conviction, I find it almost impossible but that his soteriology was shaped in some fashion by the metanarrative of sin–exile–return,[16] and thus an understanding of Israel's situation before the coming of Christ as one frustrated by lack of prophetic fulfillment and that required immanent redemption. There is simply no other probable framework available from which Paul could make the sort of claims he does concerning the inauguration of the new covenant via God's act in Christ (cf. 2 Cor. 3.3ff.; 1 Cor. 11.23ff.), that is, the realization of the exilic promises in Scripture (see further here pp. 168ff. below).

In Paul's theology, however, he transforms the promise of the land into the promise of the whole world (cf. Rom. 4.13[17]; 8.18–25; 1 Cor.

---

the hope that God's faithfulness to his people will in the end overcome their unfaithfulness to God; cf. pp. 113ff. above.

14. It is important, however, to recognize that there were a complexity of ways in which this notion could be conceived (cf. Fuller 2006: 24; Vanderkam 1997), not excluding a sense in which the presence of Jews as well as a second temple in the land marked an inaugurated fulfillment of the prophetic promises of restoration, much in the same way early Christ followers understood the significance of Christ's resurrection. The failure to do this is problematic in Wright's extensive use of the theme of "exile and return" in his reading of the New Testament, as correctly noted in Michael Fuller's study of Israel's restoration in Luke-Acts (2006: 208–9).

15. A positive view of the Diaspora seems to be evident, for example, in the writings of Philo (cf. Fuller 2006: 86–100; Halpern-Amaru 1986).

16. Cf. Neusner 1987, 1997; he asserts that the "paradigm of exile and return contains all Judaisms over all times to the present" (1997: 221).

17. Observing the similarity between Rom. 4.13 and Sir. 44.19–21, Johnson-Hodge (2007: 188) comments that "both entail the fertility of Abraham, the inclusion of the gentiles in his progeny, and the ultimate inheritance of the earth for his descendants. This passage illustrates a point that is also true for Paul: the blessing and incorporation of the gentiles are necessary parts of this particular understanding of God's promise. The author of the Wisdom of Sirach sees an implicit connection between the ancestor Abraham (the 'father of many nations'), the incorporation of the gentiles, and universal inheritance. This same connection forms the basis of Paul's argument in Romans 4."

3.21–23; Sir. 44.19–21; Ps. 36.9, 11, 22, 29, 34 LXX; *Jub.* 17.3; 22:14–15, 27–30; 32:18–19; *1 En.* 5.6–7; 4 Ezra 6.55–59; *2 Bar.* 14.13; 51.3; Philo, *Moses* 1.55; *Somn.* 1.175)—the "new creation" of Isaiah's prophecy[18] (cf. 2 Cor. 5.17; Gal. 6.15).[19] In the consummation of God's redemptive program already begun with the resurrection of Christ, Paul holds that this promise will be quite literally fulfilled (cf. Rom. 8.18–25; 1 Cor. 6.2; 15.20–28; Col. 1.15–20; Eph. 1.7–14; see also Heb. 1.2; Matt. 5.5; 2 Pet. 3.10–14; Rev. 21–22).[20] Thus, he can allude in Rom. 8.18–25 to a "new exodus" presently taking place for all creation (cf. Keesmaat 1994, 1999).[21] And if indeed Paul thought in terms of extended exile brought to an end through God's act in Christ, he suggests something of an extended and overlapping "Diaspora" during the interim period between Christ's resurrection and the final gathering together of Christ followers at the eschaton (cf. 2 Thess. 2.1; see also Mark 13.27; Matt. 24.31). Jews and gentiles in Christ are thus exhorted to endure faithful lives in the midst of an unbelieving world (cf. 1 Cor. 5.9–10; 1 Thess. 1.6–10; see also 1 Pet. 1.1ff.; Heb. 4; 12.1ff.), as a testimony to the truth of the one creator God, the God of Israel.[22]

---

18. Cf. Isa. 2.1–4; 9.6–7; 11.1–9; 25.6–10; 27.6; 40.3–5; 42.1, 6; 45.8; 49.6; 51.4–6; 54; 56.6–8; 60; and esp. 65.17–25; 66.22–23; see also Zech. 9.10; Ps. 72.8–11.

19. Cf. Cranfield 1975: 239–40; Dahl 1977: 129–30; Dunn 1988: 213; Stowers 1994: 244–55; Byrne 1996: 143; Wright 2001a: 495; Witherington 2004: 126–27; Johnson-Hodge 2007: 88, 188; Jewett 2007: 325–26; Williams 1988: 717; he rightly notes that for Paul "Canaan is but a type of the *world*."

20. As found in Isaiah 40–66, and similarly understood by the author of *Jubilees* (cf. 1.23–29; 4.26; 19.21–25; 22), inextricably linked for Paul are the establishment of the new covenant and new creation, and fulfillment of the original promise to Abraham.

21. The motif of a "second exodus" for God's people following the judgment of exile permeates Isaiah, especially chs. 40–66; cf. 4.2–6; 10.24–26; 11.11, 15–16; 35.5–10; 40.3–5; 41.17–20; 42.14–16; 43.1–3, 14–21; 48.20–21; 49.8–12; 51.9–10; 52.11–12; 55.12–13; 58.8; 60.2, 19; 63.1ff; see also Hos. 2.14ff.; 12.9; Mic. 7.14ff.

22. For Paul, irrespective of whether one is a Jew or gentile, it is not possible to live faithfully outside the sphere of Christ faith, as it is ultimately here that the truth of God has been revealed, and covenant and creation renewal is accomplished (cf. 1 Cor. 1.18–25). This conviction is in no way intrinsically triumphalistic, as Yoder (1996, 1997) and Harink (2003: 183–203) suggest, because it is rooted in a theology of the cross (cf. Phil. 1.27—2.18; 1 Cor. 4). But to the extent that this conviction has been distorted, and has thus led to various forms of ecclesiastical triumphalism, it should be pointed out that any such attitudes and actions are directly contrary to the faithfulness demanded of the Christ follower, as exhorted by Paul.

APOCALYPTIC AND SALVATION HISTORY

This leads to the false dichotomy that several contemporary scholars, e.g., Martyn, Douglas A. Campbell, and Harink, have created between apocalyptic and salvation history readings of Paul (cf. p. 81 n. 52 above). A feature of the more recent apocalyptic approaches of Campbell and Harink is their distancing from the perceived supersessionism of salvation history approaches. There is here, however, an astonishing irony in condemning salvation history interpretations as supersessionist and, as Harink suggests, "anti-Jewish" when the logic of apocalyptic interpretations can be easily be viewed as even more so—a notion that Harink himself nearly concedes (cf. 2005: 26).

But more to the point, I propose that such interpretations simply cannot, in any case, be divorced from a salvation history context, lest rendering the God of Scripture to which Paul testifies utterly arbitrary and inexplicable. As Dunn (1994: 384) rightly notes, "[F]or Paul the revelation [of Christ] was one which showed him how the ancient promises and hopes were to be fulfilled. It was new in that it focused in Jesus, but the new gospel was simply the new but also foretold way of completing the old purpose" (cf. p. 37 n. 9 above; Scroggs 1991).[23]

Indeed, the intelligibility of Harink's position, as with apocalyptic approaches generally, is difficult to locate. The following statement is illustrative:

> What binds the stories of creation, Israel, Christ, and the church is not a linear historical causality or progression, but God's creating and recreating action. For Paul there is a singular recreative act of God—to which Israel's scriptures everywhere bear witness, and which they prefigure and eagerly anticipate, but which they do not "lead up to"—God's apocalypse in the death of and resurrection of Jesus Christ and the gift of the Holy Spirit. God's deed in Christ is a direct and original act of God, an act of invasion, deliverance and new creation, eagerly anticipated and prefigured

---

23. It may be observed here that Jewish apocalyptic texts themselves do *not* reject Israel's salvation history. Rather, "an apocalypse was ... a way of reaffirming the continuity of the past with the future as both God's." And such a reaffirmation was of crucial importance when Israel found herself "suffering persecution and could see no other way for the covenant and its promises to be sustained" (Dunn 1994: 383). Further, as Wright (1997: 152–53) points out, Paul's "new creation" language is found precisely in covenantal contexts; cf. esp. 2 Cor. 3–5. Indeed, the origin of such language found in Isaiah (cf., e.g., 43.18ff.; 65.17ff.; nn. 18, 21 above) is concerned in the first place with the fulfillment of God's covenantal promises to Israel (cf. 54.9–10).

in the law and the prophets, but comparable only to God's act of creation in the beginning. This radical new-creation act of God is necessary because for Paul, as we have seen, the story of creation is, almost from the beginning, a story of God's creatures in slavery as a result both of their own action (their idolatry and disobedience) and of God's action (his handing them over, subjecting them to futility). (2005: 11)

To propose here that Israel's scriptures "bear witness," "prefigure," "anticipate," but do *not* "lead up to" Christ is a distinction with little actual substance, and seemingly the product of an inadequate grasp of what salvation history is. I am fully persuaded that Paul thinks along the lines of Oscar Cullmann's classic thesis (1956), in which the biblical *Heilsgeschichte* is represented by a double movement that unfolds first in a progressive reduction from all humanity to Israel in particular, and from Israel to the single individual, Christ; and then enlarges from Christ, the center point, to encompass once more all humanity. But despite the frequent critique from proponents of apocalyptic readings, this in no way implies that each step in the salvific program, however dependent upon one another,[24] is of equal weight. Christ, as the center, is the *decisive* redemptive moment (cf. Gal. 4.4-6).

Salvation history cannot, then, be accurately characterized as the smooth, linear escalation from problem to solution. Quite the contrary: indispensable (and not counter) to the unfolding story of redemption that began with the call of and promises to Abraham is the seeming impasse, and thus unrealized hope, brought about in the subsequent dispensation of Torah (cf. Gal. 3.19ff.; Rom. 7.9ff.; see also p. 128 n. 12 above). While perhaps rightly characterized as reaching a "dead end" (Harink 2005: 11), this phase of the story is nevertheless understood by Paul as the necessary prelude and means of preparation for the final, dramatic redemptive resolution attained *solely* through Christ (cf. Gal. 3.24; Rom. 10.4)—"the apocalyptic climax of the salvation-history which constituted the heart of [Paul's] gospel" (Dunn 1994: 388; cf. Wright 1997: 152-53).

While not completely rejecting the notion of salvation history in Paul, as with Harink (however inconsistent his position may be), Douglas A. Campbell similarly sets out in his *The Quest for Paul's Gospel* (2005) to subordinate it to an apocalyptic approach (cf. pp. 56-68, 132-45). After

---

24. In other words, just as there can be no church without first the coming of Christ, so too there is no Christ without first the calling of Israel (cf. Rom. 1.3; 9.4-5; 15.8).

pointing to charges levied against apocalyptic readings of Paul's gospel on the basis that such radical discontinuity occludes both the affirmation of God's original creation (thus the danger of gnosticism) and the people of Israel (thus the danger of anti-Judaism), he explains:

> In response to the foregoing anxieties in relation to discontinuity, many interpreters are tempted to shift their criteria—what is properly basic—to a non-christological, and usually an earlier, point or points. This move then seems to safeguard any concerns with continuity; at least these earlier stable commitments will surely be preserved through any discontinuous process of salvation. So some elements from creation, or from salvation-history, or from within the person, are affirmed in advance of any later, specifically Christian, revelation, as fundamental, inalienable, and non-negotiable (a common choice is some notion of 'covenant'). These affirmations also then serve as criteria for discerning the validity of everything else that follows; we can now understand creation, the history of Israel, and even the meaning of the Christ event itself, which unfolds later in fulfillment of this earlier criterion. (p. 66)

He then concludes that such a "prospective strategy" represents a "grievous error that must be resisted, and on numerous accounts" (p. 66). But the specific reasons he offers as to why this approach should be abandoned are wholly unconvincing and largely dependent upon an anachronistic notion that Paul left one religious system behind for a superior one (pp. 136-42). In my view, Campbell's position suffers from being both reductionistic and predicated almost entirely upon philosophical and theological abstraction with little regard for historical reconstruction.[25]

I do agree that Paul, especially in his letter to the Galatians, argues retrospectively. Because Christ is the means by which God has accomplished salvation, providing entrance into God's family, all that had gone before is only *comparatively* negative in light of the new (eschatological) reality that God has made possible (cf. Phil. 3.5-11; 2 Cor. 3.7-12). But to press this by suggesting that Paul's gospel does not presuppose equally significant prospective elements (cf. p. 134) invariably results

---

25. The latter is particularly exemplified in his claim that the "independent" and "objective" observation that Judaism is inferior to Christianity—which he supposes to be inherent in a salvation history approach—is unethical, and therefore cannot represent the center of Paul's gospel.

in an idiosyncratic/ahistorical Paul who is detached from the pervasive Jewish hope that God would soon intervene in history and bring about, in total, deliverance in accordance with the promises of Scripture (cf. Rom. 11.26–27). While there is surely coherence to Paul's gospel, concerted attention must be given to the contextual nature and complexity of Pauline thought, which I submit is not evidenced here.[26]

THE CHARACTER OF ELECTION

The question of the continuity of God's purposes comes to a critical juncture when one considers the central matter of divine election. A great deal of the basis for readings that understand a sharp distinction between the church and Israel rests upon the notion of Israel's historical election. It is proposed that this, rather than allegiance to Christ, is the foundation of Israel's status as God's people and forever remains the guarantee of their redemption. However, I suggest that such views misunderstand the very character of Israel's special election, which I argue is understood by Paul in representational and vocational terms, and as being interdependent upon human response. And it is from within this context that he is able to conceive of the church as continuous with Israel. In other words, as I have already asserted (pp. 120ff.), the church is in one sense for Paul not a distinct or wholly new entity, but the one and same people—however now transformed in Christ—whom God has called.[27]

Election: Representational and Vocational

In addressing the question of how Paul interpreted Israel's election and, in turn, how this was mutually informed by both his Christology and ecclesiology, I first turn to other Jewish texts that betray an important aspect of this seminal conviction of early Judaism, namely, that the dominion of Adam in creation has been uniquely reaffirmed to God's chosen people, Israel.[28]

The following from 4 Ezra 6.53–59 is illustrative:

---

26. However, D. A. Campbell (1994: 316–18) rightly points to Paul's varied hortatory purposes as a controlling factor in the interpretation of his letters.

27. As already suggested in the previous chapters, it is in my view the failure to recognize this double sense of what it means to be "Israel" that has created such difficulty and intense debate among Pauline scholars addressing the matter at hand.

28. I follow here much of the line of thought proposed in Wright 1991: 18–40; 1992: 262–68.

> On the sixth day you commanded the earth to bring forth before you cattle, wild animals, and creeping things; and over these you placed Adam, as ruler over all the works that you had made; and from him we have all come, the people whom you have chosen. All this I have spoken before you, O Lord, because you have said that it was for us that you created this world. As for the other nations that have descended from Adam, you have said that they are nothing, and that they are like spittle, and you have compared their abundance to a drop from a bucket. And now, O Lord, these nations, which are reputed to be as nothing, domineer over us and devour us. But we your people, whom you have called your firstborn, only-begotten, zealous for you, and most dear, have been given into their hands. If the world has indeed been created for us, why do we not possess our world as an inheritance? How long will this be so?

A similar perspective is found in *Jub.* 22.11–13, 14. The author presents Isaac as pronouncing this blessing upon Jacob:

> Blessed be my son Jacob and all the sons of God Most High, unto all the ages; may God give unto you a seed of righteousness; and some of your sons may he sanctify in the midst of the whole earth; may nations serve you, and all the nations bow themselves before your seed. Be strong in the presence of men, and exercise authority over all the seed of Seth. Then your ways and the ways of your sons will be justified, so that they will become a holy nation. May the Most High God give you all the blessings with which he has blessed me and with which he blessed Noah and Adam; may they rest on the sacred head of your seed from generation to generation forever. . . . And may you inherit the whole earth.

Likewise, the *Testament of Moses* claims that God "has created the world" not for the gentiles, but "on behalf of his people" (1.12–13). Much of the same understanding is also represented in the Qumran writings. It is asserted in 1QS 4.22–23; CD 3.19–20; 1QH 17.14–15; 4Q171 3.1–2 that to their sect in the eschaton would come "all the glory/inheritance of Adam." In keeping with these examples, the Wisdom of Solomon declares (in the context of God's original purpose for, and yet the subsequent corruption of, humanity) that the righteous who keep Torah, in contradistinction to the foolish/ungodly, "will govern nations and rule over peoples" (3.8). And finally, *Psalms of Solomon* says that God's "love is toward the seed of Abraham, the children of Israel," and God's "chastisement is upon [them] as a first-born, only-begotten son" (18.4).

A premise seemingly shared among these texts is that Israel is what may best be described as God's "true humanity"; a special lineage descended from Adam[29] that had been set apart from the midst of a fallen creation.[30] The Torah is suggestive of this worldview. Here, Israel is effectively presented as a paradigm of God's original intentions for all humanity in creation.[31] This is most evident in the numerous parallels between the role of humanity in creation and that of Abraham and his descendents (compare Gen. 1.28 with 12.2–3; 17.2, 6, 8; 22.16–18; 26.3–5; 28.3; 35.11; 47.27; 48.3–4; see also Exod. 1.7; 32.13; Lev. 26.9; Deut. 1.10–11; 7.13; 8.1; 28.63; 30.5, 16). Birch, Brueggemann et al. (1999: 171) point out that the very shape of the Pentateuch further speaks to this parallel with the beginning and closing chapters forming an inclusio: "Just as Adam and Eve are created in the image of God and commanded to have dominion in God's creation, so also Israel as God's covenant partner is given responsibilities to further the divine purposes for the life and well-being of the creation."[32]

But what this broader self-understanding would actually indicate for Israel vis-à-vis the nations finds different conclusions among the various Jewish sources. One interpretive track that is demonstrable in the texts quoted above could be properly deemed a "supersessionist"

---

29. The understanding that Adam is the first patriarch of Israel is demonstrable throughout much of the rabbinic literature; cf., e.g., b. ʿErub. 18b; Pirqe R. El. 12; Tanḥ. B. Toledot 12; Gen. Rab. 24.2; 58.4. See Scroggs 1966: 38–46.

30. Regardless of how the passage was originally read, that Jews of the late Second Temple period understood Gen. 3 as depicting the "fall" of humanity into sin and death is so thoroughly attested in the relevant Jewish literature (cf., e.g., 4 Ezra 3.7; 7.11ff., 116–26; Wisd. 2.23–24; 2 Bar. 17.3; 19.8; 23.4; 54.15; 56.6, 8ff.; Sir. 14.17; 25.24; 40.1; 41.10; T. Lev. 18.10) it is strikingly peculiar for Stowers (1994: 90), Harink (2003: 162–63) and Johnson-Hodge (2007:110) to argue that Paul did not understand it so, especially in light of Rom. 5, 7, and 1 Cor. 15 (it is especially peculiar in Harink's case, as it otherwise contradicts his apocalyptic reading of Paul). It seems to me that they make a serious error in judgment not to consider here the post-70 CE Jewish literature. It is in my mind far more likely that this understanding derives from a much older interpretive tradition, rather than representing an entirely new theological development.

31. It is important to point out that there is no primordial command for humans to rule over one another in the Genesis creation narrative. Human dominion is strictly over the non-human order, however other Jewish texts may have reinterpreted this God-given mandate for polemical reasons (cf. n. 33 below).

32. The rabbinic literature likewise portrays this relationship between humanity at large and Israel; cf. esp. Gen. Rab. 14.6: "I will make Adam first . . . and if he goes astray I will send Abraham to sort it all out" (see also Num. Rab. 13.2).

ideology. Here, Israel's divine election is interpreted in terms of abiding privilege over the other nations (cf. *Tg. Isa.* 28.9).[33] In other words, the dominion entrusted to all humanity in creation (cf. Gen. 1.26-28; Ps. 8.3-8[34]) has become the sole possession of Israel, which, if not presently enjoyed, will ultimately be realized in the future when God acts to redeem his people (cf. Dan. 7.27;[35] *1 En.* 90.30; *2 Bar.* 72.2-6; *Jub.* 32.19; *T. Mos.* 10ff.). Thus, the other nations, however they might experience some form of blessing through and/or in relation to Israel—not excluding eschatological salvation—as per the original promise to Abraham, nevertheless occupy an inferior role.[36] A second interpretive track for which one finds evidence is that Israel's election functions foremost in service to the other nations. That is, Israel is God's chosen agent through which God will work to fully restore all nations.[37]

It is without question that the prophetic literature presents the destiny of the nations, as well as the entire created order, as inextri-

33. I leave to the side here the socio-political context and motivation, e.g., Israel's persecution and subjugation by foreign powers, which led to the various expressions of such a view in the relevant literature. For the present purposes it is sufficient to observe that this self-understanding—among others (see below)—existed within Second Temple Judaism. However, it would be most *improper* to over-emphasize/distort this perspective in terms of a "cultural imperialism" characterizing the worldview of the majority of Jews in Paul's time, and further conclude that Paul is consumed with its refutation in his letters to the Galatians and Romans (cf. pp. 68-71, esp. n. 29 above).

34. Though not in the present context, in light of Dan. 7 (cf. n. 35 below), it is evident that the democratized royal ideology characteristic of Ps. 8.4-9 was eventually interpreted eschatologically, and as having Israel specifically in view (cf. Caird 1994: 378). The messianic interpretation of Ps. 8 (in conjunction with Ps. 110.1) in 1 Cor. 15.25-27; Eph. 1.20-22; Heb. 1.13—2.9 is also very relevant here; see further below.

35. Much of the book of Daniel carries unmistakable overtones of Adamic dominion as being the rightful possession of Israel. One may observe, for example, the description of King Nebuchadnezzar in 2.36-38, followed by his ironic transformation in 4.32-33. In ch. 7, "one like a son of man" (vv. 13-14), representative of (the people of) the holy ones of the most high" (vv. 18, 27)—i.e., Israel, regains dominion over the "beasts," the nations who had oppressed them.

36. It should be emphasized that even in the literature portraying the most ardent forms of this worldview there are seemingly admissions to the reality of righteous gentiles, either as a present phenomenon or in the eschaton (cf., pp. 68-71, esp. n 30 and p. 122 n. 2 above). However, the perceived relative status of these in relation to Israel, outside of Paul/the New Testament, is not precise.

37. This notion may have been interpreted among at least some first-century Jews as a basis for which to seek and/or fully accept proselytes (cf. Matt. 23.15; Gal. 5.11; also Rom. 2.19; see further p. 33 n. 7 and p. 70 n. 32 above), or foster in some respect various levels of gentile associations with the synagogue.

cably linked to God's providential purposes within and for Israel (cf., e.g., Isa. 2.2-4; 9.6-7; 11.1ff.; 14.1-2; 19.16-24; 25.6-10; 42.1-6; 45.8; 49.6; 51.4-6; 55.3-5; 56.6-8; 60.1ff.; 65.17-25; 66.18-23; Jer. 3.16-17; Ezek. 47.7-12; Mic. 4.1-4; Zeph. 3.9; Zech. 2.11; 8.20-21; 14.8-19). Nevertheless, the prophets are divided and often ambiguous as to which of the above interpretive options they envisage (cf. p. 122 n. 2 above). Yet at least one text in particular, the servant song of Isa. 52.13—53.12, is strongly suggestive of the latter, and places in proper context all other assertions in Isaiah regarding the relationship of Israel to the nations.[38]

A great deal of scholarship has surrounded the issue of whether the Suffering Servant is presented here as an individual or a corporate entity (i.e., the Jewish community), the latter reading being the dominant one within rabbinic Judaism. However, there is little reason not to accept that the fourth song in its present canonical placement intertwines on some level both these identities. It seems quite prudent to conclude with R. E. Clements (1998: 41) that the "literary background to all four passages concerning the identity of the Servant would undoubtedly support the claim that we are faced here with a figure who fulfills some form of representational collective role."[39] Understanding similarly, the following comments of Christopher R. Seitz (2001: 462) highlight the point critical to the matter at hand:

> The dual mission of the servant—restoration of the survivors of Israel and as "Israel," a light to the nations (49:6)—is here confessed . . . as fully accomplished. . . . [I]n this poem the servants come to acknowledge the life and death of the servant, as an individual, as expiatory for themselves. But because the servant,

---

38. Cf. Hanson 1995: 166: "[I]t is through the Servant's humiliation and suffering that God accomplishes the redemption of God's people from bondage to sin. . . . Even that act, though, is preliminary. Israel's redemption prepares the way for God's salvation to reach the ends of the earth. For by being restored to spiritual wholeness Israel becomes the fitting instrument through which God can teach the tôrāh to all nations as a reliable basis for universal peace. The Servant Songs of Second Isaiah thus complete the picture in the second chapter of Isaiah of the nations streaming to Zion to learn God's way as the basis for an alternative to war. God has now appointed the teacher who will instruct the nations in this path to universal harmony. The teacher is the Servant."

39. Clements proposes here multiple interpretive backgrounds from Israelite tradition (e.g., the royal, prophetic and Mosaic traditions [cf. on this last background Seitz 2001: 464]) that provide a basis for the interplay of individual and collective elements in the songs. He explains: "In this fluctuation the fate of one individual in some way both embodies, yet redeems, the fate of the larger group" (p. 42).

as an individual, has understood himself as the embodiment of "Israel, in whom I will be glorified" (49:3), especially with a vocation to the nations, the poem functions at yet another level. The individual servant's suffering and death are Israel's on behalf of the other nations.

Convincingly demonstrated by Wagner (1998, 2002), Hofius (2004: 175–83)[40] and Watson (2007b), there is much evidence to suggest that Paul was greatly influenced by this text. Paul directly quotes from the LXX passage in Rom. 10.16 and 15.21 (cf. Gal. 3.2), and textual echoes from it are found in Paul's ὑπὲρ ἡμῶν formula (cf., e.g., 1 Thess. 5.10; Rom. 5.8; 8.32; Gal. 3.13). His understanding of Christ's vicarious death for "our sins" (ἁμαρτιῶν ἡμῶν) also seems to be dependent on Isa. 53 (cf. Gal. 1.4; 1 Cor. 15.3; also Rom. 4.25), as is Paul's language of Christ being "given up" (παρέδωκεν) (cf. Rom. 8.32; 4.25; 1 Cor. 11.23). Although Paul's use of this text denotes an association of the Servant with Jesus Christ, surely he was well aware of the identification of the Servant as Israel elsewhere in Second Isaiah (cf. Isa. 44.1; 45.4; 49.3; also 42.18ff.) and was thoroughly considerate of this relationship.

Comporting with this observation, I propose along the lines of Wright's central thesis that Paul did conceive of Jesus as Israel's inclusive representative who had in himself fulfilled Israel's elect purpose as God's true humanity: the willing self-sacrificial exercise of God-given agency and power on behalf of the other (cf. Hanson 1995: 166).[41] Though drawing different implications from Wright, Kinzer (2005: 217–23) similarly refers to this connection between Jesus and Israel, seen also in the Gospel of Matthew (cf. 2.14–15; 3.15–17; 4; 19.28; 24.30; 25.31), as "Yeshua as One-Man Israel." That is, "Yeshua as representative and

---

40. Though he does demonstrate the influence of Isa. 53 upon Paul, the focus of Hofius's argument is not primarily this, but concerns, rather, the nuanced distinction between "exclusive" and "inclusive" place-taking with respect to the role of the servant in the original context of the passage as compared to its reception in the New Testament. I suggest here neither support nor rejection of this hypothesis, which is unnecessary to my argument.

41. If Paul also aligned himself with the servant of Yahweh, as per Isa. 42.6-7, 11 and 49.1, 6 (cf. Gal. 1.15-17; 2 Cor. 4.4-12), this would resonate with his understanding that he along with other Jewish Christ followers represent the righteous remnant of Israel (cf. Rom. 9.27; 11.5) who as such are fulfilling Israel's task to be "a light to the nations," particularly in view of the dawn of the eschatological age when, according to the prophets, the nations would turn in worship of Israel's God. See further Kim 2002: 101–12.

individual embodiment of the entire people of Israel."[42] Wright (1991: 25) remarks,

> [A] Messiah, if one is envisaged, draws on to himself the hope and destiny of the people itself.[43] He, like the nation, is called the son of God. There is a fluctuation between the king and his people, seen for instance in the Davidic overtones of the Abraham stories, in the solidarity expressed in e.g. 2 Samuel 5.1-2; 19.41-20.2, and the transference of royal promises to the people at large (Isaiah 55). In subsequent writings, we find such promises again referred to the whole nation (cf. Jubilees 1.24) or to the righteous remnant (4qFlorilegium 1.18f.; 1QS 8.4-10).

One should further consider here Rev. 2.26-28, in which the messianic interpretation of Ps. 2.8-9, proclaiming his universal dominion, is simultaneously applied to the people of the Messiah (cf. Rev. 5.10). This notion of shared dominion is similarly suggested by Paul in Rom. 5.17 and 1 Cor. 6.2 (cf. 2 Tim. 2.12; Eph. 2.6).

It is in light of all the above that the assertion found in Gal. 6.15-16 may properly function for Paul. The "Israel of God"—God's elect people—are all those "in Christ" (cf. Gal. 3.28-29[44]) who as such likewise represent God's true humanity. They are those destined for the new cre-

---

42. I would point out here that Wright (cf. 2001a: 549ff., 643) is certainly correct in his assertion that, for Paul, it was always God's plan that Israel's representative Messiah would be the means through which the problem of sin and death would be resolved (cf. also Rom. 3.21-26; 8.1-4; 2 Cor. 5.21; Gal. 2.19-21; 3.13; 4.4-5). However, I find no real support for Wright's suggestion that God firstly focused the sins of the world in Israel, the representative nation of the world, by means of the Torah (as the Torah reveals sin for what it is; cf. Rom. 3.20; 5.20-21; 7.13; Gal. 3.19; 1 Cor. 15.56). Paul nowhere suggests a precursory role in salvation history in this respect via Israel's Torah transgressions.

43. Cf. similarly Mowinckel 2005: 56-95 for an analysis of the "ideal of kingship in ancient Israel," as it provides a basis for later messianic speculation, including the monarchy's representative function for the nation at large; see also Clement 1998: 44-45.

44. See also 2.19-21; Rom. 6.4-5; 16.7; Col. 2.9-13; Phil. 3.9; 1 Cor. 1.30; 2 Cor. 1.21; 5.17, 21.

ation (cf. 2 Cor. 5.14–17; Col. 3.10–11; 1 Cor. 15.20–22, 42–57; Rom. 5.12–21;[45] see also Eph. 2.15;[46] 4.24). As Paul writes in Rom. 8.18–30,

> For the creation waits with eager longing for the revealing of the children of God. . . . For those whom he foreknew [cf. Rom. 11.1–2] he also predestined to be conformed to the image of his Son, in order that he might be the firstborn within a large family. And those whom he predestined he also called; and those whom he called he also justified; and those whom he justified he also glorified.

The vital corollary to this representational understanding of election is clearly demonstrated in the paraenetic material throughout the Pauline corpus, especially Phil. 1.27—2.18, whereby the servant role of Christ is portrayed as being fundamentally normative for the Christ community (cf. similarly Gal. 5.13ff.). In short, Paul's theology of election is definitively vocational—and ultimately cross-shaped; election is a phenomenon that does *not* simply find its end in divine caprice. While not excluding any sense of intrinsic privilege, it is abundantly evident that for Paul it is a serious perversion to collapse election into this category. This finds agreement not only with the Jesus tradition recorded in the Gospels (cf. esp. Mark 10.42–45; see also Rom. 15.3, 8; 2 Cor. 8.9), but discernable strands of thought in both the Torah (cf. Gen. 12.3; 18.18; 22.18; 26.4; 28.14; Exod. 19.5–6; Lev. 19.9–17, 33–36; Deut. 4.5–8; 10.12–22; see also

---

45. Much scholarly debate has surrounded the origin of Paul's Adam Christology (cf., e.g., Scroggs 1966; Wright 1992: 18–40; Dunn 1996: 98–128; Kim 2002: 165–213). Though I agree with Wright that Israel, as firstly occupying the role of the second Adam in at least some strands of Jewish tradition, is implicit in these texts, it is nevertheless not necessary to argue the point here. It suffices to take notice that in these passages Paul understands Christ as the inclusive representative of a renewed humanity inaugurated by the resurrection (cf. 2 Cor. 3.18; 4.4ff.; Col. 1.15ff.). The more explicit connection between this role and Israel is strongly suggested by Paul in Gal. 6.15–16, a point that has been generally missed by scholars.

46. It seems evident to me that the "abolishing" (καταργέω) of the Torah's "commandments" (ἐντολή) and "ordinances" (δόγμα)—integral to the creation of a unified "new humanity"—cannot be understood here in an unmitigated sense. First, the encoded audience of this passage are explicitly "gentiles" (2.11)—those who were formerly excluded from the people of God on the basis of Torah. Their inclusion is now made possible through Christ (2.13), and thus at the complete expense of their submission to the Torah *as an entrance requirement*. Second, 6.2 makes it otherwise clear that the Torah still forms a basis for the praxis of the Christ community (cf. 5.3–5; see also esp. 2.10).

Birch, Brueggemann et al. 1999: 133)[47] as well as the Prophets outside of Second Isaiah, the frequent basis of whose critique of Israel was the implicit mistaking of the covenant, particularly among the aristocracy, in terms of an election unto privilege rather than an election unto vocation (cf., e.g., Isa. 5; Jer. 7.1–8.3; see also Sanders 1997: 44).[48]

It should not be inferred here, however, that historical Israel's role as God's elect agent of redemption on behalf of all nations, if being fulfilled through Israel's Messiah and his people, spells the end of historical Israel, anymore than Paul's assertion that the church is the body of Christ (1 Cor. 12.27) means that the church displaces the person of Christ.[49] I suggest only that, in one important sense, for Paul to be "Israel" is synonymous with being genuinely human and thus bearing the primordial and Abrahamic task of bringing blessing to the rest of creation, even at the cost of self-sacrifice; a notion that might be succinctly expressed in the axiom, "Israel is as Israel does" (cf. p. 88 n. 62 and p. 121 n. 1 above).

Election: God's Sovereign Purposes and Human Volition

But what of the certainty of the promises made to historical Israel? Consideration must be given here to Campbell's assertion (1992: 172) that Paul in Rom. 9–11 is precisely addressing a potential objection to his gospel regarding "the reliability of a God who allows one covenant or one set

---

47. While there clearly are texts within the Pentateuch that stand in tension to this view, it is important to stress that "election" and "blessing" are not, in any case, synonymous (however the former necessarily includes the latter; cf. pp. 113ff. above). Especially in the Genesis narrative, it can be seen that because God chooses Israel it does *not* mean that God's blessing foremost rests upon Israel at the expense of the other nations (cf., e.g., Gen. 17.19-21; see further Westermann 1995: 270). Rather, Israel is chosen and subsequently blessed so that they in turn can be a blessing to the rest of creation. It is thus the "mediatorship of blessing," and not the blessing itself that in the first place defines "election." Brueggemann (1997: 168) comments: "Israel is given significance and responsibility well beyond itself. And the world of nations is recharacterized as an arena in which God's faithful power for life is being enacted. In these traditions of promise, Israel, by its life and obedience, is entrusted with the well-being of the nations."

48. I suggest that it is perhaps the most seminal theological insight in all of Scripture that divine election is *always* vocationally oriented (cf., e.g., the various "call narratives": Gen. 12.1-3; Exod. 3.7-12; Judg. 6.11-24; 2 Sam. 7.8-29; Isa. 6.1-10; Jer. 1.4-10; Ezek. 2.1—3.11), a notion which Paul no doubt understood well (cf. Gal. 1.15-16).

49. Indeed, the Messiah's people consist of historical Israel, as redeemed through him, and those likewise from the other nations. What one finds, then, could be explained as an "Israel" within an "Israel," though it is perhaps doubtful that Paul would himself articulate it as such.

of promises to fail, reject one people in favor of another in what could be construed as an arbitrary fashion." If God has made specific promises to a specific people, whom Paul clearly recognizes as a contemporary ethnic group with which he personally identifies (cf. Rom. 9.3; 11.1; Phil. 3.5; Gal. 1.14; 2.15), is it not imperative, then, that such promises are enjoyed by none other than this same group? Both Gaston and Harink (2003: 197, 203–7) similarly suggest that the promises made to historical Israel are guaranteed by singular virtue of God's sovereign election. And therefore, it cannot be that such promises are in the end made available only to those who choose to embrace Paul's Christ gospel.

However, I suggest once more that such views simply misunderstand the character of election, as Paul understood it. For him, and as consistent with the dominant understanding in Second Temple Judaism, God's elective purpose does not mean the irrelevancy of human choice (cf. p. 110 n. 46 above).[50] To insist upon acceptance of Jesus as Messiah, and to hold Israel accountable for this, is not contrary to the language of election, however inexplicable the relationship of the two may be (cf. Rom. 11.23).[51]

---

50. The Scripture in which Paul's worldview was deeply imbedded presents far more ambiguity on this matter than for which both Gaston and Harink allow. The Davidic covenant, for example, is portrayed at several points as unconditional (cf. 2 Sam. 7.15-16; Jer. 33.17-22; 2 Chron.13.5; Ps. 89.20-37), and yet it is also spoken of as being ultimately dependent upon human response (cf. 1 Kgs. 2.4; 8.25; 9.4-5; Isa. 7.9b; Ps. 132.11-12; Ps. 89.38-52: note that Ps. 89, after claiming the covenant to be unconditional, affirms that it has nevertheless been broken, though it does not offer disobedience as a reason; the absence of such an admission of guilt being a common feature of psalms of lament). Still further, 1 Sam. 2.27-36 first presents the priestly covenant with the house of Eli as seemingly unconditional (vv. 27-30a), but the covenant is then interpreted as being conditional (vv. 30b-36). Brueggemann (1997: 419) suggests accordingly that (a) "Israel, as Yahweh's covenant partner, is expected to order its way of life in ways that are appropriate to this relationship," and (b) "if this relationship is indeed one of passionate commitment, as it surely is, it is undoubtedly the case (by way of analogy) that every serious, intense, primary relationship has within it dimensions of conditionality and unconditionality that play in different ways in different circumstances."

51. Harink (2003: 171-79) resists any implication that Israel's actual response to God is significant in Paul's theologizing here. But Paul's stress upon God's sovereignty and faithfulness does not intend to reduce Israel to merely a corporate *object* of God's affection, as if Israel is not a subjective covenant partner, and that Jews (unlike gentiles) possess no personal responsibility (cf. the discussion of Israel's covenantal obligation in Brueggemann 1997: 417-34). Such a reading cannot be sustained in this section, and is utterly foreign to not only the letter in its entirety but the Pauline corpus in general.

The Torah itself declares that the promised covenant blessings are predicated upon Israel's continued obedience (cf. Deut. 27–29). Deuteronomy 30 (cf. 32.15ff.) presumes Israel's eventual failure (as a testimony to the plight of sin they share with the rest of humanity, which will require a decisive act of God to rectify; cf. Rom. 3.20ff.; 4.13ff.; 5.12ff.; 7.7ff.; Gal. 3.21ff.) and the consequential covenant curse of exile. And yet it also presumes God's promised restoration of his people in the land, whereby a repentant Israel by means of God's spirit would then keep Torah from the heart (cf. Ezek. 11.19-20; 36; Jer. 3.6ff.; 31; 32.39-40; Isa. 32.15; 44.3; 59.21; see also 1 Kgs. 8.46-53).

Many later Jewish writings reflected upon the implications of Deut. 30ff. (cf., e.g., 4 Ezra 7.20-24; 119ff.; Pseudo-Philo 19; *T. Mos.* 1.1ff.), and understood this repentance and subsequent restoration of Israel eschatologically (cf. Bar. 2.27ff.; 4.1ff.; *Jub.* 1.14-23; 23.26; 4QMMT C 12-32; see also 2 Bar. 78.6-7; *T. Mos.* 1.18; *T. Jud.* 23.5; *T. Iss.* 6.4 ; *T. Zeb.* 9.7-8; *T. Dan* 5.4-13; 6.4; *T. Naph.* 4.3-5; Tob. 13.5ff.; 14.4-7; 4 Ezra 4.38-39; Sanders 1997: 48-49).[52] Thus, for Paul to assert that God has finally made possible Israel's redemption (and therefore a means by which gentiles too can be saved) through their obedient submission to Christ, the τέλος of Torah (10.3-4), is consistent with Jewish tradition,[53] however christologically transformed (cf. 9.25-26; 15.8-12; n. 4 above).[54]

---

52. Sanders (1985: 57–117; 1992: 289-303) has suggested that "'Jewish eschatology' and 'the restoration of Israel' are almost synonymous" (1985: 97; cf. Nickelsburg 1981: 18). He remarks: "[T]he expectation of the reassembly of Israel was so widespread, and the memory of the twelve tribes remained so acute, that '*twelve*' would necessarily mean '*restoration*'" (1985: 98)—and so Paul's reference in 1 Cor. 15.5 (cf. Matt. 29.28).

53. Wagner (2002: 136-57) persuasively argues that Rom. 9.30—10.4 evokes the greater context of Isa. 8.14 and 28.16, which are quoted in 9.33. As in the Isaiah passages, the "motif of faith/trust is central to Paul's criticism of Israel in Romans 9.30—10.4. . . . Isaiah 8 and 28-29 LXX offers Paul an important precedent for his insistence that Israel's lack of faith/trust stems not from their adherence to the Law, but rather from their failure to understand the Law rightly and so pursue it ἐκ πίστεως" (p. 151); that is, I suggest, to understand the Torah as invariably leading to his Christ gospel (cf. pp. 79ff., esp. n. 49 above).

54. While Davidic messianic expectations (derived from texts such as, e.g., Isa. 9.6-7; 11.1-12; Jer. 23.5-8; 33.14-26; Ezek. 34.23ff.; 37.24-28; Amos 9.11ff.; Hos. 3.4-5; Mic. 5.2-3; Zech. 3.8; 6.11-13) are by no means monolithic in the postbiblical literature, Fuller (2006: 184) points out that when such a figure is envisaged "it is usually within the exilic model of restoration. For those Jews who sustained the hope for his coming, the messiah's arrival was understood to be pivotal to Israel's restoration" (cf., e.g., *Pss. Sol.* 17–18; *1 En.* 37-71; 4 Ezra 7.25-44; 12.31-34; 13.25-50; 2 Bar. 26.1—30.5; 36.1—40.4; 53.1—76.5; 4Q252 5.1-6; 4Q161 3.11ff.; 4Q285 frg. 5; 4Q174 1).

It is this new covenant theology that Paul has already affirmed in Rom. 2.25-29; 8:1-11, and which he further elaborates upon in Rom. 10.5-11 (cf. 2 Cor. 3.3-16). Contrary to some readings, vv. 5-6 do not set Lev. 18.5 and Deut. 30 in opposition with one another, as if the latter negates the former (so Dodd 1932: 166; Käsemann 1980: 286; cf. more recently Watson 2004: 314-53), but rather Paul interprets Lev. 18.5 in light of Deut. 30. He maintains, therefore, that the "doing of the law" through which one attains the status of righteousness and finds "life" is ultimately accomplished by means of the gospel of Christ (cf. Rom. 1.17; 5.18ff.). And as such, it is now available not only for Jews qua Jews, but also gentiles qua gentiles. Wright (2001a: 662) comments:

> This, taken as a whole, explains v. 4, and thereby, in turn, explains how salvation is now available for all who share this faith. In other words, while opening the promise to those of any and every ethnic background, Paul is more specifically showing how his prayer in 10:1 is to be answered. This is how God is restoring the fortunes of Israel. Just as MMT urged its readers to make their status in the renewed people of God secure by particular temple regulations, and just as Baruch urged his readers to seek the divine Wisdom, so Paul urges people of every race [cf. p. 69 n. 28 above] to discover the risen Lord Jesus as Messiah and find thereby the renewed covenant membership of which Deuteronomy spoke.

This is, moreover, the exact basis for Paul's argument in Gal. 2.15-3.14. The curse of death suggested in 2.19; 3.10, 13 evokes the covenant curses of the closing chapters of Deuteronomy (cf. 27.26), the zenith of which is exile from the land of promise, a reversal of the exodus (cf. Deut. 28.58-68) that would be realized by virtue of Israel's corporate idolatry/covenant disobedience (cf. Isa. 24.4-6). Metaphorically it represents death (Deut. 30.19-20; cf. Ezek. 37; Hos. 6.2), i.e., separation (in a certain sense) from God's presence (cf. Gen. 2.15-3.24; Lev. 26.11ff.). This experience of "death" was thus a reality for the Deuteronomist's vision of Israel. And in Paul's theology this was a continuing reality for Israel, as well as the nations by default (cf. pp. 80 n. 50; 128 nn. 12, 13; 158-66 above), until the coming of Christ[55] and inauguration of the new

---

55. That is, the coming of "faith" (Gal. 3.23; cf. pp. 78-83, esp. n. 49 above), through which one "will live" (Gal. 3.11; cf. 2.19-21). Paul assumes here, and does not argue for, the reality of Christ—"apart from the Torah [cf. Gal. 3.12] ... [yet] attested by the Torah and prophets" (Rom. 3.21)—as the means through which God has brought

covenant and new creation (cf. my expanded translation of Gal. 2.16-21 in pp. 129-30 above).[56]

In sum, there is no foundation here for any claim that Paul, understood so, has turned his back on historical Israel because of an insistence upon trusting in Christ for the Jew, as with the gentile. It is, in my mind, incontrovertible that such a call for repentance, in harmony with other Jewish voices of the period[57] and implicit throughout Rom. 9-11, was fundamental to Paul's mission and theology; the non-negotiable basis for the nations' and Israel's salvation alike.[58]

---

about covenant and creation renewal (cf. Rom. 4.13-16). Read in this light, Gal. 3.10-14 makes abundant sense.

56. Though I do not follow all the exegetical conclusions here of either scholar, cf. Wright 1991: 137-56, Scott 1993; see also Elliot 1994: 134-38; contra Esler 1998: 190-91, Longenecker 1998: 138-39; Kim 2002: 136-52.

57. For Qumran, who believed that their community represented the beginning realization of the promises of national restoration, such repentance was a condition of membership; cf. 1QS 1.24ff.; 3.8-9; 5.1ff.; 8.3ff.; 10.20; 1 QH 2.9; 6.6; 14.24; 16.17-18; 18; CD 4.2; 6.4f.; 8.16; 19.16; 20.17. Of course, one should similarly note here the New Testament gospel portrayals of the kingdom of God proclamation to Israel of both John the Baptist and Jesus (cf., e.g., Matt. 3.1-2; Mark 1.4, 14-15; and esp. Luke 13.3-5: "[U]nless you repent, you will all perish. . . ."). See Wright 1996: 246-58.

58. If Luke's account of Paul's mission in Acts is to be given any historical credence, such a conclusion is difficult to avoid.

7

Conclusion

THE PRECEDING HAS DEMONSTRATED the variety of ways in which the question of the relationship of church and Israel has been addressed in contemporary scholarship, resulting in forceful arguments for two main, perhaps seemingly irreconcilable, perspectives. Yet, the conclusion reached here is that the Pauline corpus demonstrates support for both of these perspectives, though with qualification.

MULTIPLE PERSPECTIVES

The first consists in the understanding that the church of Jews and gentiles *is* Israel. It has been seen that in Rom. 2.29 Paul extends the name "Jew" to all Christ followers. Given the tight connection between the names Ἰουδαῖος and Ἰσραήλ, his willingness to identify both Jewish and gentile members of the Christ community as the former, particularly in a letter that seeks overall to preserve subgroup identities (see below), speaks loudly to the seminal nature of his conviction regarding the identity of the church as "Israel." And while Paul does not in Romans apply the latter title to Christ followers, he does exactly this in his letter to the Galatians.

Asserting in the strongest possible terms that gentile Christ followers have obtained equal status in the covenant solely on the basis of

Christ, Paul thinks here of God's people as a single eschatological entity that has been brought into fruition via the apocalypse of Christ—and this was in accordance with the providential plan and purpose of God, as foretold in Scripture. It is this eschatological people that will inhabit the new creation, which has for Paul already been inaugurated by Christ's own resurrection. Thus, irrespective of ethnic background, those "in Christ" (3.28-29) are "Abraham's offspring" (3.29), the "family of faith" (6.10), and "heirs" of the promises (3.16, 29; 4.7). They, the "church of God" (1.13), are none other than the "Israel of God" (6.16).

But consideration must be given here to the high probability that this claim is made in the context of a reform group that, even if comprised mostly of gentiles, largely functioned as an extension of the greater Jewish community. *It need not—nor should not—be read as a sectarian slogan, expressing a determined effort to define the Christ community over against the synagogue, or attempting to usurp the heritage of the Jewish people.* Indeed, I have attempted to demonstrate in chapter 5 above that Paul would not have perceived the communities he founded as a necessarily independent social entity from the synagogue, as he himself remained personally connected to it. There is for Paul no inconsistency between membership in the Christ community as well as the synagogue.

Nowhere in any of Paul's letters does he demand that his addressees sever existing ties to the synagogue, despite his firm rhetoric that gentiles in Christ should remain non-Jews and not entertain proselyte conversion. Further, Paul nowhere suggests that Jews should relinquish their cultural practices, including full Torah obedience, and in effect become non-Jews. It is these convictions that are requisite aspects of the second perspective clearly evidenced in the Pauline corpus.

This second perspective suggests that the church is *not* to be identified with Israel. However, rather than an entirely distinct community from the Jewish people, for Paul, the church is a larger entity that includes the redeemed of Israel, along with repentant representatives from the other nations (cf. 1 Thess. 1.9), in accordance with the eschatological pilgrimage expectations of Scripture and Jewish tradition.[1] This is pre-

---

1. This is what Tomson (1990: 268-69) refers to as Paul's "pluriform ecclesiology." Though I do not follow all of the implications he draws from it, Kinzer (2005: 151-79) similarly employs the phrase "bilateral ecclesiology" to describe "the one ekklesia of the Messiah [that] consists of two distinct but united communal networks, one Jewish and one Gentile" (p. 177).

cisely what Paul claims in Rom. 9–11, culminating in the conclusion he reaches in 11.26. Despite appearances, God is through Christ (however paradoxically) bringing about the promised restoration of his covenant people, and through Israel God is restoring the other nations as well.[2] Accordingly, Jewish and gentile participants in salvation retain their ethnic distinctions, yet both groups are therein transformed, having experienced covenant and creation renewal.[3] In this regard, attention must be given to the central and thoroughly testified Pauline conviction that, *for both Jews and gentiles alike, the only ground for membership in God's people is Jesus Christ, through whom the world has been reconciled to God* (2 Cor. 5.19).

But if it be the case that Paul's letters collectively present both perspectives, does this indicate that he is at best inconsistent, if not hopelessly incoherent? It does not. What allows these two seemingly contrary notions to be held together is the recognition that the title "Israel," though carrying an inextricable ethnic connotation, is nevertheless employed by Paul in a multifaceted way; the impact of its meaning is contingent upon the context in which Paul employs it. I observe three primary referents for the term: (a) the historical nation in its entirety, (b) the elect from within the historical nation, and (c) the elect from both the Jewish and gentile world, i.e., the church. And I would further claim that, for Paul, (a) will give way to (b) in the eschaton, and thus only (b) and (c) will remain in perpetuity.

Of all nine scholars investigated in chapter 2 above, it would seem, therefore, that Donaldson's overall view, despite my specific criticisms, is the closest to the position I have argued.[4] Even a surface reading of Paul's letters reveals that ethnic particularities continue to be presupposed by him. And these ethnic distinctions carry enormous theological significance. God is not the God only of Jews, for this would violate the central tenet of Jewish understanding, the Shema, in which Paul is resolutely

---

2. It is the resurrection of Christ that inaugurates Israel's restoration, but, as argued in ch. 4 above, such restoration is brought to its fullness only by means of the consequential redemption of the gentiles. Thus, each group is necessarily dependent upon the other in this salvific program made possible by the Christ event.

3. The single fullest articulation of this transformation in Paul, intertwining the notions of both covenant and creational renewal, is perhaps found in Rom. 8.

4. This is also despite the fact that Donaldson (1997: 55) errs in his assessment that membership in "Israel" in first-century Judaism indicated a purely religious affiliation divorced from other aspects of ethnicity.

grounded. In light of the Christ event, he can therefore assert, "Is he not the God of gentiles also? Yes of gentiles also, since God is one; and he will justify the circumcised on the ground of faith, and the uncircumcised through that same faith" (Rom. 3.29b-30). And it is ultimately the salvation of the gentiles qua gentiles alongside Jews qua Jews in Christ that Paul finds to be contained in the promise(s) of God to Abraham (cf. Rom. 4; Gal. 3).

However, in as much as "Israel" is a representative people, a "true humanity"—which is a self-understanding reflected in the Pentateuch and in many postbiblical Jewish writings of Paul's time and thereafter, and of which Paul was no doubt aware—then it cannot be but that all people groups have a share in this: "For there is no distinction between Jew and Greek; the same Lord is Lord of all and is generous to all who call on him. For, 'Everyone who calls on the name of the Lord shall be saved'" (Rom. 10.12-13; cf. Gal. 3.26-29; see also Eph. 2.11-22; 3.5-6; 4.1-6).[5] This is, once more, what is indicated in Gal. 6.15-16, which connects the "Israel of God" with the "new creation" brought into being through God's act in Christ (cf. 2 Cor. 5.17); both expressions encompassing all Christ followers, Jewish and gentile, who await their final transformation "into the body of [Christ's] glory" (Phil. 3.21; cf. 1 Cor. 15.20-28, 50-57; Rom. 6.1-5; 8.18-23; 1 Thess. 4.13-17; 2 Cor. 4.14—5.5; Col. 3.4).

Additionally significant here is the importance Paul places upon the continuity of God's people—from exodus to eschaton; the salvation history that is Paul's worldview. As Robin Scroggs (1991: 215) remarks, "Paul knows himself to be part of a grand story, the past which he reads out of the Torah (from the perspective of his present faith); the present, from his experience of the Christ event and the church; and the future, from his hope in the constancy of the God he has come to know out of the past and present." Because of this, I suggest that he could not have effectively appropriated the Scripture as a present and living resource in shaping the Christ community's self-understanding, praxis, and hope (cf. Rom. 15.4) except by making such an association of it with Israel (cf. esp. 1 Cor. 10; see also 5.1, 9-13; 12.2).[6]

---

5. This is decidedly *not* "replacement theology," but "inclusion theology."

6. Cf. Hays 1989: 84-121; he rightly asserts, "The church discovers its true identity only in relation to the sacred story of Israel, and the sacred story of Israel discovers its full significance—so Paul passionately believed—only in relation to God's unfolding design for salvation of the Gentiles in the church" (pp. 100-101).

MULTIPLE IDENTITIES

But to fully appreciate Paul's negotiation of the identity of Israel in relation to the church, it is necessary to take into account the notion of nested or multiple identities. As has been demonstrated by both Esler (2003: 49ff.) and Johnson-Hodge (2007: 117-20, 126-35), building upon well-established research in the social sciences, ethnic identities are by no means static or mutually exclusive. Rather, identity is a dynamic phenomenon subject to negotiation. As such, individuals and/or groups in possession of multiple identities may emphasize one affiliation over another as situations demand. This social phenomenon is implicitly understood and taken advantage of by Paul.

Basic to both his theological conviction and missionary agenda was the need to establish unity; a uniform purpose and hope within and among the multiethnic churches he established and/or addressed in his letters (as well as unity between these communities and the Jerusalem church). For Paul, the success of his gospel program depended upon the extent to which this could be actualized. It is in this light that Paul—particularly in Romans and Galatians—addresses communities that were in some respect failing to embody the full implications of the gospel.[7]

For the Galatian churches this failure lie among gentile Christ followers who were contemplating proselyte conversion, and thereby denying the legitimacy of membership in the people of God solely on the basis of Christ and thus independent in many integral respects of traditional Jewish communal norms. For the churches in Rome it was primarily the failure of gentile Christ followers to recognize the continuing validity of Jewish identity, and to fully appreciate that they were

---

7. This is also clearly the case in 1 Corinthians, in which Paul at several points seems to presuppose the identity of Israel for members of the Christ community (cf. 5.1, 9–13; 1 Cor. 10; 12.2). However, I have chosen to focus attention here on Romans and Galatians, which are more directly consumed with matters of ethnicity and the impact this has on unity. But for an excellent analysis of how Paul negotiated identity in order to reconcile the various factions in Corinth, cf. Tucker 2007. The letter to the Philippians is also concerned with issues of unity, as well as Jewish ethnicity. But it is not clear that the disunity to which Paul alludes here is connected to matters of ethnicity, as they are in Romans and Galatians.

I would additionally note that the "failure" in question suggested in each of these letters is relative. The situation in Galatia is of a more serious concern for Paul; he does not view the Christ community in Rome in such a state of crisis (cf. Rom. 15.14), marked especially by the absence of a thanksgiving in the opening of his letter to the Galatians.

indelibly part of a decidedly Jewish movement (cf. esp. Rom. 11.13ff.; 15.8-12).[8] Though they clearly have distinctive purposes, in both letters *Paul must overcome misperceptions of identity that had already been the cause of at least some communal disruption and disharmony and would, if left unchecked, impede the advance of his gospel mission.*[9]

In terms informed by social identity theory, then, the fundamental premise that lay behind Paul's rhetoric in both letters can be formulated as a new eschatological reality making possible a shared and primary ingroup identity attained solely through Christ. This identity is in continuity with (though not identical to) the historical Jewish people, indicative of a particular praxis, and singularly equivalent to membership in God's people, Israel. Within this larger group there necessarily reside subordinate group identities, relativized by their shared superordinate identity, but nevertheless abiding and significant and allowing for some difference in appropriate communal behavior. Still further, Paul asserts that it is precisely on the grounds of their common ingroup identity that each member of the community must accept and respect the salience of subordinate identities found therein.

THE POLITICS OF INTERPRETATION

But what of the serious claim that a definition of Israel based on any other than traditional ethnic terms effectually opens the door for the annulment of Jewish identity, and perhaps inevitable anti-Jewish sentiment (cf. Campbell 2006: 51)? I would point out here that "open doors" need not be walked through. For example, the very notion of salvation

---

8. That there were as well tensions arising from the other direction, i.e., animosity directed towards gentiles from Jews, cannot be dismissed, and much of Paul's explicit exhortations regarding the proper relationship between these subgroups in the Roman Christ community swing in both directions (cf., e.g., 12.3; 14.3; 15.7). However, it would seem that Paul is more concerned with the collective attitude of the non-Jewish faction, which probably represented the majority among the churches of the city (cf. esp. Rom. 9–11).

9. With respect to Romans, Paul suggests in 15:22–29 that he would like to secure a new base of operation in Rome for his mission to Spain. It was thus imperative for him to see his addressees unified under the gospel that he believed had been commissioned to him. Esler's explanation of leadership from a social-scientific approach (2003: 38), as it provides a lens for understanding Paul, is particularly relevant here: "In short, leaders must be 'entrepreneurs of identity', capable of turning 'me' and 'you' into 'us' in relation to a particular project in a particular context that will bestow on the shared social identity meaning, purpose, and value."

through Christ alone "leaves the door open" for the conclusion that human behavior is ultimately irrelevant. This, in turn, could result in a careless attitude towards responsible ethics, and general immorality (cf. Rom. 6.1, 15; Gal. 5.13; 1 Cor. 6.12). But should the conviction of the total sufficiency of Christ be therefore abandoned? Clearly, this would be a false deduction.[10]

That the history of the church and Pauline interpretation has evidenced anti-Judaism does not mean that such is the intent or inevitable consequence of Paul's teaching or, specifically, of readings that observe an identification of the church as "Israel." Rather, such anti-Judaism indicates that one aspect of Paul's theologizing has often been distorted at the expense of other important aspects, and with dire consequences. Undoubtedly, it is imperative to recognize the latent anti-Judaism of certain doctrinal formulations, to which large segments of the church have historically held and which many Christian interpreters have ignorantly perpetuated.

Yet, much of the explicit anti-Jewish sentiment and action exercised in the name of Christianity throughout the centuries was surely not in the absence of a preconceived prejudice and agenda, however exasperated and/or falsely justified by negative views and stereotypes of Judaism/Jewish people fostered by gross misinterpretations of New Testament teaching. The co-opting of Scripture to serve nefarious ends will never cease to be a dangerous possibility just as it has been, all too often, an unfortunate reality (this side of the resurrection).

Notwithstanding, as suggested above, the extent to which the ongoing significance of historical Israel has been wrongfully ignored in the history on interpretation,[11] the necessary correction lay not in committing the same type of error in reverse, refusing to observe the addi-

---

10. This false implication of Paul's teaching had actually taken hold in the church at Corinth (cf. esp. 1 Cor. 5–6), and apparently his mission was being wrongly characterized in precisely this way (cf. Rom. 3.8; 6.1, 15; see also Furnish 1968: 99–106; Elliot 1990: 97–98). But this, of course, did not lead Paul to fundamentally alter his gospel message.

11. Cf. Kinzer 2005: 266–302 for notable exceptions to this and Christian self-understanding vis-à-vis Judaism, including the dispensational system of theology held in conservative evangelical and fundamentalist Christianity and presupposed in much American popular theology (especially in regard to biblical eschatology). Yet, this acritical reading of the Bible has led for many to the equally problematic consequence of an entirely uncritical, and frequently unethical, perception of the present-day Middle Eastern crisis along with general anti-Palestinian sentiment.

tionally indispensable strand of Pauline thought identifying the church with Israel. Rather, if truth remains the goal of all such inquiry, it is incumbent upon interpreters to faithfully represent the full spectrum of Paul's teaching.[12] Whatever the degree of success, this has in fact been the objective of the present study.

---

12. To be clearly differentiated are subjective judgments about what Paul may have taught, and subjective judgments about the teaching itself. Such is far too often blurred in contemporary scholarship. The possibility must always be held open that one will not agree with what one interprets Paul to have written.

Bibliography

Abegg, Martin C.
1997   "Exile and the Dead Sea Scrolls," in *Exile: Old Testament, Jewish, and Christian Conceptions* (ed. James M. Scott; JSJSup 56; Leiden: Brill), 111–26.

Achtemeier, Paul J.
1985   *Romans* (IBC; Atlanta: John Knox).
1996   *1 Peter* (Hermeneia; Minneapolis: Fortress).
1997   "Unsearchable Judgments and Inscrutable Ways: Reflections on the Discussion of Romans," in *Pauline Theology*, vol. 4: *Looking Back, Pressing On* (eds. E. Elizabeth Johnson and David M. Hay; Atlanta: Scholars), 3–21.

Ackroyd, Peter R.
1968   *Exile and Restoration: A Study of Hebrew Thought of the Sixth Century BC* (OTL; Philadelphia: Westminster).

Allison, Dale C.
1985   "The Background of Romans 11:11–15: A Suggestion," *PRSt* 12.1: 23–30.

Barclay, John M. G.
1988   *Obeying the Truth: A Study of Paul's Ethics in Galatians* (Edinburgh: T. & T. Clark).
1996   *Jews in the Mediterranean Diaspora: From Alexander to Trajan (323 BCE–117 CE)* (Edinburgh: T. & T. Clark).
2007   "Constructing Judean Identity after 70 CE: A Study of Josephus's *Against Apion*," in *Identity and Interaction in the Ancient Mediterranean: Jews, Christians and Others: Essays in Honour of Stephen G. Wilson* (ed. Zeba A. Crook and Philip A. Harland; NTM 18; Sheffield: Sheffield Phoenix), 98–112.

Barrett, C. K.
1991   *The Epistle to the Romans* (2nd ed.; Peabody, MA: Hendrickson).

Bibliography

Barth, Karl
1956   *Church Dogmatics*, vol. 4/1: *The Doctrine of Reconciliation* (trans. Geoffrey W. Bromiley; Edinburgh: T. & T. Clark).
1957   *Church Dogmatics*, vol. 2/2: *The Election of God the Command of God* (trans. Geoffrey W. Bromiley; Edinburgh: T. & T. Clark).
1968   *The Epistle to the Romans* (trans. Edwyn C. Hoskyns; Oxford: Oxford University Press).

Bassler, Jouette M.
1982   *Divine Impartiality: Paul and a Theological Axiom* (SBLDS 59; Chico, CA: Scholars).
1984   "Divine Impartiality in Paul's Letter to the Romans," *NT* 26: 43–58.

Baur, F. C.
1876   *Paul the Apostle of Jesus Christ: His Life and Works, His Epistles and His Doctrines: A Contribution to a Critical History of Primitive Christianity* (2nd ed.; trans. Eduard Zeller, rev. Allan Menzies; London: Williams and Norgate).

Beale, G. K.
1999   "Peace and Mercy upon the Israel of God: The Old Testament Background of Galatians 6,16b," *Bib* 80: 204–23.

Beckwith, Roger T.
1981   "Daniel 9 and the Date of Messiah's Coming in Essene, Hellenistic, Pharisaic, Zealot and Early Christian Computation," *RevQ* 40: 521–42.

Beker, J. Christiaan
1984   [1980] *Paul the Apostle: The Triumph of God in Life and Thought* (Philadelphia: Fortress).
1990   "Romans 9–11 in the Context of the Early Church," *PSBSup* 1: 40–55.

Bell, Richard H.
1994   *Provoked to Jealousy: The Origin and Purpose of the Jealousy Motif in Romans 9–11* (Tübingen: Mohr).

Betz, H. D.
1977   *Galatians* (Hermeneia; Philadelphia: Fortress).

Birch, Bruce C., Walter Brueggemann, Terrence E. Fretheim, and David L. Petersen
1999   *A Theological Introduction to the Old Testament* (Nashville: Abingdon).

Boyarin, Daniel
1994   *A Radical Jew: Paul and the Politics of Identity* (Contraversions 1; Berkley: University of California Press).

Brändle, Rudolf, and Ekkehard W. Stegemann
1998   "The Formation of the First 'Christian Congregations' in Rome in the Context of the Jewish Congregations," in *Judaism and Christianity in First-Century Rome* (eds. Karl P. Donfried and Peter Richardson; Grand Rapids: Eerdmans), 117–28.

Bruce, F. F.
1982 *The Epistle of Paul to the Romans* (TNTC 6; Grand Rapids: Eerdmans).
1982 *The Epistle to the Galatians* (NIGTC; Grand Rapids: Eerdmans).

Brueggemann, Walter
1997 *Theology of the Old Testament: Testimony, Dispute, Advocacy* (Minneapolis: Fortress).

Bryan, Christopher
2000 *A Preface to Romans: Notes on the Epistle in Its Literary and Cultural Setting* (Oxford: Oxford University Press).

Buell, Denise Kimber
2005 *Why This New Race: Ethnic Reasoning in Early Christianity* (New York: Columbia University Press).

Burke, Trevor J.
2006 *Adopted into God's Family: Exploring a Pauline Metaphor* (Downers Grove, IL: InterVarsity).

Burton, Ernest DeWitt
1921 *A Critical and Exegetical Commentary on the Epistle to the Galatians* (ICC; Edinburgh: T. & T. Clark).

Byrne, Brendon
1996 *Romans* (SP 6; Collegeville, MN: Liturgical).

Caird, George Bradford
1994 *New Testament Theology* (ed. L. D. Hurst; Oxford: Oxford University Press).

Calvin, John
1961 *The Epistles of Paul to the Romans and to the Thessalonians* (trans. Ross Mackenzie; eds. David W. Torrance and Thomas F. Torrance; London: Oliver & Boyd).

Campbell, Douglas A.
1994 "Determining the Gospel through Rhetorical Analysis in Paul's Letter to the Roman Christians," in *Gospel in Paul: Studies on Corinthians, Galatians and Romans for Richard N. Longenecker* (JSNTSup 108; eds. L. Ann Jervis and Peter Richardson; Sheffield: Sheffield Academic), 315–36.
2005 *The Quest for Paul's Gospel: A Suggested Strategy* (New York: T. & T. Clark).

Campbell, William S.
1992 *Paul's Gospel in Intercultural Context: Jew and Gentile in the Letter to the Romans* (Frankfurt: P. Lang).
1993a "Judaizers," in *Dictionary of Paul and His Letters* (eds. Gerald F. Hawthorne and Ralph P. Martin; Downers Grove, IL: InterVarsity), 512–16.
1993b "Israel," in *Dictionary of Paul and His Letters* (eds. Gerald F. Hawthorne and Ralph P. Martin; Downers Grove, IL: InterVarsity), 441–42.
1993c "Olive Tree," in *Dictionary of Paul and His Letters* (eds. Gerald F. Hawthorne and Ralph P. Martin; Downers Grove, IL: InterVarsity), 642–44.

1995 "The Rule of Faith in Romans 12:1—15:13: The Obligation of Humble Obedience to Christ as the Only Adequate Response to the Mercies of God," in *Pauline Theology*, vol. 3: *Romans* (eds. D. M. Hay and E. E. Johnson; Minneapolis: Fortress, 1995), 259-86.

2000 "Divergent Images of Paul and His Mission," in *Rereading Israel in Romans: Legitimacy and Plausibility of Divergent Interpretations* (eds. Christina Grenholm and Daniel Patte; Harrisburg, PA: Trinity), 187-211.

2004 "'All God's Beloved in Rome!': Jewish Roots and Christian Identity," in *Celebrating Romans: Template for Pauline Theology: Essays in Honor of Robert Jewett* (ed. Sheila E. McGinn; Grand Rapids: Eerdmans), 67-82.

2005 "Perceptions of Compatibility between Christianity and Judaism in Pauline Interpretation," *BibInt* 13.3: 298-316.

2006 *Paul and the Creation of Christian Identity* (New York: T. & T. Clark).

Carroll, Robert P.
1992 "Israel, History of (Post-Monarchic Period)," *ABD* 3: 567-76.

Casey, Maurice
1998 "Where Wright Is Wrong: A Critical Review of N. T. Wright's *Jesus and the Victory of God*," *JSNT* 69: 77-103.

Chilton, Bruce D.
1997 "Salvific Exile in the Isaiah Targum," in *Exile: Old Testament, Jewish, and Christian Conceptions* (ed. James M. Scott; JSJSup 56; Leiden: Brill), 239-47.

Clements, R. E.
1998 "Isaiah 53 and the Restoration of Israel," in *Jesus and the Suffering Servant: Isaiah 53 and Christian Origins* (eds. William H. Bellinger Jr. and William Farmer; Harrisburg, PA: Trinity), 39-54.

Cohen, Shaye
1999 *The Beginnings of Jewishness: Boundaries, Varieties, Uncertainties* (Berkley: University of California Press).

Combes, I. A. H.
1998 *The Metaphor of Slavery in the Writings of the Ancient Church* (JSNTSup 156; Sheffield: Sheffield Academic).

Cosgrove, Charles H.
1997 *Elusive Israel: The Puzzle of Election in Romans* (Louisville: Westminster John Knox).

Cousar, Charles B.
1982 *Galatians* (IBC; Atlanta: John Knox).

Cranfield, C. E. B.
1977 *The Epistle to the Romans*, vol. 1 (ICC; Edinburgh: T. & T. Clark).
1979 *The Epistle to the Romans*, vol. 2 (ICC; Edinburgh: T. & T. Clark).

Cullmann, Oscar
1956 *Christ and Time: The Primitive Christian Conception of Time and History* (trans. Floyd V. Filson; London: SCM).

Dahl, N. A.
1950 "Der Name Israel: Zur Auslegung von Gal. 6.16," *Judaica* 6: 161–70.
1974 "The Messiahship of Jesus in Paul," in *The Crucified Messiah and Other Essays* (Minneapolis: Augsburg), 37–47.

Das, A. Andrew
2007 *Solving the Romans Debate* (Minneapolis: Fortress).

Davies, W. D.
1948 *Paul and Rabbinic Judaism* (London: SPCK).
1969 *Invitation to the New Testament* (Garden City, NY: Doubleday).
1977 "Paul and the People of Israel," *NTS* 24: 4–39

Dodd, C. H.
1920 *The Meaning of Paul for Today* (New York: Doran).
1932 *The Epistle of Paul to the Romans* (MNTC; New York: Harper).
1951 *Gospel and Law* (New York: Columbia University Press).
1952 *Christianity and the Reconciliation of the Nations*, (London: SCM).
1953 *According to the Scriptures* (New York: Scribner).
1954 *New Testament Studies* (New York: Scribner).
1964 *The Apostolic Preaching and Its Developments* (New York: Harper & Row).
1965 *Christ and the New Humanity* (Philadelphia: Fortress).

Donaldson, Terence L.
1997 *Paul and the Gentiles: Remapping the Apostle's Convictional World* (Minneapolis: Fortress).
2006 "Jewish Christianity, Israel's Stumbling and the *Sonderweg* Reading of Paul," *JSNT* 29.1: 27–54.
2007 *Judaism and the Gentiles: Jewish Patterns of Universalism (to 135 CE)* (Waco, TX: Baylor University Press).

Donfried, Karl Paul
1991 "A Short Note on Romans 16," in *The Romans Debate* (ed. Karl Paul Donfried; rev. ed.; Peabody, MA: Hendrickson), 44–52.

Dunn, James D. G.
1988 *Romans 9–16* (WBC 38b; Dallas: Word).
1990 *Jesus, Paul, and the Law: Studies in Mark and Galatians* (Louisville: Westminster John Knox).
1993 *The Epistle to the Galatians* (Peabody, MA: Hendrickson).
1994 "How New Was Paul's Gospel?: The Problem of Continuity and Discontinuity," in *Gospel in Paul: Studies on Corinthians, Galatians and Romans for Richard N. Longenecker* (JSNTSup 108; eds. L. Ann Jervis and Peter Richardson; Sheffield: Sheffield Academic), 367–88.

1996 *Christology in the Making: A New Testament Inquiry into the Origins of the Doctrine of the Incarnation* (Grand Rapids: Eerdmans).
1998 *The Theology of the Apostle Paul* (Grand Rapids: Eerdmans, 1998).
2001 [1996] "In Search of Common Ground," in *Paul and the Mosaic Law* (ed. James D. G. Dunn; WUNT 89; Grand Rapids: Eerdmans), 309–34.
2003 *Jesus Remembered: Christianity in the Making*, vol. 1 (Grand Rapids: Eerdmans).

Ehrensperger, Kathy
2004 *That We May Be Mutually Encouraged: Feminism and the New Perspective in Pauline Studies* (New York: T. & T. Clark).

Eisenbaum, Pamela
2000 "Paul as the New Abraham," in *Paul and Politics: Ekklesia, Israel, Imperium, Interpretation: Essays in Honor of Krister Stendahl* (ed. Richard A. Horsley; Harrisburg, PA: Trinity), 130–45.

Elliot, Neil
1990 *The Rhetoric of Romans: Argumentative Constraint and Strategy and Paul's Dialogue with Judaism* (JSNTSup 45; Sheffield: JSOT Press).
1994 *Liberating Paul: The Justice of God and the Politics of the Apostle* (Maryknoll, NY: Orbis).

Elliot, Susan
2003 *Cutting Too Close for Comfort: Paul's Letter to the Galatians in Its Anatolian Context* (JSNTSup 248; London: T. & T. Clark).

Esler, Philip F.
1994 *The First Christians in Their Social Worlds: Social-Scientific Approaches to New Testament Interpretation* (London: Routledge).
1998 *Galatians* (London: Routledge).
2003 *Conflict and Identity in Romans: The Social Setting of Paul's Letter* (Minneapolis: Fortress).

Evans, Craig A.
1999 "Jesus & the Continuing Exile of Israel," in *Jesus & the Restoration of Israel: A Critical Assessment of N. T. Wright's "Jesus and the Victory of God"* (ed. Carey C. Newman; Downers Grove, IL: InterVarsity), 77–100.

Fee, Gordon
1995 *Paul's Letter to the Philippians* (NICNT; Grand Rapids: Eerdmans).

Fishbane, Michael
1988 *Biblical Interpretation in Ancient Israel* (New York: Oxford University Press).

Fitzmyer, Joseph A.
1993 *Romans: A New Translation with Introduction and Commentary* (AB 33; New York: Doubleday).

Fredriksen, Paula
1991 "Judaism, the Circumcision of Gentiles, and Apocalyptic Hope: Another Look at Galatians 1 and 2," *JTS* 42: 532–64.

Fuller, Michael E.
2006 *The Restoration of Israel: Israel's Re-gathering and the Fate of the Nations in Early Jewish Literature and Luke-Acts* (BZNW 138; New York: de Gruyter).

Fung, Ronald Y.
1988 *The Epistle to the Galatians* (NICNT; Grand Rapids: Eerdmans).

Furnish, Victor P.
1968 *Theology and Ethics in Paul* (Nashville: Abingdon).

Gager, John G.
2000a *Reinventing Paul* (New York: Oxford University Press).
2000b "Paul, the Apostle of Judaism," in *Jesus, Judaism, and Christian Anti-Judaism: Reading the New Testament after the Holocaust* (ed. Paula Fredriksen and Adele Reinhartz; Louisville: Westminister John Knox), 56–76.

Gamble, Harry
1977 *The Textual History of the Letter to the Romans: A Study in Textual and Literary Criticism* (Grand Rapids: Eerdmans).
1995 *Books and Readers in the Early Church* (New Haven: Yale University Press).

Gaston, Lloyd
1987 *Paul and the Torah* (Vancouver: University of British Columbia Press).

George, Timothy
1994 *Galatians* (NAC 30; Nashville: Broadman & Holman).

Giorgio, Jossa
2006 *Jews or Christians?: The Followers of Jesus in Search of Their Own Identity* (trans. Molly Rogers; Tübingen: Mohr/Siebeck).

Gowan, Donald E.
1977 "The Exile in Jewish Apocalyptic," in *Scripture in History and Theology: Essays in Honor of J. Coert Rylaarsdam* (eds. A. L. Merrill and T. W. Overholt; Pittsburgh Theological Monograph Series 17; Pittsburgh: Pickwick), 205–23.
1986 *Eschatology in the Old Testament* (Philadelphia: Fortress).

Grenholm, Cristina, and Daniel Patte
2000 "Overture: Receptions, Critical Interpretations, and Scriptural Criticism," in *Rereading Israel in Romans: Legitimacy and Plausibility of Divergent Interpretations* (eds. Christina Grenholm and Daniel Patte; Harrisburg, PA: Trinity), 1–56.

Gruen, Erich S.
2004 *Diaspora: Jews amidst Greeks and Romans* (Cambridge: Harvard University Press).

Guthrie, Donald
1969 *Galatians* (NCBC; London: Nelson).

Hafemann, Scott J.
1988 "The Salvation of Israel in Romans 11:25–32," *ExAud* 4: 38–58.

1996 "The 'Temple of the Spirit' as the Inaugural Fulfillment of the New Covenant within the Corinthian Correspondence," *ExAud* 12: 29–42.
1997 "Paul and the Exile of Israel in Galatians 3–4," in *Exile: Old Testament, Jewish, and Christian Conceptions* (ed. James M. Scott; JSJSup 56; Leiden: Brill), 329–72.

Halpern-Amaru, Betsy
1986 "Land Theology in Philo and Josephus," in *The Land of Israel: Jewish Perspectives* (ed. Lawrence A. Hoffmann; Notre Dame: University of Notre Dame Press).

Hanson, Paul D.
1995 *Isaiah 40–66* (IBC; Louisville: Westminster John Knox).

Harink, Douglas
2003 *Paul among the Postliberals: Pauline Theology beyond Christendom and Modernity* (Grand Rapids: Brazos).
2005 "Paul and Israel: An Apocalyptic Reading," paper presented at the Pauline Soteriology Group at the SBL Annual Meeting, Philadelphia.

Harland, Philip A.
2003 *Associations, Synagogues, and Congregations: Claiming a Place in Ancient Mediterranean Society* (Minneapolis: Fortress).

Hays, Richard B.
1983 *The Faith of Jesus Christ: An Investigation into the Narrative Substructure of Galatians 3:1—4:11* (SBLDS 56; Chico, CA: Scholars).
1989 *Echoes of Scripture in the Letters of Paul* (New Haven: Yale University Press).
2000 *The Letter to the Galatians* (NIB 11; Nashville: Abington).
2004 "Major Reviews: 'Paul among the Postliberals: Pauline Theology beyond Christendom and Modernity' by Douglas Harink," *Int* 58.4: 399–402.
2005 *The Conversion of the Imagination: Paul as Interpreter of Israel's Scriptures* (Grand Rapids: Eerdmans).

Hendriksen, William
1981 *Exposition of Paul's Epistle to the Romans* (2 vols; Grand Rapids: Baker).

Hofius, Otfried
1986 "Das Evangelium und Israel. Erwägungen zu Röm 9–11," *ZTK* 83: 297–324.
1990 "'All Israel Will Be Saved': Divine Salvation and Israel's Deliverance in Romans 9–11," *PSBSup* 1: 19–39.
2004 "The Fourth Servant Song in the New Testament Letters," in *The Suffering Servant: Isaiah 53 in Jewish and Christian Sources* (eds. Bernd Janowski and Peter Stuhlmacher; Grand Rapids: Eerdmans).

Horne, C. M.
1978 "The Meaning of the Phrase 'And Thus All Israel Will Be Saved' (Romans 11:26)," *JETS* 21: 329–34.

Howard, George
1990 *Paul: Crisis in Galatia: A Study in Early Christian Theology* (2nd ed.; Cambridge: Cambridge University Press).

Hvalvik, Reidar
1990 "A 'Sonderweg' for Israel: A Critical Examination of a Current Interpretation of Romans 11.25–27," *JSNT* 38: 87–107.

Jeremias, Joachim
1977 "Einige vorwiegend sprachliche Beobachtungen zur Römer 11.25–36," in *Die Israelfrage nach Röm 9–11* (ed. Lorenzo DeLorenzi; SMB 3; Rome: Abbazia S. Paolo), 193–203.

Jewett, Robert
1970–71 "The Agitators and the Galatian Congregation," *NTS* 17: 198–212.
1982 *Christian Tolerance: Paul's Message to the Modern Church* (Philadelphia: Westminster).
2007 *Romans* (Hermeneia; Minneapolis: Fortress).

Jobes, Karen H.
1993 "Jerusalem Our Mother: Metalepsis and Intertextuality in Galatians 4:21–31," *Westminster Theological Journal* 55: 299–320.

Johnson, Dan G.
1984 "The Structure and Meaning of Romans 11," *CBQ* 46: 91–103.

Johnson, E. Elizabeth
1989 *The Function of Apocalyptic and Wisdom Traditions in Romans 9–11* (SBLDS 109; Atlanta: Scholars).

Johnson, Luke Timothy
1999 "A Historiographical Response to Wright's Jesus," in *Jesus & the Restoration of Israel: A Critical Assessment of N. T. Wright's "Jesus and the Victory of God"* (ed. Carey C. Newman; Downers Grove, IL: InterVarsity), 206–24.

Johnson-Hodge, Caroline
2007 *If Sons, Then Heirs: A Study of Kinship and Ethnicity in the Letters of Paul* (Oxford: Oxford University Press).

Käsemann, Ernst
1969 *New Testament Questions of Today* (trans. W. J. Montague; London: SCM).
1971 *Perspectives on Paul* (trans. Margaret Kohl; Philadelphia: Fortress).
1980 *A Commentary on Romans* (trans. and ed. Geoffrey W. Bromiley; Grand Rapids: Eerdmans).

Kaylor, R. David
1988 *Paul's Covenant Community: Jew and Gentile in Romans* (Atlanta: John Knox).

Keck, Leander E.
1977 "The Function of Rom. 3.10–18. Observations and Suggestions," in *God's Christ and His People: Studies in Honour of Nils Alstrup Dahl* (ed. Jacob Jervell and Wayne A. Meeks; Oslo: Norwegian Universities Press) 141–57.
2005 *Romans* (ANTC; Nashville: Abingdon).

Keesmaat, Sylvia C.
1994 "Exodus and the Intertextual Transformation of Tradition in Romans 8.14–30," *JSNT* 16: 29–56.
1999 *Paul and His Story: (Re)interpreting the Exodus Tradition* (Sheffield: Sheffield Academic).

Kim, Seyoon
1982 *The Origin of Paul's Gospel* (Grand Rapids: Eerdmanns).
2002 *Paul and the New Perspective: Second Thoughts on the Origin of Paul's Gospel* (Grand Rapids: Eerdmans).

Kinzer, Mark S.
2005 *Post-Missionary Messianic Judaism: Redefining Christian Engagement with the Jewish People* (Grand Rapids: Brazos).

Knibb, Michael A.
1976 "The Exile in the Literature of the Intertestamental Period," *HeyJ* 17: 253–72.
1987 *The Qumran Community* (CCWJCW 2; Cambridge: Cambridge University Press).

Kraabel, A. T.
1987 "Unity and Diversity among Diaspora Synagogues," in *The Synagogue in Late Antiquity* (ed. Lee I. Levine; Philadelphia: American Schools of Oriental Research).

Kramer, Werner R.
1966 *Christ, Lord, Son of God* (trans. Brian Hardy; Studies in Biblical Theology 1/50; London: SCM).

Lampe, Peter
1989 *Die Stadtrömischen Christen in den ersten beiden Jahrhunderten* (WUNT 18; 2nd ed.; Tübingen: Mohr/Siebeck).

Lane, William L.
1998 "Social Perspectives on Roman Christianity during the Formative Years from Nero to Nerva: Romans, Hebrews, *1 Clement*," in *Judaism and Christianity in First-Century Rome* (ed. Karl P. Donfried and Peter Richardson; Grand Rapids: Eerdmans), 196–244.

Lenski, R. C. H.
1945 *The Interpretation of St. Paul's Epistle to the Romans* (Columbus, OH: Wartburg).

Levine, Amy-Jill
2007 *The Misunderstood Jew: The Church and the Scandal of the Jewish Jesus* (New York: HarperOne).

Lieu, Judith M.
1996 *Image and Reality: The Jews in the World of the Christians in the Second Century* (Edinburgh: T. & T. Clark).
2002a "'Impregnable Ramparts and Walls of Iron': Boundary and Identity in Early 'Judaism' and 'Christianity,'" *NTS* 48: 297–313.

2002b *Neither Jew nor Greek? Constructing Early Christianity* (New York: T. & T. Clark).
2006 *Christianity in the Jewish and Graeco-Roman World* (New York: Oxford University Press).

Longenecker, Bruce W.
1998 *The Triumph of Abraham's God: The Transformation of Identity in Galatians* (Nashville: Abingdon).

Longenecker, Richard N.
1990 *Galatians* (WBC 41; Dallas: Word).

Malina, Bruce J.
1993 *The New Testament World: Insights from Cultural Anthropology* (rev. ed.; Louisville: Westminster John Knox).

Martyn, J. Louis
1991 "Events in Galatia: Modified Covenantal Nomism versus God's Invasion of the Cosmos in the Singular Gospel: A Response to J. D. G. Dunn and B. R. Gaventa," in *Pauline Theology*, vol. 1: *Thessalonians, Philippians, Galatians, Philemon* (ed. Jouette M. Bassler; Minneapolis: Fortress), 160–79.
1997a *Galatians: A New Translation with Introduction and Commentary* (AB 33A; New York: Doubleday).
1997b *Theological Issues in the Letters of Paul* (Nashville: Abingdon).

Mason, Steve
1994 "'For I Am Not Ashamed of the Gospel' (Rom. 1.16): The Gospel and the First Readers of Romans," in *Gospel in Paul: Studies on Corinthians, Galatians and Romans for Richard N. Longenecker* (JSNTSup 108; eds. L. Ann Jervis and Peter Richardson; Sheffield: Sheffield Academic), 254–87.
2007 "Jews, Judaeans, Judaizing, Judaism: Problems of Categorization in Ancient History," *JSJ* 38: 457–512.

Matera, Frank J.
1988 "The Culmination of Paul's Argument to the Galatians: Gal. v.1-vi.17," *JSNT* 32: 79–91.
1992 *Galatians* (Sacra pagina 9; Collegeville, MN: Liturgical).

Matlock, R. Barry
1996 *Unveiling the Apocalyptic Paul: Paul's Interpreters and the Rhetoric of Criticism* (Sheffield: Sheffield Academic).

Meeks, Wayne A.
1983 *The First Urban Christians: The Social World of the Apostle Paul* (New Haven: Yale University Press).
1985 "Breaking Away: Three New Testament Pictures of Christianity's Separation from the Jewish Communities," in *"To See Ourselves as Others See Us": Christians, Jews, "Others" in Late Antiquity* (ed. Jacob Neusner and Ernst S. Frerichs; Scholars Press Studies in the Humanities; Chico, CA: Scholars), 93–116.

Merkle, Ben L.

2000 "Romans 11 and the Future of Ethnic Israel," *JETS* 43.4: 709–21.

Middleton, J. Richard, and Brian Walsh
1995 *Truth Is Stranger Than It Used to Be: Biblical Faith in a Postmodern Age* (Downers Grove, IL: InterVarsity).

Miller, David A.
2007 "What's in a Name?" Blog discussion in 6 parts, December 21–26, 2007 (online: http://gervatoshav.blogspot.com)

Moo, Douglas J.
1996 *The Epistle to the Romans* (NICNT; Grand Rapids: Eerdmans).

Moore, George F.
1921 "Christian Writers on Judaism," *HTR* 14: 197–254.

Mowinckel, Sigmund
2005 [1956] *He That Cometh: The Messiah Concept in the Old Testament and Later Judaism* (trans. G. W. Anderson; Grand Rapids: Eerdmans).

Moxnes, Havlor
1980 *Theology in Conflict: Studies in Paul's Understanding of God in Romans* (NovTSup 53; Leiden: Brill).

Munck, Johannes
1959 *Paul and the Salvation of Mankind* (trans. Frank Clarke; London: SCM).
1967 *Christ and Israel: An Interpretation of Romans 9–11* (trans. Ingeborg Nixon; Philadelphia: Fortress).

Murphy-O'Connor, Jerome
1996 *Paul: A Critical Life* (Oxford: Clarendon).

Mussner, Franz
1976 "'Ganz Israel wird gerettet werden' (Röm 11,26): Versuch einer Auslegung," *Kairos* 18: 241–55.
1977 *Der Galaterbrief* (HTKNT 9; 3rd ed.; Freiburg: Herder).

Nanos, Mark D.
1996 *The Mystery of Romans: The Jewish Context of Paul's Letter* (Minneapolis: Fortress).
1998 "The Inter- and Intra-Jewish Political Contexts of Paul and the Galatians," paper presented at the Paul and Politics Group at the SBL Annual Meeting, Orlando.
2000 "Challenging the Limits That Continue to Define on Paul's Perspective on Jews and Judaism," in *Reading Israel in Romans: Legitimacy and Plausibility of Divergent Interpretations* (eds. Christina Grenholm and Daniel Patte; Harrisburg, PA: Trinity), 212–24.
2002a *The Irony of Galatians: Paul's Letter in First Century Context* (Philadelphia: Fortress).
2002b "The Inter- and Intra-Jewish Political Contexts of Paul and the Galatians," in *The Galatians Debate: Contemporary Issues in Rhetorical and Historical Interpretation* (ed. Mark D. Nanos; Peabody, MA: Hendrickson).

2005a "A Torah-Observant Paul?: What Difference Could It Make for Christian/Jewish Relations Today?," paper presented at Christian Scholars Group on Christian-Jewish Relations, Boston.
2005b "Rethinking the 'Paul and Judaism' Paradigm," paper presented at Yale University.
2008 "Paul's *Reversal* of Jews Calling Gentiles 'Dogs' (Philippians 3:2): 1600 Years of an Ideological Tale Wagging an Exegetical Dog?," paper posted at http://www.marknanos.com.

Neusner, Jacob
1987 *Self-Fulfilling Prophecy: Exile and the Return of Judaism* (Boston: Beacon).
1997 "Exile and Return as the History of Judaism," in *Exile: Old Testament, Jewish, and Christian Conceptions* (ed. James M. Scott; JSJSup 56; Leiden: Brill), 221–38.

Nickelsburg, George W. E.
1981 *Jewish Literature between the Bible and the Mishnah: A Historical and Literary Introduction* (Philadelphia: Fortress).

Pearson, B. A.
1971 "1 Thessalonians 2.14–16: A Deutero-Pauline Interpolation," *HTR* 64: 79–94.

Ponsot, Hervé
1982 "Et Ainsi Tout Israël Sera Sauvé: Rom., XI, 26a," *RB* 89: 406–17.

Räisänen, Heikki
1986 *Paul and the Law* (Philadelphia: Fortress).
1988 "Paul, God, and Israel: Romans 9–11 in Recent Research," in *The Social World of Formative Christianity and Judaism: Essays in Tribute of Howard Clark Kee* (eds. Jacob Neusner et al.; Philadelphia: Fortress), 178–206.

Rajak, Tessa
1984 "Was There a Roman Charter for the Jews?," *JRS* 74: 107–23.
1985 "Jewish Rights in the Greek Cities under Roman Rule: A New Approach," in *Studies in Judaism and Its Greco-Roman Context* (ed. William Scott Green; AAJ 5; Atlanta: Scholars), 19–35.

Refoulé, François
1984 "... *Et ainsi tout Israel sera sauvés*": *Romans 11.25–32* (LD 117; Paris: Cerf).

Richardson, Peter
1969 *Israel in the Apostolic Church* (SNTSMS 10; Cambridge: Cambridge University Press).

Ridderbos, Herman N.
1953 *The Epistle of Paul to the Churches of Galatia* (NICNT; Grand Rapids: Eerdmans).
1975 *Paul: An Outline of His Theology* (trans. John Richard DeWitt; Grand Rapids: Eerdmans).

Robinson, D. W. B.
1965 "The Distinction between Jewish and Gentile Believers in Galatians," *ABR* 13: 29–48.

Robinson, J. A. T.
1902 "ΠΩΡΩΣΙΣ AND ΠΗΡΩΣΙΣ," *JTS* 3: 81–93.

Rollins, W. G.
1987 "Greco-Roman Slave Terminology and Pauline Metaphors for Salvation," in *SBLSP 1987* (ed. K. Richard; Atlanta: Scholars), 100–110.

Ruether, Rosemary Radford
1974 *Faith and Fratricide: The Theological Roots of Anti-Semitism* (New York: Seabury).

Runesson, Anders
2008 "Inventing Christian Identity: Paul, Igantius, and Theodosius I," in *Exploring Early Christian Identity* (ed. Bengt Holmberg; WUNT 226; Tübingen: Mohr/Siebeck), 59–92.

Sanders, E. P.
1977 *Paul and Palestinian Judaism: A Comparison of Patterns of Religions* (Philadelphia: Fortress).
1983 *Paul, the Law, and the Jewish People* (Philadelphia: Fortress).
1985 *Jesus and Judaism* (Philadelphia: Fortress).
1990 *Jewish Law from Jesus to Mishnah: Five Studies* (London: SCM).
1991 *Paul* (Oxford: Oxford University Press).
1992 *Judaism: Practice and Belief 63 BCE–66 CE* (London: SCM).
2008 "Comparing Judaism and Christianity: An Academic Autobiography," *Redefining First-Century Jewish and Christian Identities: Essays in Honor of Ed Parish Sanders* (ed. Fabian E. Udoh; Notre Dame: University of Notre Dame Press, 2008), 11–41.

Sanders, James A.
1997 "The Exile and Canon Formation," in *Exile: Old Testament, Jewish, and Christian Conceptions* (ed. James M. Scott; JSJSup 56; Leiden: Brill), 37–62.

Schmithals, Walter
1975 *Der Römerbrief als historisches Problem* (SNT 9; Gutersloh: Gerd Mohn).

Schoeps, Hans-Joachim
1961 *Paul: The Theology of the Apostle in the Light of Jewish Religious History* (trans. Harold Knight; Philadelphia: Westminister).

Schrenk, Gottlob
1949 "Was bedeutet 'Israel Gottes'?" *Judaica* 6: 81–94.

Schüssler Fiorenza, Elisabeth
2000 "Paul and the Politics of Interpretation," in *Paul and Politics: Ekklesia, Israel, Imperium, Interpretation: Essays in Honor of Krister Stendahl* (ed. Richard A. Horsley; Harrisburg, PA: Trinity), 40–57.
2001 *Jesus and the Politics of Interpretation* (New York: Continuum).

Schweitzer, Albert
1950 [1912] *Paul and His Interpreters* (London: Black).
1968 [1931] *The Mysticism of the Apostle Paul* (New York: Seabury).

Scott, James M.
1993 "'For as Many as Are of Works of the Law Are under a Curse' (Galatians 3.10)," in *Paul and the Scriptures of Israel* (ed. Craig A Evans and James A. Sanders; Sheffield: JSOT), 187–221.
1997 "Exile and the Self-Understanding of Diaspora Jews in the Greco-Roman Period," in *Exile: Old Testament, Jewish, and Christian Conceptions* (ed. James M. Scott; JSJSup 56; Leiden: Brill), 173–220.
2001 "'And Then All Israel Will Be Saved' (Rom 11:26)," in *Restoration: Old Testament, Jewish, and Christian Perspectives* (ed. James M. Scott; JSJSup 56; Leiden: Brill), 489–528.

Scroggs, Robin
1966 *The Last Adam: A Study in Pauline Anthropology* (Philadelphia: Fortress).
1991 "Salvation History: The Theological Structure of Paul's Thought (1 Thessalonians, Philippians, and Galatians)," in *Pauline Theology*, vol. 1: *Thessalonians, Philippians, Galatians, Philemon* (ed. Jouette M. Bassler; Minneapolis: Fortress), 212–26.

Segal, Alan F.
1990 *Paul the Convert: The Apostolate and Apostasy of Saul the Pharisee* (New Haven: Yale University Press).

Seitz, Christopher R.
2001 *Isaiah 40–66* (NIB 6; Nashville: Abington).

Silva, Moisés
2001 *Interpreting Galatians: Explorations in Exegetical Method* (Grand Rapids: Baker Academic).

Slingerland, H. Dixon
1997 *Claudian Policymaking and the Early Imperial Repression of Judaism in Rome* (South Florida Studies in the History of Judaism 160; Atlanta: Scholars).

Smail, Thomas
1980 *The Forgotten Father* (London: Hodder & Stoughton).

Soulen, Kendall
1996 *The God of Israel and Christian Theology* (Minneapolis: Fortress).

Staples, Jason A.
2008 "All Israel—What Do the Gentiles Have to Do with It? A Fresh Look at Romans 11:25–27," paper presented at the Pauline Epistles Group at the SBL Annual Meeting, Boston.

Stanley, Christopher D.
1993 "'The Redeemer Will Come εκ Σιων': Romans 11.26–27 Revisited," in *Paul and the Scriptures of Israel* (ed. Craig A Evans and James A. Sanders; Sheffield: JSOT Press), 118–42.
1996 "'Neither Jew nor Greek': Ethnic Conflict in Graeco-Roman Society," *JSNT* 64: 101–24.
2004 *Arguing with Scripture: The Rhetoric of Quotations in the Letters of Paul* (New York: T. & T. Clark).

Steck, O. H.

1967 *Israel und das gewaltsame Geschick der Propheten: Untersuchungen zur Überlieferung des deuteronomistischen Geschichtsbildes im Alten Testament, Spätjudentum und Urchristentum* (WMANT 23; Neukirchen-Vluyn: Neukirchener).

1968 "Das Problem theologischer Strömungen in nachexilischer Zeit," *EvT* 28: 445–58.

Stendahl, Krister

1976a *Paul among Jews and Gentiles and Other Essays* (Philadelphia: Fortress).

1976b "In No Other Name," in *Christian Witness and the Jewish People* (ed. A. Sovik; Geneva: Lutheran World Federation), 48–53.

1995 *Final Account: Paul's Letter to the Romans* (Minneapolis: Fortress).

Stibbe, Mark

1999 *From Orphans to Heirs: Celebrating Our Spiritual Adoption* (Abingdon: Bible Reading Fellowship).

Stowers, Stanley K.

1994 *A Rereading of Romans: Justice, Jews, Gentiles* (New Haven: Yale University Press).

Stuhlmacher, Peter

1971 "Zur Interpretation von Römer 11.25–32," in *Probleme biblischer Theologie* (ed. H. W. Wolff; Munich: Kaiser), 555–70.

1994 *Paul's Letter to the Romans: A Commentary* (trans. Scott J. Hafemann; Louisville: Westminster John Knox).

Tajfel, Henri, ed.

1978 *Differentiation between Social Groups: Studies in the Social Psychology of Intergroup Relations* (New York: Academic).

Tajef, Henri, and John C. Turner

2001 "An Integrative Theory of Intergroup Conflict," in *Intergroup Relations: Essential Readings* (ed. D. Abrams and M. A. Hogg; Key Readings in Social Psychology. Philadelphia: Psychology), 94–109.

Theron, D. J.

1956 "'Adoption' in the Pauline Corpus," *EvQ* 28: 6–14.

Thielman, Frank

1989 *From Plight to Solution: A Jewish Framework for Understanding Paul's View of the Law in Galatians and Romans* (Leiden: Brill).

1994 *Paul & the Law: A Contextual Approach* (Downers Grove, IL: InterVarsity).

Thiselton, Anthony C.

2000 *The First Epistle to the Corinthians: A Commentary on the Greek Text* (NIGTC; Grand Rapids: Eerdmans).

Tomson, Peter J.

1990 *Paul and the Jewish Law: Halakha in the Letters of the Apostle to the Gentiles* (Minneapolis: Fortress).

Tucker, J. Brian
2007 "Negotiating Identity and Paul's Rhetoric: The Use of Social Identity and Self-Categorization Theory in the Corinthian Correspondence to Support the Pauline Mission," paper presented at the Rhetorics of Social Formation conference, University of Redlands.

Van der Horst, Pieter W.
2000 "'Only Then Will All Israel Be Saved': A Short Note on the Meaning of καὶ οὕτως in Romans 11:26," *JBL* 119.3: 521–26.

Vanderkam, James C.
1997 "Exile in Jewish Apocalyptic Literature," in *Exile: Old Testament, Jewish, and Christian Conceptions* (ed. James M. Scott; JSJSup 56; Leiden: Brill), 89–110.

Wagner, J. Ross
1997 "The Christ, Servant of Jew and Gentile: A Fresh Approach to Romans 15:8–9," *JBL* 116: 473–85.
1998 "The Heralds of Isaiah and the Mission of Paul: An Investigation of Paul's Use of Isaiah 51–55 in Romans," in *Jesus and the Suffering Servant: Isaiah 53 and Christian Origins* (eds. William H. Bellinger Jr. and William Farmer; Harrisburg, PA: Trinity), 193–222.
2002 *Herald of the Good News: Isaiah and Paul in Concert in the Letter to the Romans* (Leiden: Brill).

Walters, James C.
1993 *Ethnic Issues in Paul's Letter to the Romans: Changing Self-Definitions in Earliest Roman Christianity* (Valley Forge, PA: Trinity).
1998 "Romans, Jews, and Christians: The Impact of the Romans on Jewish/Christian Relations in First-Century Rome," in *Judaism and Christianity in First-Century Rome* (ed. Karl P. Donfried and Peter Richardson; Grand Rapids: Eerdmans), 175–95.

Wasserberg, Günter
2000 "Romans 9–11 and Jewish-Christian Dialogue: Prospects and Provisos," in *Rereading Israel in Romans: Legitimacy and Plausibility of Divergent Interpretations* (eds. Christina Grenholm and Daniel Patte; Harrisburg, PA: Trinity), 174–86.

Watson, Francis
1986 *Paul, Judaism, and the Gentiles: A Sociological Approach* (SNTSMS 56; Cambridge: Cambridge University Press).
2004 *Paul and the Hermeneutics of Faith* (London; New York: T. & T. Clark).
2007a *Paul, Judaism, and the Gentiles: Beyond the New Perspective* (rev. ed.; Grand Rapids: Eerdmans).
2007b "The Hermeneutics of Salvation: Paul, Isaiah, and the Servant," paper presented at the Pauline Soteriology Group at the SBL Annual Meeting, San Diego.

Weima, Jeffrey A. D.
1993 "Gal. 6.11–18: A Hermeneutical Key to the Galatian Letter," *CTJ* 28: 90–107.

Welborn, L. L.
1984 "On the Date of First Clement," *BR* 24: 34–54.

Westermann, Claus
1995 *Genesis*, vol. 2: *Genesis 12–36* (Minneapolis: Augsburg Fortress).

Wiefel, Wolfgang
1991 "The Jewish Community in Ancient Rome and the Origins of Roman Christianity," in *The Romans Debate* (ed. Karl Paul Donfried; rev. ed.; Peabody, MA: Hendrickson), 85–101.

Williams, Sam K.
1980 "The 'Righteousness of God' in Romans," *JBL* 99: 241–90.
1997 *Galatians* (Nashville: Abingdon).

Witherington, Ben, III
1998 *Grace in Galatia: A Commentary on Paul's Letter to the Galatians* (Grand Rapids: Eerdmans).
2004 *Paul's Letter to the Romans: A Socio-rhetorical Commentary* (Grand Rapids: Eerdmans).

Wrede, William
1907 *Paul* (London: Green).

Wright, N. T.
1991 *The Climax of the Covenant: Christ and the Law in Pauline Theology* (Edinburgh: T. & T. Clark).
1992 *The New Testament and the People of God*, vol. 1 of *Christian Origins and the Question of God* (Minneapolis: Fortress).
1996 *Jesus and the Victory of God*, vol. 2 of *Christian Origins and the Question of God* (Minneapolis: Fortress).
1997 *What Saint Paul Really Said: Was Paul of Tarsus the Real Founder of Christianity?* (Grand Rapids: Eerdmans).
1998 "Romans and the Theology of Paul," in *Pauline Theology*, vol. 3: *Romans* (eds. D. M. Hay and E. E. Johnson; Minneapolis: Fortress), 30–67.
1999 "In Grateful Dialogue: A Response," in *Jesus & the Restoration of Israel: A Critical Assessment of N. T. Wright's "Jesus and the Victory of God"* (ed. Carey C. Newman; Downers Grove, IL: InterVarsity), 244–77.
2000 "Paul's Gospel and Caesar's Empire," in *Paul and Politics: Ekklesia, Israel, Imperium, Interpretation: Essays in Honor of Krister Stendahl* (ed. Richard A. Horsley; Harrisburg, PA: Trinity), 160–83.
2001a *The Letter to the Romans* (NIB 10; Nashville: Abingdon).
2001b [1996] "The Law in Romans 2," in *Paul and the Mosaic Law* (ed. James D. G. Dunn; WUNT 89; Grand Rapids: Eerdmans), 131–50.

Yoder, John Howard
1996 *The Jewish-Christian Schism Revisited: A Bundle of Old Essays* (Notre Dame: Shalom Desktop).
1997 *For the Nations: Essays Evangelical and Public* (Grand Rapids: Eerdmans).

Zetterholm, Magnus
2003   *The Formation of Christianity in Antioch: A Social-Scientific Approach to the Separation between Judaism and Christianity* (New York: Routledge).

Zoccali, Christopher
2008   "'And So All Israel Will Be Saved': Competing Interpretations of Romans 11:26 in Pauline Scholarship," *JSNT* 30.3: 289–318.

Index of Ancient Documents

OLD TESTAMENT

Genesis
1.26–28	161
1.28	160
1–2	69
2.15—3.24	169
6.6–7	114
12.1–3	166
12.2–3	160
12.3	125, 165
15.16	108
17.2	160
17.5	125
17.6	160
17.8	160
17.19–21	166
18.18	165
22.16–18	160
22.18	165
26.3–5	160
26.4	165
28.3	160
28.14	165
35.11	160
48.3–4	160
48.19	97

Exodus
1.7	160
3.7–12	166
19.5–6	165
19.6	86
32.13	160
32.14	114

Leviticus
18.5	169
19.9–17	165
19.33–36	165
26.9	160
26.11ff.	169
26.41	66

Numbers
25.6–18	127

Deuteronomy
1.10–11	160
4.5–8	62, 165
7.13	160
8.1	160
9.4ff.	63
10.12–22	165
10.15	66

Deuteronomy (continued)

27–29	168
27–32	152
27.26	169
28.58–68	169
28.63	160
29.4	107–8, 152
30	66, 108, 168–69
30ff.	168
30.5	160
30.6	64, 66
30.12–14	152
30.16	160
30.19–20	169
32.4	152
32.15ff.	168
32.21	152
32.26	114
32.31	152
32.43	152

Judges

6.11–24	166

Joshua

7.25	92

1 Samuel

2.27–30a	167
2.27–36	167
2.30b–36	167
7.5	92
15.11	114
15.35	114
25.1	92

2 Samuel

5.1–2	164
7.8–29	166
7.15–16	167
16.22	92
19.41—20.2	164

1 Kings

2.4	167
8.25	167
8.46–53	168
9.4–5	167
12.1	92
18–22.40	133
18.40	127
19.10	127

2 Chronicles

12.1	92
13.5	167

Ezra

	153
3.11	75

Nehemiah

	153

Psalms (MT)

2.8–9	164
8	161
8.3–8	161
8.4–9	161
69.22–23	109
72.8–11	154
89.20–37	167
89	167
89.38–52	167
110.1	161
132.11–12	167

Psalms (LXX)

36.9	154
36.11	154
36.22	154
36.29	154
36.54	154
84	77
84.7	77
84.8–9	75
84.9	77, 85
84.11	75
84.1	75
124.5	75
127.6	75

Isaiah

1.9	152	30.18–26	88
2	162	32.15	64, 66, 108, 168
2.1–4	154	32.15–17	88
2.2–4	62, 123–24, 162	32.15–18	77
2.3	96	35.5–10	154
4.2–6	154	37.31–32	77
5	166	40–66	77, 154
5.1–4	88	40.3–5	154
5.7	71	40.7–8	77, 152
6	108	40.13	77, 152
6.1–10	166	40.21	77, 152
6.9–10	77, 107–8, 152	40.28	77, 152
7.9b	167	41.17–20	154
8	168	42.1	62, 154
8.14	77, 152, 168	42.1–6	162
8.22	77	42.1–9	71, 123
9.6–7	154, 162, 168	42.6	62, 154
10–12	147	42.6–7	163
10.22	103	42.11	163
10.22–23	77, 152	42.14–16	154
10.24–26	154	42.18ff.	163
11.1ff.	162	43	77
11.1–9	154	43.1–3	77, 154
11.1–12	168	43.14–21	154
11.9–10	62	43.18ff.	155
11.10	77, 147, 152	44.1	163
11.11	154	44.1–4	88
11.11–12	147	44.3	64, 66, 108, 168
11.15–16	154	45.4	163
14.1–2	123, 162	45.8	77, 154, 162
18.7	123	45.9	77, 107, 152
19.16–24	162	45.14	123
24.4–6	169	45.23	77
25.6–10	123–24, 154, 162	48.20–21	154
27.6	77, 152, 154	49.1	163
27.9	77, 96, 101, 113, 152	49.3	163
28–29	168	49.6	62, 123, 154, 162–63
28.16	77, 107, 152, 168	49.8–12	154
28.22	77, 152	50.8	77
29	108	51.1	77
29.10	77, 107–8, 152	51.3	77
29.16	77, 152	51.4–6	123, 154, 162
29.18–19	108	51.9–10	154
30.1–17	88	52.5	59–60, 77
		52.7	77, 152

Index of Ancient Documents

Isaiah (continued)

52.7–10	60
52.11–12	154
52.13—53.12	162
52.15	77
53	163
53.1	77, 152
53.6	77
53.11–12	77
53.12	77
54	77, 85, 154
54.1	77–78
54.5	85
54.9–10	155
54.10	75, 77
54.15	85, 122
55	164
55.3–5	162
55.10–13	77
55.12–13	154
56.1	77
56.3	77
56.6–8	85, 122, 154, 162
58.8	154
58.11	77
59.7–8	77
59.20	94, 96, 113
59.20–21	77, 100, 152
59.21	64, 66, 77, 88, 108, 168
60	123, 154
60.1ff.	162
60.2	154
60.19	154
60.21	77
61.6	86
63.1ff.	154
64.10	77
65	77
65.1	77
65.1–2	152
65.2	77, 114
65.8	77
65.17ff.	155
65.17–22	77
65.17–25	154, 162
66.6–11	77
66.18–21	122
66.18–23	162
66.22–23	154

Jeremiah

1.4–10	166
3.16–17	162
3.17	123
3.18	97
4.4	66
7.1—8.3	166
7.5–7	71
9.23	68
9.25–29	66
16.5	75, 77
18.1–6	107
18.8	114
18.10	114
23.5–8	168
26.13	114
30.3	97
31	66, 108, 168
31.31–34	27, 66, 97
31.33	64
31.34	96
32.39–40	64, 168
33.14–26	168
33.17–22	167
50.41	109

Ezekiel

2.1—3.11	166
11.19–20	64, 168
34.23ff.	168
36	66, 108, 168
36.20–21	59
36.22–32	64
36.27	64
37	97, 169
37.24–28	168
39.25	75
39.29	64
44.7–9	66
47.7–12	162

Daniel

2.36–38	161
4.32–33	161
4.34	69
6.26–27	69
7	161
7.13–14	161
7.18	121, 161
7.27	121, 161
9.11	92
9.15–27	152

Hosea

1–2	152
1.9–10	97
1.10	152
2.14ff.	154
2.23	75, 97, 152
3.4–5	168
6.2	169
7.8	97
8.8	97
12.9	154

Joel

2.28	64
2.32	96

Amos

5.15	75
9.11–12	85, 121
5.21–25	71

Jonah

3.10	114

Micah

4.1–3	123
4.1–4	124, 162
4.2	96
5.2–3	168
7.14ff.	154

Habbakkuk

1.6	109

Zephaniah

3.9	123, 162

Haggai

2.6–7	123
2.21–22	123

Zechariah

2.11	123, 162
3.8	168
6.11–13	168
8.20–21	123, 162
8.20–23	124
9.10	154
11.16	109
12.10	64
14.8–19	162

Malachi (LXX)

3.22	94

APOCRYPHA

Tobit

1.8	33
13.5ff.	112, 152, 168
13.11	62
13.11–14	123
14.4–7	112, 152, 168
14.5–7	123
14.6	62

Judith

14.10	33

Esther (Gk.)

16.15–16	70

Wisdom of Solomon

1.1–2	70
2.23–24	160
3.8	159
6.9–11	70
7.26	80

Wisdom of Solomon (continued)

10.17	80
11.4	80
12.9–27	108
15.7	107
18.4	62
19.4–5	108

Sirach

14.17	160
24.8	80
24.23	80
25.24	160
33.13	107
36	152
36.11–12	123
40.1	160
41.10	160
44.19–21	153–54
44.20	110
45.23–24	127
48.2	127
48.10	152

Baruch

2.27ff.	112, 168
2.30–35	63
3.8	152
3.29–30	80
3.37—4.1	80
4.1ff.	112, 168
4.5—5.9	152

4 Ezra

3.7	160
3.28–36	80
4.35–37	112
4.38–39	112–13, 168
6.25–28	123
6.53–59	158
6.55–59	154
7.11ff.	160
7.22	109
7.19–24	80
7.20–24	168
7.25–44	168
7.37–38	80, 109
7.79–82	80
7.116–26	160
7.119ff.	168
8.55–58	80
8.56–58	109
9.10–12	80
12.31–34	168
13.25–50	168
13.39–50	152

1 Maccabees

1.15	79
1.44–48	79
1.60–61	79
2.15–28	127
2.54	127
2.58	127
2.45–46	79

2 Maccabees

1–2	152
3.1–3	69
3.12	69
3.33–39	69
5.16	69
6.6	5
6.10	79
6.12–16	108
9.11–18	69
9.17	5
13.23	69

3 Maccabees

1.9	69

4 Maccabees

4.11–12	69
18.12	127

NEW TESTAMENT

Matthew

2.14–15	163
3.1–2	170

Index of Ancient Documents

3.15–17	163	3.19–20	112
4	163	6.5	33
5.5	154	8.1ff.	127
8.11–13	116	8.1–3	127
10.5–6	149	10.1–33	69
10.16–23	116	10.9–16	132
11.21–23	116	10.28–29	132
15.21–28	149	10.34–48	133
19.28	163, 168	13.16–50	69
21.42–43	116	13.43	33
23.15	33, 161	15	140
23.23–24	71	15.1	79
23.29—24.51	116	15.1ff.	131
24.30	163	15.11	132
24.31	154	15.12ff.	85
25.31	163	15.20	140
26.64	116	16.13	134
27.25	116	16.13–14	69
		16.13–15	134

Mark

		16.20	134
1.4	170	17.4	69
1.14–15	170	17.11–12	69
7.19b	132	17.16–17	69
10.42–45	165	18.2	136
13	116	18.4–7	69
13.27	154	21.17–26	132
14.62	116	22.3–5	127
		26.4–5	127
		28	136

Luke

		28.21	131
3.38	81		
7.2–5	69		
10.13–15	116		

Romans

11.42	71	1.1	110
13.3–5	170	1.1–4	117, 149
13.34–35	116	1.1–15	56
17.22–37	116	1.3	156
19.41–44	116	1.5	46, 140
21	116	1.5–6	56–57
23.27–31	116	1.7	57, 110, 121
		1.13	57

John

		1.13–15	56
12.20	69	1.15	99, 111
		1.16	61, 80–81, 98, 117, 125, 149

Acts

2.11	33	1.16–17	79, 140, 147

Index of Ancient Documents

Romans (continued)

1.17	169	3.1	15, 67
1.18ff.	129	3.1–4	59, 113
1.18–32	59	3.2	62
1.18—2.16	62	3.3–7	146
1.18—2.29	64	3.8	132, 177
1.18–3.20	58, 61	3.9	62
1.24	65	3.10–18	62
1.26	65	3.15–17	77
1.26–27	63	3.16–20	62
1.26–32	71	3.19–20	103, 128
1.28	65	3.20	15, 63, 65, 128, 164
2	64	3.20ff.	168
2.1	59	3.20–21	129
2.1–5	61	3.21	169
2.1–11	108	3.21ff.	60
2.2–16	64	3.21–22	79, 103
2.3–5	62	3.21–26	26, 110, 128, 145, 164
2.8–9	92, 129	3.21–31	103
2.9	77	3.22	105, 146
2.11	71	3.23	62
2.12	61–62, 129	3.25–26	65
2.12–13	61	3.26	79
2.13	64	3.27	70, 125, 147
2.13–16	62	3.27–29	68
2.14	128	3.28–30	81, 110
2.14ff.	128	3.28–31	65
2.17	71	3.29–30	102
2.17ff.	64	3.29b–30	174
2.17–20	61	3.30	68, 78, 80, 125–26, 147
2.17–24	58–59, 61	3.31	15, 140
2.17–29	58, 60–62, 64, 68, 71, 102	4	20, 45–46, 70, 124–25, 147, 153, 174
2.19	161	4.1	7
2.21–23	59, 62	4.1ff.	69
2.23	59	4.1–8	110, 125
2.24	59–60, 77, 109	4.3ff.	62
2.25	62, 67, 128	4.9–10	125
2.25f.	79	4.9–17	124
2.25–29	56, 58, 63, 65–67, 103, 133, 169	4.11ff.	128
		4.11–12	45, 69–70, 78
2.27	63	4.11–16	125
2.28–29	66, 131	4.11–17	104
2.29	19, 20, 45, 54–55, 57–58, 64, 97, 116, 121, 129, 171	4.12–13	147
		4.13	153
3	64	4.13ff.	168

Index of Ancient Documents

4.13–15	125	7.1	56, 128
4.13–16	170	7.1–6	65, 69
4.13–22	110	7.1—8.4	80
4.13–25	35	7.6	65, 128
4.14ff.	92	7.7	15
4.14–16	126	7.7ff.	168
4.15	128–29	7.9ff.	156
4.16	45, 65, 68, 70, 78, 80, 109, 125, 147	7.10	128
		7.7–13	62, 103
4.17–18	125	7.12	15
4.18	110	7.13	128, 164
4.18ff.	70	7.24	128
4.19	139	8	128, 173
4.22–25	69	8.1–4	65, 103, 128, 145, 164
4.25	77, 163	8.1–11	65–66, 169
5	160	8.1–17	64, 128
5–8	101	8.2	128
5.6–11	113	8.12–30	48
5.8	163	8.14–17	104
5.11	68	8.14–23	81
5.12	111	8.15	81
5.12ff.	168	8.18–21	41
5.12–14	62, 103	8.18–23	65, 174
5.12–21	37, 128, 165	8.18–25	69, 153–54
5.15	111	8.18–30	165
5.18ff.	169	8.23	81
5.18–19	111	8.28–30	65, 110
5.18–21	103	8.32	77, 163
5.20	128	8.33–34	77
5.20–21	164	8.35	77
5.21	111	9	104–5, 110
6	128	9–10	104
6.1	177	9–11	2, 10, 12, 20, 30, 41, 46, 50–51, 59, 68, 71, 78, 82, 88, 91–92, 97, 104, 108, 114, 124, 151, 166, 170, 173, 176,
6.1ff.	64, 71, 128		
6.1–5	65, 174		
6.1–11	128		
6.17–18	128		
6.4	111	9.1–5	27, 103–5, 131
6.4–5	164	9.3	167
6.5	81	9.3ff.	7
6.5–6	65	9.4	15, 81, 97, 103
6.11	111	9.4–5	62, 109, 117, 124, 149, 156
6.15	177		
6.19	111	9.4–13	110
7	20, 80, 127–29, 160	9.5	113

208 *Index of Ancient Documents*

Romans (*continued*)
9.6	47, 72, 77, 96–97, 104–5, 152	10.11	77, 152
		10.11–13	81
9.6–8	104, 106, 114	10.12	105
9.6–13	35	10.12–13	174
9.7–8	112	10.13	96, 105, 138
9.7–13	114	10.14–21	106, 110, 114
9.8	48, 121, 125	10.15	77, 152
9.12	110	10.16	152, 163
9.14	152	10.16–21	65
9.14–16	107	10.18	100
9.15–18	147	10.18–19	77, 152
9.17–18	108	10.19	97, 99
9.20	77, 111, 152	10.19–20	109
9.22–26	109	10.19–21	152
9.22–23	110	10.20	77
9.24	80, 125	10.20–21	152
9.24–26	104	10.21	77, 97, 112, 114
9.24–29	47	11	27, 39, 45, 101, 104–6, 116, 121, 136, 149
9.25–26	47, 97, 109–10, 152, 168	11.1	7, 15, 41, 97, 103, 105, 117, 167
9.27	97, 103, 163		
9.27–28	77, 152	11.1–2	62, 127, 131, 165
9.27–29	47, 104	11.1–5	103, 111, 149
9.29	77, 152	11.1–10	112
9.30	146	11.2	97
9.30–31	77	11.2–4	133
9.30—10.4	52, 69, 80, 103, 128, 168	11.5	80, 92, 95, 106, 111, 163
9.30—10.13	65	11.5–6	70, 110, 127
9.31	15, 97, 102	11.7	93, 95, 97, 102, 109, 115
9.32	138	11.7ff.	52
9.33	77, 113, 152, 168	11.8	77, 107, 152
10	104	11.9–10	109
10.1	103, 105	11.11	41, 97, 101, 103, 105, 138
10.2–4	27	11.11–14	152
10.3	68	11.11–15	60, 103, 110, 112–13
10.3–4	103, 168	11.11–24	111
10.4	26, 65, 68, 81, 126, 148, 156, 169	11.12	109, 112
		11.13	56
10.5–6	169	11.13ff.	80, 127, 147, 176
10.5–11	169	11.13–14	106, 109
10.6	80, 111	11.13b–14	99
10.6ff.	63	11.14	103
10.8–10	103	11.15	112–13
10.9	103, 138	11.16–18	117, 149
10.9–13	125	11.16–24	124

Index of Ancient Documents   209

11.17–21	101	14.3	176
11.17–24	101	14.5–6	139
11.18	146	14.9	138
11.19–20	71, 109	14.10–11	138
11.21	63	14.11	77
11.21–22	110	14.13	77
11.22	101	14.13ff.	128
11.23	97, 101, 109, 167	14.13–23	67
11.24	63, 111, 113, 125	14.14	132, 138
11.25	35, 92, 97–98, 113	14.14b	139
11.25b	107, 115	14.15–23	140
11.25–26	96–99	14.18	138
11.25b–26	107, 111	14.20	132
11.25–27	46, 96, 111	14.21	77
11.25–36	41	15	99
11.26	15, 20, 48, 54–55, 62, 72,	15.1	56, 140
	91, 93, 95–98, 105, 111,	15.3	138, 165
	114–16, 121, 129	15.4	174
11.26a	115	15.5–6	138
11.26–27	65, 77, 113, 152, 158	15.3–12	104
11.26b–27	96	15.4–12	129
11.26–28	113	15.5–12	41, 81
11.26–29	149	15.7	176
11.26–36	94	15.8	113, 156, 165
11.27	97, 103, 115	15.8a	146
11.28	15, 111, 113	15.8b	146
11.28a	106, 113	15.8–9	65, 68, 109, 145–46
11.28–29	96, 101	15.8–12	20, 97, 117, 149, 168, 176
11.28–32	147	15.9a	146–47
11.28b–29	114	15.9b–12	147
11.29	41, 96	15.10–12	152
11.30–32	65, 111, 147	15.12	77, 113, 147
11.31	106, 111	15.14	99, 175
11.32	62, 65, 103, 114–15	15.14–33	129
11.33–36	100, 107	15.19	98
11.34	77, 152	15.20	99, 111
12.3	176	15.21	77, 163
12.5	111	15.22–29	176
13.8–10	66	15.24	100
13.8–14	64, 71, 128, 140	15.25–31	103
13.11	77	15.29	98
13.11–12	105	15.33	73
14	20, 131, 136, 138, 140	16	56–57
14.1	139	16.3–16	56
14.1—15.13	78, 146	16.7	164

Index of Ancient Documents

Romans (*continued*)
16.16	57
16.17–20	139
16.20	105
16.25	95
16.25–27	41
16.26	46, 140

1 Corinthians
1.2	110, 121
1.10	129
1.18–25	145, 154
1.22–24	57, 80, 125, 128
1.24	80, 110
1.26	110
1.30	164
1.31	68
2.1	95
2.7	95
2.10ff.	66, 129
3.16	83
3.21–23	154
4	116, 154
4.1	95
5–6	177
5.1	63, 85, 121, 126, 174–75
5.1ff.	71
5.9–10	126, 154
5.9–13	63, 85, 121, 126, 174–75
6.2	154, 164
6.9–11	71
6.12	177
7.7	49
7.16	103
7.17–20	21, 57, 67, 128
7.18	110, 128
7.18f.	79
7.18–19	66
7.19	64, 69, 71, 83, 128–29
8–10	140
8.6	80
8.9–13	140
9.19–23	140, 146
9.20–21	57, 78
9.21	66, 128
9.22	103
10	174–75
10.1	7
10.1ff.	85, 117, 121, 126
10.4	80
10.11	146
10.18	121
10.20	63, 121
10.23–24	140
10.27	126
10.32	8, 74
10.32—11.1	140
11.23	163
11.23ff.	63, 65, 121, 153
11.26	107
12.2	63, 85, 121, 126, 174–75
12.12–13	81, 129
12.27	166
13.13	74
14.25	111
15	81, 160
15.3	163
15.3–4	151
15.5	168
15.9	8, 74
15.20–22	165
15.20–28	65, 154, 174
15.25–27	161
15.42–57	129, 165
15.50–57	65, 81, 174
15.54–57	128
15.51–52	95, 105
15.56	128–29, 164
16.1–3	129
16.20b	57

2 Corinthians
1.1	121
1.21	164
2.17	148
3	148
3–5	155
3.3ff.	63, 65, 121, 146, 153
3.3–16	108, 169
3.4–18	37

3.6	65	1.13–14	20, 117, 127
3.7–11	128–29	1.14	7, 167
3.7–12	157	1.15	80, 110
3.14ff.	15	1.15–16	166
3.14–15	109	1.15–17	163
3.16	109	2	83, 141
3.18	65, 129, 165	2.1–14	86
4.4	80	2.3	79
4.4ff.	165	2.4	131
4.4–12	163	2.7	79
4.7–12	148	2.7–10	132
4.14	81	2.9	79
4.14—5.5	65, 174	2.11–14	132
5.10	138	2.12	79
5.12	68	2.13–16	63
5.14–21	128	2.14	133
5.14–17	165	2.15	7, 58, 63, 70, 128, 132, 167
5.17	77, 81, 154, 164, 174		
5.17–21	145	2.15–16	63, 80, 82, 102–3, 125–26, 145, 147
5.19	173		
5.19–21	146	2.15—3.14	169
5.21	164	2.16	63
6.16	83	2.16–21	129, 170
7.10	114	2.16b	70
8.9	165	2.19	169
9	129	2.19–20	79
9.5	110	2.19–21	164, 169
9.13	140	2.21—3.5	144
10–13	133	3	20, 45–46, 70, 73, 124–25, 174
10.15–16	99		
10.17	68	3–6	141
11	131	3.1–5	66, 70, 84, 126
11.18	68	3.2	77, 163
11.24	42, 135	3.5	166
13.11	73	3.5–6	83
13.12	57	3.6ff.	69
13.13	74	3.6–9	82
		3.7	70
Galatians		3.8	73, 78, 80, 125
1.4	163	3.8a	79
1.6	82–83, 110	3.8b–18	79
1.6ff.	143	3.10	77, 169
1.6–10	83	3.10ff.	35
1.8–9	83	3.10–11	15
1.13	8, 74, 82–83, 171	3.10–14	170

Galatians (continued)

3.11	169	5	83
3.11–14	65	5–6	84
3.12	169	5.1—6.17	83
3.13	163–64, 169	5.2–12	83
3.13–14	144	5.3	79, 83–84
3.14	80	5.4	83
3.15	83	5.6	52, 84
3.15–18	35	5.8	83, 110
3.15–29	82	5.10b	83
3.16	78, 82, 110, 171	5.11	70, 84, 128, 161
3.19	128, 164	5.12	83
3.19ff.	156	5.13	110, 177
3.21	15	5.13ff.	64, 128, 165
3.21ff.	168	5.13–26	140
3.21–22	62, 103	5.13—6.2	66, 71
3.21–23	128	5.13—6.10	84
3.22	128–29	5.14	142
3.22–25	144	5.16ff.	79
3.22ff.	81	5.22–25	77–78
3.23	80, 169	5.22–26	88
3.23–29	65	5.25	77
3.24	79, 156	6.10	79, 83, 171
3.25	80	6.11–18	83
3.26–29	145, 174	6.12	84, 135, 142
3.26—4.7	79	6.13	68, 84, 142
3.28	81, 104, 129	6.14–15	52, 69
3.28–29	125, 147, 164, 171	6.15	15, 73, 78, 84, 154
3.29	35, 70, 72, 81–82, 84, 110, 121, 171	6.14–16	125
		6.15–16	82, 88, 164–65, 174
4.1–7	80	6.16	19, 20, 45, 54–55, 71, 73–78, 82–86, 88, 96, 116, 121, 129, 131, 171
4.1–11	144		
4.3	52, 80–81		
4.4–5	164	Ephesians	
4.4–6	77, 156	1.7–14	154
4.5	80–81	1.9–10	95
4.7	171	1.20–22	161
4.8	52, 63	2.3	63
4.12	135	2.6	164
4.21–31	37	2.10	165
4.25	144	2.11	165
4.25–26	77	2.11–22	81, 105, 129, 145, 174
4.26	78	2.13	165
4.27	77	2.15	165
4.30–31	135	3.3–9	95

3.5–6	81, 105, 129, 145, 174
3.14–19	73
4.1–6	81, 105, 129, 145, 174
4.24	165
5.3–5	165
5.32	146
6.19	95
6.23f.	74
6.23–24	73

Philippians

1.1	121
1.3–13	134
1.27–28	134
1.27–30	134
1.27—2.18	154, 165
2.6	80
2.5–8	79
2.8	134, 146
2.9–11	145
2.10–11	138
2.12	134
2.15	134
2.16	134
2.17	134
3	20, 69, 127–28, 131, 133
3.1–16	134
3.2	133
3.2ff.	96
3.3	65, 68, 97, 116, 121
3.3ff.	69
3.4ff.	133
3.3–6	79
3.4–9	27
3.5	7, 167
3.5–6	117
3.5–11	157
3.9	68, 164
3.14	110
3.17	94, 134
3.20	133–34
3.20–21	65, 81, 135
3.21	129, 174
4.1	134–35
4.9	73
4.21	57

Colossians

1.2	121
1.15ff.	165
1.15–16	80
1.15–20	145, 154
1.26–27	95
2.2	95
2.9–13	164
2.11–15	121
3.4	65, 81, 174
3.10–11	165
3.11	81, 129
3.15	110
4.3	95
4.15–16	57

1 Thessalonians

1.4–10	110
1.6–10	154
1.9	171
1.10	92, 129
2.12	110
2.14–16	92, 108, 116
2.15–16	27
2.16	103, 127
3.13	121
4.1–8	64, 71, 128
4.3–8	140
4.5	85, 121, 126
4.7	110
4.13ff.	81
4.13–17	65, 174
4.15	63
4.15–17	105
4.17	111
5.1–11	92
5.9	129
5.10	163
5.23	73
5.24	110
5.26–27	57

2 Thessalonians

1.10	121
1.11–12	110
2.1	154
2.1–4	116
2.13–14	110
3.16	73

1 Timothy

1.2	73

2 Timothy

1.3	73
2.12	164

Hebrews

	137
1.4	154
1.13—2.9	161
4	154
12.1ff.	154

1 Peter

1.1ff.	154
2.9–12	85

2 Peter

3.10–14	154

2 John

3	73

Jude

2	73

Revelation

2.26–28	164
5.9–10	86
5.10	164
6–19	116
6.11	112
7.4	112
14.1	112
21–22	154

PSEUDPIGRAPHA

Apocalypse of Abraham

31.1–8	109
31.6	80

2 Baruch

13.1–12	80
14.13	154
17.3	160
19.8	160
23.4	160
23.4–5	112
26.1—30.5	168
30.4–5	109
36.1—40.4	168
41.1–6	109
41.4	33
44.15	109
48.20–24	62
48.40–47	80
51.3	154
51.6	109
53.1—76.5	168
54.15	160
56.6	160
56.8ff.	160
57.1–2	110
68.5–6	69
68.5–7	152
72.2–6	123, 161
78.2	75
78.6–7	112, 168
78.7	152
82.3–9	109

1 Enoch

5.6–7	154
10.21—11.2	123
37–71	168
48.4–5	123
63.1–12	80
85–90	152
90.30	123, 161
91.11–17	152

Index of Ancient Documents

93.1–10	152	8.34	152
105.1	62	9.19	75
		11	152
Jubilees		11.9	75
1.9–18	152	17	152
1.14–23	112, 168	17–18	168
1.21–24	64	17.29–35	123
1.21–25	78	17.51	75
1.23	67	18.14	159
1.23–29	154		
1.24	164	*Pseudo-Philo*	
1.27–28	78	11.1–2	80
4.26	78, 154	19	168
15.25–34	79	22.1	92
17.3	154	23.1	92
19.21–25	78, 154		
22	78, 154	*Sibylline Oracles*	
22.9	75	3.195	62, 80
22.11–13	159	3.545–50	70
22.14	78, 159	3.556–72	123
22.14–15	154	3.624–31	70
22.15	78	3.710–23	123
22.27–30	154	3.757–75	123
22.30	78	4.24–39	70
23.6	112, 168		
24.11	110	**Testament of the Twelve** Patriarchs	
32.18–19	154	*Testament of Asher*	
32.19	123, 161	7.2–7	152
50.9	92		
		Testament of Benjamin	
Letter of Aristeas		10.3–11	123
4–7	69	10.11	92, 94
16	70		
140	70	*Testament of Dan*	
		5.4–13	112, 152, 168
Odes of Solomon		6.4	112, 168
11.1–3	67		
		Testament of Issachar	
On Jonah		6	152
216–19	70	6.4	112, 168
Psalms of Solomon		*Testament of Joseph*	
4.29	75	20.5	92
6.9	75		
8.33–34	75		

Index of Ancient Documents

Testament of Judah

23	152
23.5	112, 168
24.4–6	123
25.5	123

Testament of Levi

10	152
14–18	152
14.3ff.	62
14.4	80
17.5	92
18.2–9	123
18.10	160

Testament of Naphtali

4.1–5	152
4.3–5	168
8.3–4	123

Testament of Simeon

6.2–7	112

Testament of Zebulun

9.5–9	152
9.7–8	112, 168
9.8	123

Testament of Moses

1.1ff.	168
1.12–13	159
1.18	112, 168
10ff.	161

QUMRAN DOCUMENTS

CD

1.3–11	152
3.10ff.	64
3.10–14	152
3.19–20	159
4.2	170
4.7–12	109
6.4f.	170
8.16	170
14.4–5	109
19.16	170
20.17	170

1Q14 frg. 10

7	110

1Q28b

4.27	62

1Q34

2.5–7	64

1QH

2.9	170
2.18	66
5.11f.	64
6.5–10	110
6.6	170
7.6ff.	64
9.32	64
12.12	64
13	78
13.11	75
13.15–18	78
13.23–25	78
13.24–25	64
14.8ff.	64
14.13	64
14.24	170
15.13–19	110
16.1ff.	110
16.7–15	64
16.15	64
16.17–18	170
17.14–15	159
17.15	78
18	66, 170

1QM

1.2–3	152

1QpHab

11.13	66

1QS
1.16—2.25	64
1.24ff.	170
3.8–9	170
4.22–23	159
5.1ff.	170
5.5	66
8.3ff.	170
8.4–10	164
10.20	170
11.17–22	107

4Q161
3.11ff.	168

4Q171
3.1–2	159

4Q174
1	168
1.18f.	164

4Q252
5.1–6	168

4Q285 frg. 5
	168

4Q504
5.6ff.	64
5.7–21	152

4QMMT
C 12–32	112
C 27–31	63

TARGUMS

Targum Isaiah
25.6–10	123
28	152
28.9	161

Targum Hosea
14.7–8	152

Targum Micah
5.1–3	152

RABBINIC WRITINGS

Mishnah
ʾAbot
1.12	33

Bikkurim
1.4	33

ʿEduyyot
5.2	79

Kiddushin
14.4	110

Sanhedrin
10.1	92, 94, 114

Talmud (Babylonian)
ʿAbodah Zarah
3b	109

ʿErubin
18b	160

Pesaḥim
8.8	79
87b	33

Šabbat
31a	33
118b	113

Sanhedrin
97b	33, 113
98a	113

Index of Ancient Documents

Yebamot
24b	109
47b	79

Talmud (Jerusalem)
Megillah
3.2.74d	79

Other Rabbinic Works
Genesis Rabbah
14.6	160
24.2	160
58.4	160

Exodus Rabbah
30.12	79

Numbers Rabbah
13.2	160

Mekilta
20.10	33

Pesiqta Rabbati
161a	109

Pirqe Rabbi Eliezer
12	160

Sipra
86b	80

Sipre Numbers
108	33

Sipre Deuteronomy
41	113

Tanḥuma B. Toledot
12	160

EARLY CHRISTIAN WRITINGS

Barnabas
87

1 Clement
	137
29.2—30.1	86

Diognetus
87

Eusebius
Preparation for the Gospel
13.12.6–7	70

Justin Martyr
Dialogue with Trypho
122	33
123.7	76
124.1ff.	76

Ignatius
To the Magnesians
10.2–3	87

To the Philadelphians
6.1	87

Tertullian
Apology
40.1–5	142

OTHER GRECO-ROMAN WRITINGS

Dio Cassius
Roman History
37.17.1	33
57.18.5	33
60.6.6	136
67.14.1–3	33

Diodorus Siculus
World History
1.55	79

Epictetus
Diatribal
2.19.19	60

Index of Ancient Documents   219

3.7.17	60
4.8–9	60
24.40–43	60

Horace
Satires

1.4.142–43	33
1.9.60–72	79

Josephus
Against Apion

2.137	79
2.140–42	79
2.168	70
2.255–57	70
2.279–84	69
2.45	69
2.48	69

Jewish Antiquities

1.192	79
3.318–19	69
8.116–17	69
11.3–5	69
11.87	69
11.103	69
11.120–32	69
11.331–36	69
12.11–18	69
12.22	70
13.69–71	69
13.78	69
13.172	110
13.242–44	69
13.318–19	79
14.110	69
14.213–16	141
16.14	69
16.162–66	141
18.13	110
18.34–48	79
18.82	33
18.83–84	141
18.122	69
18.286	69
18.288	69
18.309	69
20.34–53	33
20.38	79
20.195	69
20.41	70

Jewish War

2.162–63	110
2.201	69
2.340–41	69
2.409–17	69
4.181	69
4.275	69
5.15–18	69
5.562–64	69

Juvenal
Satires

14.96	33
14.96–106	79

Martial
Epigrams

7.35.3–4	79
7.35.82	79
11.94	79

Maximus of Tyre
The Philosophical Orations

33.2b-c	60

Orosius
History Against the Pagans

7.6.15–16	136

Paulus
Sententiae

5.22.3–4	79

Persius
Satires

5.179–84	79

Petronius
Satyricon
68.8	79
102.13–14	79

Philo
De somniis
1.175	154

Embassy
157	69
245	70
291	70
294–97	70
309–10	70
317–20	70
291–320	69

Good Person
62	70
72–74	70

Legum allegoriae
2.86	80

Moses
1.55	154
2.17–43	69

On the Migration of Abraham
92	79

On the Special Laws
1.1–11	79
1.51–52	33
1.305	66
2.42–48	70
4.178	33

On the Virtues
102	33

Questions and Answers on Exodus
2.2	66

Strabo
Geography
16.2.37	79

Suetonius
Augustus
32.1–2	141

Claudius
25.4	136

Domitian
12	79

Julius
42.3	141

Tacitus
Annales
15.44	137

Histories
5.5	137
5.5.2	79
5.5.8–9	79

Index of Modern Authors

Achtemeier, Paul J., 58, 63, 86–87, 137
Ackroyd, Peter R., 152
Allison, Dale C., 112

Barclay, John M. G., 6, 73, 84, 136–37, 142, 144
Barrett, C. K., 63, 92–93, 106, 110–12, 114
Barth, Karl, 95
Bassler, Jouette M., 58, 62–63
Baur, F. C., 2, 137,
Beale, G. K., 73–75, 77–78
Beker, J. Christiaan, 25, 104
Bell, Richard H., 92–95, 104, 106
Betz, H. D., 72, 75, 80, 84, 135
Birch, Bruce C., 160, 166
Boyarin, Daniel, 17
Brändle, Rudolf, 135–36
Bruce, F. F., 58, 72, 80, 92
Brueggemann, Walter, 3, 117, 160, 166–67
Bryan, Christopher, 110
Buell, Denise Kimber, 7, 69
Burke, Trevor J., 80, 143
Burton, Ernest DeWitt, 72

Byrne, Brendon, 58–59, 92–94, 111–12, 154

Caird, George Bradford, 161
Calvin, John, 95
Campbell, Douglas A., 9, 79, 155–58
Campbell, William S., 4, 19, 40–50, 67, 71, 76, 83, 88, 92, 104, 109, 121–23, 126, 138 39, 166, 176
Carroll, Robert P., 152
Chilton, Bruce D., 152
Clements, R. E., 162
Cohen, Shaye, 4–6, 8
Combes, I. A. H., 81
Cosgrove, Charles H., 10–14, 55
Cousar, Charles B., 73
Cranfield, C. E. B., 57–58, 62–63, 92–93, 95–96, 104, 106, 111–12, 114–15, 128, 154
Cullmann, Oscar, 156

Dahl, N. A., 73, 154
Das, A. Andrew, 56–57, 92, 135–37, 141–42
Davies, W. D., 2, 72, 80, 88

Dodd, C. H., 1-2, 4, 9, 17-18, 23-31, 37-39, 58, 63, 94, 104, 119-20, 145, 150, 169
Donaldson, Terence L., 18-19, 31, 32-37, 39-40, 43-46, 48, 58, 63, 69-71, 73, 80, 92, 102-4, 109, 112-13, 120-22, 124, 126, 131, 146, 149-50, 173
Donfried, Karl Paul, 56, 99
Dunn, James D. G., 4, 18-19, 31-35, 37-40, 43-45, 48, 53, 58, 62-63, 65, 67-68, 71-73, 80-81, 92-95, 104, 106, 109, 111-12, 120-21, 123, 135, 138, 149, 154-56, 165

Ehrensperger, Kathy, 3-4, 10-12, 104, 139
Eisenbaum, Pamela, 4, 17
Elliot, Neil, 58, 61, 64, 152, 170, 177
Elliot, Susan, 79
Esler, Philip F., 4-6, 18, 56, 58, 61, 69, 73, 84, 92, 99, 104, 106, 123, 126, 128, 134, 136-39, 170, 175-76
Evans, Craig A., 152

Fee, Gordon, 134
Fishbane, Michael, 89
Fitzmyer, Joseph A., 56, 58-59, 63, 92-96, 104, 109, 112
Fredriksen, Paula, 122
Fuller, Michael E., 152-53, 168
Fung, Ronald Y., 73, 85
Furnish, Victor P., 177

Gager, John G., 4, 13-15, 56, 100, 149, 151
Gamble, Harry, 56, 59
Gaston, Lloyd, 4, 17, 19, 49-53, 58, 60, 70, 72, 80, 92-93, 96, 100-105, 117, 145, 147-51, 167
George, Timothy, 73, 135
Giorgio, Jossa, 127, 131-33, 136

Gowan, Donald E., 152
Grenholm, Cristina, 12, 14
Gruen, Erich S., 136-37
Guthrie, Donald, 73

Hafemann, Scott J., 64-65, 73, 106, 112, 128, 152
Halpern-Amaru, Betsy, 153
Hanson, Paul D., 162-63
Harink, Douglas, 9, 19, 49-52, 71-72, 92, 117, 149-51, 154-56, 160, 167
Harland, Philip A., 126, 141-42
Hays, Richard B., 16, 59, 73, 79, 82, 102, 113, 127, 147-49, 151-52, 174
Hendriksen, William, 104
Hofius, Otfried, 92-95, 163
Horne, C. M., 104
Howard, George, 132
Hvalvik, Reidar, 93-94, 105, 113

Jeremias, Joachim, 96
Jewett, Robert, 56, 58-59, 62-63, 65, 70-71, 92-96, 100-101, 103-4, 106, 111-12, 114, 128, 139-40, 143-44, 154
Jobes, Karen H., 77-78
Johnson, Dan G., 106, 112
Johnson, E. Elizabeth, 108
Johnson-Hodge, Caroline, 4, 6-7, 70, 79-81, 104, 117, 120, 123-25, 149, 151, 153-54, 160, 175

Käsemann, Ernst, 9, 15-16, 18, 24-31, 37-39, 53, 58-59, 63, 65, 92-95, 106, 111-12, 114, 119-20, 128, 140, 145, 148, 150, 169
Keck, Leander E., 58, 62-63
Keesmaat, Sylvia C., 154
Kim, Seyoon, 163, 165, 170
Kinzer, Mark S., 4, 148, 163, 172, 177
Knibb, Michael A., 152
Kraabel, A. T., 153

Lampe, Peter, 135
Lane, William L., 86
Lenski, R. C. H., 104
Levine, Amy-Jill, 6
Lieu, Judith M., 7-8, 43, 87, 88, 131
Longenecker, Bruce W., 170
Longenecker, Richard N., 73, 83-84, 135

Malina, Bruce J., 142
Martyn, J. Louis, 71, 73, 80-82, 135, 155
Mason, Steve, 4-6, 137
Matera, Frank J., 73, 83-84, 135
Matlock, R. Barry, 25-26
Meeks, Wayne A., 127, 135
Merkle, Ben L., 104, 106-7
Middleton, J. Richard, 12
Miller, David A., 4
Moo, Douglas J., 56, 58, 63, 65, 92-95, 104, 106, 109, 111-12, 115, 128
Moore, George F., 2
Mowinckel, Sigmund, 164
Munck, Johannes, 2, 20, 92-93, 106
Murphy-O'Connor, Jerome, 137
Mussner, Franz, 72, 92, 94

Nanos, Mark D., 4, 8, 17, 19, 40-46, 48, 50, 53, 67, 71, 79, 91, 93, 98-101, 107, 111-12, 122-24, 126-27, 132-33, 135-44
Neusner, Jacob, 153
Nickelsburg, George W. E., 168

Patte, Daniel, 12, 14
Pearson, B. A., 116
Ponsot, Hervé, 96

Räisänen, Heikki, 10, 58, 62-63, 65, 104
Rajak, Tessa, 141-42
Refoulé, François, 104
Richardson, Peter, 72, 74-76, 85, 87
Ridderbos, Herman N., 73, 104
Robinson, D. W. B., 72

Robinson, J. A. T., 108
Rollins, W. G., 81
Ruether, Rosemary Radford, 17
Runesson, Anders, 88

Sanders, E. P., 2-3, 10, 34, 42, 58, 62-64, 66, 68, 92, 94, 110, 112, 114, 127, 133, 168
Sanders, James A., 166, 168
Schmithals, Walter, 135
Schoeps, Hans-Joachim, 2
Schrenk, Gottlob, 72
Schüssler Fiorenza, Elizabeth, 16, 148
Schweitzer, Albert, 2, 9, 26, 36
Scott, James M., 92, 111, 152, 170
Scroggs, Robin, 17, 73, 155, 160, 165, 174
Segal, Alan F., 17
Seitz, Christopher R., 162
Silva, Moisés, 73
Slingerland, H. Dixon, 136-37
Smail, Thomas, 81
Staples, Jason A., 97
Stanley, Christopher D., 59, 94, 106, 109
Steck, O. H., 152
Stegemann, Ekkehard W., 135-36
Stendahl, Krister, 2, 4, 11, 15, 17, 100
Stibbe, Mark, 81
Stowers, Stanley K., 4, 56, 58, 60, 62-63, 65-67, 80, 100, 102-3, 151, 154, 160
Stuhlmacher, Peter, 58, 92-94, 112, 128

Tajfel, Henri, 18
Theron, D. J., 81
Thielman, Frank, 58, 73, 152
Thiselton, Anthony C., 129
Tomson, Peter J., 132, 139-40, 172
Tucker, J. Brian, 175
Turner, John C., 18

Van der Horst, Pieter W., 93, 111
Vanderkam, James C., 152-53

Wagner, J. Ross, 56, 59, 77, 92, 94, 107–9, 112, 137, 146–47, 151–52, 163, 168
Walters, James C., 87, 135–36, 141
Walsh, Brian, 12
Wasserberg, Günter, 17
Watson, Francis, 10, 104, 127, 133, 135–36, 163, 169
Weima, Jeffrey A. D., 73, 84
Welborn, L. L., 86
Westermann, Claus, 166
Wiefel, Wolfgang, 136
Williams, Sam K., 62, 70, 73, 79, 120, 146–47, 154

Witherington III, Ben, 58, 63, 73, 80, 83–84, 92, 104, 110–12, 127, 135–36, 154
Wright, N. T., 4, 17–19, 31–40, 43–48, 50, 53, 58–59, 62–66, 68–69, 71, 73, 80, 86, 92–93, 95–97, 101, 104–14, 120–21, 140, 147, 149–51, 153–56, 158, 163–65, 169–70

Yoder, John Howard, 154

Zetterholm, Magnus, 4, 86, 135, 137, 140

www.ingramcontent.com/pod-product-compliance
Lightning Source LLC
Chambersburg PA
CBHW062021220426
43662CB00010B/1421